WALKING IN TWO WORLDS

MIXED-BLOOD INDIAN WOMEN SEEKING THEIR PATH

WALKING IN
TWO WORLDS
MIXED-BLOOD INDIAN WOMEN
SEEKING THEIR PATH

NANCY MAYBORN PETERSON

CAXTON PRESS
Caldwell, Idaho
2006

ISBN 978-0-87004-450-8

Library of Congress Cataloging-in-Publication Data

Peterson, Nancy M., 1934-
 Walking in two worlds : mixed-blood Indian women seeking their path / by Nancy Mayborn Peterson.
     p. cm.
 Includes bibliographical references and index.
 ISBN 0-87004-450-8
 1. Indian women--North America--Biography. 2. Indians of North America--Mixed descent. 3. Indian women--North America--Ethnic identity. 4. North America--Ethnic relations. I. Title.

 E98.W8P47 2006
 305.4092'30597--dc22
 [B]

                                    2006014478

Lithographed and bound in the United States of America by

CAXTON PRESS
Caldwell, Idaho
173763

DEDICATION

To Britney, Alex and Ryan,
seeking paths of their own.

TABLE OF CONTENTS

ILLUSTRATIONS

NANCY MAYBORN PETERSON

ACKNOWLEDGMENTS

I first learned of Susan Bordeaux Bettelyoun's poignant story when I was researching my Platte River history, *People of the Moonshell.* I worked from a photocopy of her manuscript housed at the Nebraska State Historical Society. I also spent days transcribing part of the LaFlesche Family Papers so I could write of Susette LaFlesche Tibbles. While I also was charmed by the letters Susan LaFlesche (Picotte) sent home from medical school, I was alerted to the discord between full and mixed bloods.

Later in the decade, I was in Helena, Montana, researching my second Missouri River history, *People of the Old Missury,* when I happened on a small display about Helen Clarke. That led me to her papers, and again I was intrigued by the dichotomy inherent in her heritage.

Over the years, I have sought more stories of mixed-blood Indian women, trying to understand how they dealt with the disparate positions into which they were born. I learned how others, such as Gertrude Bonnin and Mary Little Bear Inkanish, struggled painfully with their dual identities. The result is this volume, in which I have attempted to pay tribute to the spirit of these women, who accomplished so much despite formidable obstacles.

I am deeply indebted to the many scholars who have already delved into the lives of these women. Valerie Sherer Mathes is deservedly the recognized authority on the LaFlesche sisters. Emily Levine has made the Bordeaux-Waggoner manuscript accessible to a world-wide audience. Alice Marriott detailed the life of Mary Little Bear Inkanish. Charlotte Gray and A. LaVonne Brown Ruoff have written of E. Pauline Johnson, and Ruoff has also probed the life of Jane Johnston Schoolcraft. Lalla Scott recorded Annie Lowry's memories. These historians led the way.

In studying Roberta Lawson, I have been assisted by her grandson, Edward Campbell Lawson, and Morgan Davis of the General Federation of Women's Clubs who shared generously from their archives. Thomas E. Young of the Philbrook Museum of Art also was exceptionally generous in his response for information, as were Frances A. Donelson of the Bacone College Library and the McFarlin Library of the University of Tulsa. Head Archivist Bill Welge and the staff of the Oklahoma State Historical Society have assisted me with information on both Lawson and Mary Little Bear Inkanish. I have benefitted greatly from the knowledge of Clark and Garth Inkanish, grandsons of Mary. Eva Williams, curator of the Southern Plains Indian Museum has been helpful and LaVerna Capes, manager of the museum's gift shop, shared personal memories of Mary Inkanish. The Nevada Historical Society supplied material on Annie Lowry, and grandson Alfred Happy also sought information on my behalf.

The Nebraska State Historical Society answered my requests for further information on the LaFlesche family. Susan Bordeaux Bettelyoun's great niece, Margi Morrison, willingly shared family information, and LaVera Rose of the South Dakota State Historical Society offered much information on the Sioux. I enjoyed meeting Joyce Turvey Clarke, Helen's great niece, in East Glacier Park, who readily shared her extensive collection of family history. The staff of the Montana State Historical Society supplied many requests. Thanks to McMaster University of Hamilton, Ontario, which makes its Pauline Johnson Archive available on the internet.

I am ever indebted to the helpful staff of the Denver Public Library's Western History Department, especially Colleen

Nunn and Phil Panum, and the staff of the Arapahoe Regional Library System's Interlibrary Loan Department who have made enormous efforts to answer my many requests. My heartfelt thanks to all.

Lastly, I thank friends Ron Dreher for assistance with a photograph; Linda Berry, Bonnie McCune, Betty Swords, and Barbara Fleming, who encouraged me in the beginning, Beverly Chico, who often directs her fount of information my way, and my husband, Jim, for his patient, continuing support.

Introduction

Their fathers were often called "squaw men" with all the derision the title implied. The white fur trader's union with a native American woman was looked on as merely a necessity of doing business. Often they were part of a second family, unacknowledged back East. Trader James McKenzie called the mixed-blood family "a most wretched species . . . neither one thing nor the other." Fur man Alexander Fisher called the resulting family "a spurious breed." If they were boys, they sometimes became fearsome fighters like the Bent brothers, Charles and George, who exemplified the belief that "half breeds" inherited only the most savage inclinations of both races. They could inflict their anger on anyone in their way, and say with their full-blooded brothers when resistance was doomed, "It's a good day to die!" Or, they could watch the collapse of their culture with the fatalism of Squamish Chief Seattle, who wrote to President Franklin Pierce in 1854, "It matters little where we spend the rest of our days. They are not many."

But if they were girls . . . if they were women, they were born to give new life—to nurture and protect it. Women in Indian society had held central positions in their culture before the white perspective reduced them to menial servants. They were the keepers of tradition, the personification of Mother Earth, who not only were essential to help feed, clothe and house the people, but to keep the essence of tribal beliefs alive. These girls' mothers were their husband's helpmates; they essentially took white men into their families and enabled them to live in the wilderness. They were bridges of communication, of mediation and negotiation. They had no doubts about who they were and what their role was.

Their daughters, steeped in the tradition of their Indian mothers but forced into the world of their white fathers, found they did not belong in either world. Poet Mary Tall Mountain, whose father was Scot and mother Athabascan, said, "But I know who I am. Marginal person, misfit, mutant. . . ." Present-day writer Diane Glancy describes hearing "voices in the grass. Two Dresses, they say in the wind. And truly, I have the feeling of being split between two cultures, not fully belonging to either one."

Writer Joy Harjo, a blend of French, Cherokee and Creek, echoes the feeling. "I used to see being born of this mixed blood/ mixed-vision a curse, and hated myself for it. . . . The only message I got was not belonging anywhere, not to any side." Even those with marginal Indian blood feel the dichotomy, the tug of war.

Diane Glancy, only one-eighth Cherokee, asks, "How can the influence of one be as strong as seven together? Yet in my writing, as well as in my life for the past several years, it is my Indian heritage that emerges again and again."

If these modern women still struggle with their true identity, imagine the trauma of the first generation of mixed-blood daughters, who moved from the family lodge to the glaring, regimented din of school life, where everything obviously Indian was stripped away as one would skin an animal. The remaining inner core of their identity was continually attacked and belittled. And then, minds awash with incredible new knowledge, they were returned to the family fire their teachers disparaged. They had no role models. They had no support system. At times their own people considered them traitors. They had to find their own way, make their own place. That the women whose stories are told in this volume surmounted the difficulties of their lives and earned their places as leaders in both white and Indian societies speaks to their courage, their intelligence, their heart. Some of them never could put the pain inflicted by white schools behind them; others gratefully accepted the learning they were offered. Some, even with fractional native blood, always identified themselves as Indian. Others had to reject their Indian heritage before they could make peace with it.

All these women, in the end, took the tools and training whites had provided, and instead of melding into white society—accepting white values—used those tools to help their people. They found differing paths—medicine, music, crafts, the classroom, the lecture hall, the stage, the written word— and walked strong and tall. Each woman did, as Paula Gunn Allen says in *The Sacred Hoop*, "what Indian matrons have always done: knit old ways to the new circumstances in such a way that the fundamental world-view of the tribe will not be distorted or destroyed." The Iroquois Great Law of Peace contains this truth: "The chain of culture is the chain of women linking the past with the future."

Chief Seattle believed that his people were at "The end of living and the beginning of survival." These women did far more than survive; they reached a hand to help their people find a place in a hard new future.

Introduction Bibliography

Allen, Paula Gunn. *The Scared Hoop*, Beacon Press, 1986.
Green, Rayna. *Women in American Indian Society,* Chelsea House Publishers, 1992.
Katz, Jane, ed. *Messengers of the Wind,* One World, Ballantine Books, 1995.
McGaa, Ed., Eagle Man. *Mother Earth Spirituality,* Harper Collins, 1990.
Saum, Lewis O. *The Fur Trader and the Indian,* University of Washington Press, 1965.
Swann, Brian and Arnold Krupat, editors. *I Tell You Now - Autobiographical Essays of Indian Writers,* University of Nebraska Press, 1987.

Bently Historical Library, University of Michigan

Jane Johnston Schoolcraft

Chapter One

LINES WRITTEN UNDER AFFLICTION

Jane Johnston Schoolcraft, 1800-1841
Chippewa - Irish

It was mid-June of 1820 when twenty-year-old Jane
Johnston, child of an Ojibwa mother and Irish father, first
became aware of Henry Ward Schoolcraft, former glass
manufacturer, explorer, mineralogist and scholar. The thirty-
eight-man government expedition the twenty-seven-year-old
geologist accompanied tied up their boats near Jane's home
on the Saint Mary's River in Michigan Territory. The sound of
the St. Marys waters, churning and boiling east in their nearly
mile-wide channel, as they made their way from Lake Superior
to Lake Huron, was a constant in her life in the small Ojibwa
village of Sault Ste. Marie. Her mother's people depended on
its turbid waters for the white fish which were a staple of their
diet. And, with their location on the trails of fur commerce, the
Ojibwas were accustomed to entertaining passers-by.

But the group Schoolcraft, son of an Albany County, New
York, pioneering family, accompanied was different. It was
headed by General Lewis Cass, governor of the Territory of
Michigan, who had the blessing of the United States secretary
of war. The expedition planned to take a long, hard look at the
mineral resources of the Lake Superior area. The lake which
the natives called Gitche Gumee, or Great Water, had long
centered the Ojibwas' lives.

1

These Algonquin people, also known as Chippewas, lived along Lake Superior's southern shore and frequented its islands. Its soaring cliffs and the long stretches of sand beach that framed its cold, greenish waters were home. The land and water provided a living that often was only marginal. Wild rice from the marshes, berries, maple syrup and sugar were supplemented with occasional deer, moose and bear, but fish were their mainstay. Their light and supple birch bark canoes, expertly balanced by their standing occupants, bobbed in the river's rushing waters from early spring to late fall. The fishermen stood in their bouncing craft and maneuvered to dip their nets into the teaming flood and flip fish into the boats. When dried, the fish sustained them through the lengthy winters.

Thus far white men had come mainly to seek the sleek furs of the north country's animals, and most of these men had been from Canada—French or English. These Americans posed a new threat of lasting intrusion. The first thing they wanted was to buy enough Ojibwa land at the Sault to build an army fort, signifying their intent to extend their influence over territory they had secured from the British in the War of 1812. They would be planting the American flag where it had never before flown.

The dark-eyed, delicate Jane was not an ignorant young woman. Although she was also called Obahbam-wa-wa-ge-zheg-o-qua, which translates to 'The Sound the Stars Make Rushing Through the Skies," she had an unexpected sophistication. She was better traveled and better educated than many white women of her time. Her fur-trader father, John Johnston, had made sure of that. He had schooled his eldest daughter well in English and grammar, history and literature. She had absorbed more knowledge from his extensive library of classics. He enjoyed her company—she had been schooled to be his companion—and he had taken her with him on his business trips to towns such as Detroit, reachable by boat 350 miles southeast of the

Sault, and to French-speaking Quebec and English Montreal. When Jane was nine, in 1809, he had taken her to his northern Ireland homeland, intending to let his childless sister and her husband adopt and educate her. However, a strenuous voyage and the humid climate undermined Jane's health. When her uncle died suddenly, John Johnston had decided to take Jane back to Sault Ste. Marie.

Her mother, whose Ojibwa name meant "Woman of the Green Prairie," had been re-christened "Susan" by her Irish husband, but she had not left her Ojibwa identity behind. Susan worked, with her husband's blessing, to educate Jane and their seven other children in her own areas of expertise. Her contribution had been to school them in her people's legends and history. She was especially careful that they appreciated the power and importance of her father, Chief Waub Ojeeg, (the White Fisher) and grandfather, Ma Mongazida, who had led the Ojibwa for generations. On June 16, 1820, Jane was witness to her mother's considerable power.

Although John Johnston was away in Europe when the Americans arrived, Susan invited the officers of the delegation to take their meals with the family in their spacious log home. The grounds of the Johnston property looked as if a wealthy merchant had picked up his New England residence and moved it—complete with accouterments—to the Michigan forest. Roses, sweet william and lilacs graced the front yard, while a bountiful kitchen garden filled the back. The roomy living room, which featured a large open fireplace, was hung with portraits framed in gold. "Miss Jane," fluent in English where her mother was not, and trained to be a gracious hostess, presided at the dinner. She was dressed much as their own wives would have been, in a long gown collared with lace, as she smoothly supervised the serving of the dinner from a sideboard that sparkled with Irish-silver serving pieces.

It may have been during this dinner that Jane learned that the intense, brown-haired Henry Schoolcraft was already a published writer, having written of his travels to Missouri's lead mines the year before. The army officers marveled at and reveled in this oasis of civilization at the edge of the Michigan forest, and then retired to their tents spread along the shoreline.

General Cass had brought his three-dozen men to a shore peopled with British allies. Although hostilities of the War of 1812 were eight years in the past, loyalties had not changed. The Ojibwas were used to selling their furs to the British company headquartered on the St. Mary's north shore. They were satisfied with the presents, and especially the liquor, the giant North West Company supplied. The Americans were neither sought nor welcomed by the half-dozen French traders who remained at the Sault to trade with the 200 members of the tribe. A dozen French houses lay dilapidated and abandoned. Four dozen lodges of Ojibwa—frameworks of poles placed in a circle, bent inward and covered with birch bark or grass mats—rose beyond a small ravine. They were home to fifty or sixty warriors who had fought for the British and thought of Americans as enemies.

After the members of the expedition rose the next morning, the general called the leading Indian men to a council. Many of the braves dressed in their finest garb, and numerous British medals sparkled in the sun as they gathered to sit in a circle before the general's tent, where an American flag was prominently displayed. After the proper passing of the pipe and presentation of presents, Cass informed them through an interpreter, they now owed their allegiance to the United States. He also said the Americans intended to establish a garrisoned post right there in their village and expected them to grant the necessary land.

Immediate rumbles of dissatisfaction greeted Cass's words. Soon there was open disagreement among the Ojibwas—some in favor of accepting the inevitable, others insisting they resist. As the hours wore away, agitation increased until a chief named

Sassaba, attired in a uniform of British scarlet, leapt up, hurled his lance into the ground and harangued the assembly. He angrily rejected the American's right to rule them. Shouting defiance, he kicked away the presents and stalked off. The council dissolved in confusion and the participants withdrew to their separate camps, where the Ojibwas immediately raised the British flag.

It was an act of insolence that Governor Cass could not tolerate. Putting his troops on alert, he marched unarmed, accompanied only by his interpreter, to Sassaba's lodge. He yanked down the offending flag, stomped into the lodge and lectured the chief that two flags could not wave over the same territory and that the Americans would not tolerate the British banner. As the governor returned to his tent with the offending flag, the troops saw Indian women and children fleeing in panic. Hurriedly, the outnumbered Americans prepared for an attack that did not come.

Only later did the Americans learn that admiration for the courage of Governor Cass had made the Indians hesitate, and —more important—Woman of the Green Prairie had interceded for them. She called the leading men to meet behind her home and counseled peace, convincing them resistance was madness. She noted Cass had the greatness required to introduce the American flag throughout the area, and the time for resistance had passed. As the summer dusk thickened, the chiefs met again with the governor in one of the Johnston buildings and signed a treaty ceding four square miles along the St. Mary's for the fort. But they kept their important access to the river's fish. Thanks largely to Susan Johnston's intervention, the expedition was soon on its way, but Jane and Henry Schoolcraft were fated to meet again.

About 10:00 a.m. on July 6, 1822, another detachment of American troops rowed up to the green shores of Sault Ste. Marie. There were more soldiers this time—a battalion of men slated to garrison the newly completed Fort Brady. The Ojibwa, who had been expecting them, fired a salute and the troops flowed onto the wharf, stirring the village dogs to excited barking as Indians of all ages hurried to the water's edge. This time a blue-eyed, greying man of sixty limped forward to greet the army; he leaned slightly on his cane as he bid them formal welcome.

John Johnston had been engaged in the fur trade in the America wilderness almost thirty years by then, but he retained the manners of a gentleman. With pomp and martial music, Colonel Hugh Brady raised a flag east of the Johnston's house and as the military settled into their quarters, the roll of drums announcing meals, drills and watch changes added a new and strange tone to the clamor of the rapids.

Arriving again with the troops, but this time on a different mission, was Henry Schoolcraft. He had been appointed Indian agent for the Ojibwa at Sault Ste. Marie and tribes on west for 1,200 miles. It was a post he considered temporary, hoping he might later find a position in his field of mineralogy. The army rented one of Johnston's buildings and offered to share the twelve-by-fourteen foot whitewashed building with the new Indian agent. It had one small window in front and one in the rear with what passed for a fireplace in one corner.

Schoolcraft had no training or experience in working with Indians. But he was a fit and seasoned traveler of the wilderness. He knew how to live off the country—that one had to shoot a squirrel through the head to have useable meat, what to use to start a fire, that some berries were edible and others not, and more important, that when nature failed to provide, you tightened your belt and kept going anyway. He had an active, observant mind that probed everything he saw. He had published another well-received book, this one about the previous expedition under Governor Cass and the natural resources of the Lake Superior area. Until now, his interest had centered on minerals and his pockets were always full of specimens. Now charged with the Indians' welfare, his focus began to change.

He was amazed and bemused and charmed by the Johnston family, residing at the edge of what he thought of as "the howling wilderness." Susan Johnston, although of pure Ojibwa blood, rivaled her husband in her outgoing hospitality. A tall, robust woman, she wore her native costume of a short calico dress with beaded leggings and moccasins, her braided hair held high with a comb. Surprisingly, she welcomed and ministered to the strangers with the same affection she lavished on her large family. Her oldest son was away in the British navy, and second son, George, had fought with the British army. Even the house they lived in was a replacement for the former home the Americans had burned during the war. But the family seemed not to bear grudges.

There were three girls and two boys who ranged in age from nine to twenty. And there was the young woman called Jane who once again claimed Schoolcraft's attention. In ten days he was taking his meals with the Johnstons and in August he was occupying one of the apartments in their rambling building. As autumn turned to winter, he joined Jane and the others not only at meals, but in the spacious sitting room with its highly polished beams and large fireplace for evenings of reading and conversation.

Jane had grown up with these literary gatherings that helped to pass the long winter evenings. With the family grouped around the large table, Jane and her sisters kept their fingers busy with needlework, while their father sometimes read aloud, sometimes listened as one of his sons read a passage. Always he had comments about the material and the way it was read. The sessions were a true blending of cultures, for the Ojibwa had always passed the frigid winter nights by listening to legends and experiences of the tribal elders, and one often stopped by out of the bitter blackness to share his tales.

Jane, seeming an exotic creature whose tremulous voice echoed both the liquid vocal qualities of her mother's ancestry and her father's Irish lilt, was a ready and able translator for Henry Schoolcraft. It was an eye-opening experience for Schoolcraft, who had not credited the Ojibwas with this depth of culture and imagination. He was later to write, "Nothing has surprised me more. . . than to find that the Chippewas amuse themselves with oral tales of a mythological or allegorical character." He was entranced and began to wonder if this culture needed to be preserved. The evening invariably ended with John, a devout Catholic, reading from his Bible before he closed the night's gathering. Jane or one of his other daughters would place a pillow on the floor, where their father joined his kneeling family. By December 29, the agent was joining the family in their devotions.

Schoolcraft was to learn later that the depths of winter were the only times the storytellers would divulge their tales. It was a time of almost total isolation. Navigable waters were locked under ice. The flocks of swans, brants, cranes and ducks had made their way south weeks before. All the traders who could had withdrawn to friendlier climates—or at least to thicker walls and better stoves. Snowstorm followed snowstorm and bitter winds sculpted drifts up to the eaves. One English family remained on the American side and another English and one Scot across the river in Ontario. The nearest semblance of civilization, perhaps a dozen traders with their Indian wives and families, remained on Drummond Island, fifty miles southeast. Piles of wood disappeared into the agent's huge Montreal stove. While he put the leisure time to good use, quizzing Jane and her family about the Ojibwa language and beginning meticulous tables of vocabulary, he decided authors who wrote of the poetry of solitude had some other place in mind.

But over the long months of study and contact with Jane and the other Johnstons and their Ojibwa guests, his attitudes about Indians began to change. People he had thought before to be "bloodthirsty savages," without "feelings of pity, justice, and mercy," were amazingly human. They had religion, traditions, medicines, music, dances, birth and death rituals, and especially a language he was finding incredibly complicated. He began to see recording the details of this culture could be a life's work, and he was confident his scientific, analytical approach could be a valuable tool. What had seemed a temporary assignment became a consuming interest.

Schoolcraft was conscious of what he owed the Johnston family. "I have stumbled, as it were, on the only family in North West America who could, in Indian lore, have acted as my guide, philosopher and friend," he wrote a correspondent.

Jane, whose wide-set luminous black eyes sparkled with intelligence, was proving to be an apt, welcome partner in Henry's studies. And, with his own small library, the garrison's library housed in his quarters, and new books he ordered constantly from Detroit, Albany and New York City, he was enlarging both their horizons. Before he faced another winter, heedless of his mother's vocal stance against miscegenation, he asked The Sound of Stars Rushing Through the Skies to become his bride.

When Jane's mother had been promised to John Johnston at age sixteen, she had reacted with terror and aversion, even after entering a ten-day fast and seeing propitious visions. After the ceremony, in which she had been baptized "Susan," she fled to a dark corner and grieved her fate. Even though Johnston treated her with patient, tender care for ten days, she fled back home, only to have Waub Ojeeg thrash her and return her to her husband.

Thirty-one years later, Jane's October 1823 marriage to Henry engendered no such fears. She had experienced her white father's devotion to her mother and their children. Susan was the respected matriarch of the clan, her opinion sought and her wisdom valued. And Henry had won Jane, and most of the Ojibwa, with his fascinated interest in everything Indian. Almost immediately he had begun collecting not only stories, but the articles of their daily lives, which he kept in special cabinets at the agency building. He wanted to preserve her people, their customs, character and history, not destroy them.

Henry wrote Jane poems expressing his love of her "gentle manners, polished mind, grace, sweetness, taste, benevolence and naivete," and she replied in kind. Her mother was constantly involved with Henry's research, ready and willing to answer his questions. Jane's father, who liked to write, had a special fondness for Henry, and her brother, George, who loved to read, had become his good friend and most-skilled interpreter. A visiting parson administered their vows on October 12. Johnston added a special section onto his house for the couple.

The winter of 1824 was a happy time for the newlyweds. Jane was a gentle presence at her husband's side as they studied and compiled the beginnings of an Ojibwa dictionary. Some days for exercise they donned their snowshoes and walked the short distance to the agency, to the cantonment, to the foot of the rapids and back; when the snow allowed horses to maneuver, they took the two-wheeled cart for a drive. Often they stood watching the night sky flutter and flame with the colors of the aurora borealis. Three or four times they excitedly tore open letters, newspapers and packages that had arrived by dogsled or snowshoe. With the minister in residence, they met twice a week "for preaching." This time spring came before they had started looking for its signs. By then Jane knew they would have a child that summer.

Henry's life as agent was not as smooth. He had seen enough of the harm alcohol did to the Indians that he was discouraging its use, and many Ojibwas resented his stance. One of Jane's cousins had died in a drunken brawl his first year at the Sault. A few weeks after, Sassaba—the imposing chief who had defied the Americans in council—and four others were returning from a drinking binge when they drowned and were swept away. Despite Schoolcraft's displeasure, liquor was readily available from the traders, both in the village and across the river. The agent refused entry to his office or home to any intoxicated Indian, and his forceful ejection of one leading chief served as an object lesson that kept his door clear of drunken men. But every man carried liquor as part of his medicine bag, and the minister, who had hoped to save souls, abandoned his efforts. When the ice went out in the spring, he went with it.

Yet, Schoolcraft's marriage to the granddaughter of Waub Ojeeg gained him unexpected access to Ojibwa camps. Perhaps his open respect for his wife was a factor. On an April trip up to the Tacquimenon River Falls he was received "with a degree of confidence and cordiality by the Indians, which I had not expected." He credited this hospitality to his marriage to "an educated and intelligent lady," descended from the former ruler of the nation. On June 27, 1824, Jane gave him a son they named William Henry Schoolcraft. Three months later they boarded a schooner with the infant William Henry, Jane's younger sister and a servant, bound for Detroit, New York City and, for Henry, a trip down to the headquarters of the newly established Office of Indian Affairs in Washington, D.C.

Although New York occupied only the lower tip of the island of Manhattan, its commerce had recovered from War of 1812 stoppages. It could claim to be the country's metropolis; the Erie Canal, which was almost completed, would allow goods to be shipped west by water clear across the Great Lakes. Sewer and water service was primitive, but there was excited talk among the city's 170,000 people about the gas lines that were even then being laid to reach streets and homes below Canal Street.

Henry's growing reputation as a writer opened doors in literary circles. They moved into a boarding house and the family spent the fall seeing the city's places "of amusement and instruction" and socializing with the elite and educated. They were fascinated with Jane, whom some called "the northern Pocahontas." At least in her husband's proud eyes, she caused a sensation, an Indian princess who had been educated abroad and could write, he noted, with "ability, grammatical skill and taste." Jane dressed as a fashionable white woman, except for modest black, silk pantaloons, and wore her black hair in a high bun with cascading ringlets. But with her high cheekbones, black eyes and a complexion one observer took for Spanish ancestry, she stood out. For his part, auburn-haired, ebony-eyed William Henry excited attention as a baby of "more than ordinary beauty and mental promise." Passers-by, seeing mother and son leave their boarding house, asked questions, struck up acquaintances and became friends.

Henry, who was feeling sandwiched between the differing desires of the military and the Indian Department, left his family with friends on a country estate on Bloomsbury Road and traveled to Washington in January to resolve some difficulties. Returning with permission to erect new buildings at the agency, he soon was deep in plans with his host, two other influential friends and Jane to establish an Indian magazine when he returned to the Sault. In the meantime he prepared the manuscript of his third book for his publishers. In May he boated up the Hudson with Jane, and she delighted him by translating and telling him about the origins of Indian names they encountered. After a week with his relatives in western New York, they took steamboats back to the Sault. They began housekeeping in what was known as the Allen House on a hill west of the fort with furniture they had bought in Buffalo.

With William Henry, or Willy, now walking and agency business growing, the couple needed more space. Among the buildings he had permission to build were a sawmill and a blacksmith shop. But the most important was to be an agency and home containing a total of fifteen rooms. The foundation and basement for the two-story building were laid in the fall of

1826. Named Elmwood for the grove of trees that surrounded it, its large windows would overlook the river. There would be rooms to receive the Indians, to store annuity goods and emergency rations, apartments for temporary visitors. The grounds would be laid out with fruit trees, flowering shrubs, flower beds and a vegetable garden, as well as walks and gracious arbors.

That winter the pair began producing the first Indian magazine in the United States. They had known from the first it would be a handwritten effort—Henry had produced such a manuscript magazine in his youth—but they intended to circulate its few copies to friends such as Lewis Cass in Detroit and interested parties in New York City.

When Jane's second son was stillborn, she suffered serious physical and mental distress; for a time she lingered near death. But in December 1825 they sent out *The Literary Voyager,* No. 1. It was to average twenty-three pages in length, much of it in Jane's flowing script. The editor told his readers he wished to keep alive "the spark of literary excitement," in so remote a spot. It began by describing the Chippewas' history and Lake Superior, included short pieces on superstitions, allegories, customs, a profile of a Cherokee missionary. It featured prose and poetry by Henry, who used a variety of pseudonyms, and Jane, who wrote under the names of Leelinau and Rosa.

Leelinau promised to offer the stories and songs her mother taught her; both Waub Ojeeg and Ozha-guscoday-way-quay were renowned for their skill with words and Jane displayed similar talent. But Rosa included a poem, written to sisters on a garden walk after a shower, that spoke to her grief and loss. She spoke of "pain and care—the tear and sigh," but described it as buffered by "faith's bright calm" until the tears are banished and one is shown "light and peace." The second issue in December she wrote the poem "Resignation," in which she tried to teach her heart that faith could lead to calm acceptance when cherished hopes and dreams had "forever flown." In

January she contributed the Ojibwa legend of the robin's origin, a continued history of the rivalry between their people and the Sioux and a parable of an Indian flirt. Henry began to include essays on the Ojibwa language, which he was finding contained both subtlety and irony. It was, he wrote, "one of the most pure, clear and comprehensive forms of Algonquin."

As January closed, Rosa wrote lines of awaking to the beauties of nature, and in No. 7, February's first issue, "Lines Written Under Affliction," acknowledged that God's bitterest cup is mixed with sweetness, and that a landscape pleases only because 'Tis the union of sombre and bright."

Producing copies of these many-paged manuscripts was a chore, transcribing it a "drudgery," Henry openly admitted, but it did make the winter days pass. Henry had formed a local reading society of the Johnstons, a few officers and wives and other locals, where he read each issue before circulating it to others. Although it remained in manuscript form, Henry gave it the subtitle of *"Muzzeniegan,"* an Ojibwa word meaning printed document.

Still grieving in mid February, Rosa's "Lines Written Under Severe Pain and Sickness," indicates distress so great that "when Thy goodness wills that I should die/ This dream of life I'll leave without a sigh." Later that month her husband of five years wrote a poetic tribute on Jane's birthday, celebrating her "manners chaste/ Virtue tenderness and taste"; even its lines acknowledged their lost babe. In the next issues, Jane continued to share her knowledge of her people's legends and customs, and paid tribute with a fiery defense of her grandfather, Waub Ojeeg, who had died before she was born.

But in the issue of March 28, 1827, the couple shared a new personal grief. In little more than a day's time, two-year-and eight-month-old Willy, whose bright chatter had filled their lives, was dead of croup. Numbly they trekked a road cut through banks of snow to the garrison burying ground. John Johnston read an English service, and they lowered the small coffin into the frozen earth. Both parents, the sutler, the army doctor and friends fashioned their sorrow into poetry. Jane, now bereft of two sons, reined her grief into the disciplined lines of "To My Ever Beloved and Lamented Son William Henry." The eleven-verse lament opens with

Who was it nestled on my breast,
And on my cheek, sweet kisses prest
And in whose smile I felt so blest?
Sweet Willy.

Henry decided God had taken their son because they had loved him too much, erecting an idol in their hearts. Jane's faith, always central to her life, did not question why, only sought to accept what was and look forward to a painless afterlife. She closes

But soon my spirit will be free,
And I my lovely son shall see,
For God, I know, did this decree.
My Willy.

Finding their own home too redolent with memories, the couple again moved in with the Johnston family, where they managed one more small issue of the magazine, making fifteen in all. Jane's writing would not be published again, except as reprints in the works of her husband and other writers, but Henry kept a file of *The Literary Voyager* which he shared with interested readers for many years.

Life went on. In October they moved into the baronial agency and soon cradled a new daughter, Jane Susan Anne, whom they called Janee. With blond hair and blue eyes, she looked more European than Indian. A year later son John Johnston completed their family. Henry's welcome was restrained; his determination to maintain an emotional distance made easier because the boy's dark features were a marked contrast to their lost Willy, whom they both openly continued to mourn. Jane embraced this new opportunity for motherhood and her spirits revived, although she was plagued with ill health the rest of her life. As her mother had imbued her with Ojibwa culture, Jane spoke only Ojibwa to her children.

She was constantly called on to play hostess for elaborate dinners when the table might be laden with several meats, multiple side dishes and a wide choice of desserts. In 1828, Henry was elected to the Michigan Territorial Legislature, which met in Detroit. He spent most of the spring and summer away from home on business, returning in time to witness John Johnston's death of fever. Jane, who had always turned to her father for advice and counsel, felt his loss keenly. In the next few years, she was often left to care for the household while Henry went out on repeated expeditions to make peace between Sioux and Ojibwa and further explore the territory.

In the summer of 1832, Jane waited at home, nursing the children, who had been vaccinated for smallpox, as her husband combined his agent's duties with a side trip to satisfy his obsessive search for a wilderness icon. Married nearly ten years, he took time to write her about his adventures, addressing her as "My dearest," and expressing wishes for her welfare. She shared his excitement when he returned from the 2,800-mile expedition with plants, shells, copper and other minerals, and all manner of "queer and doubtful things." He had collected voluminous information on the native people, plants and wildlife, but the news that made his chest swell with pride was that he and fourteen others, in five small birch bark canoes, had finally discovered the source of the Mississippi River. It was a small lake the Indians had long known, but he renamed it Lake Itasca and the feat secured his national reputation. He immediately set about compiling a book describing the discovery, neglecting to mention the Indian guide who had led him there.

Then, in May 1833, Henry uprooted the family, deciding he could function better at the agency to the south on Mackinac Island, adjacent to the straits that separate Lake Michigan and Lake Huron. He could be in closer contact with the sources of power in the states, and the children would have the advantage of more schooling.

Leaving her family behind, Jane settled into the older, less-convenient agency house, situated on the side of a limestone bluff above the more populous village of Mackinac. Her health continued frail, but her husband's growing prominence made the agency a social center. A central door bore a brass knocker inscribed "United States Agency," and windows were framed with wooden shutters fastened with an "S" crafted of iron. In high-ceilinged rooms lit by candelabra, Henry and Jane entertained local military officers, fur company factors, government representatives and visiting scholars. Both parents took part in schooling their children, who also attended a missionary school on the island. Jane's dichotomy of culture must have caused her pain and seems to have caused the couple increasing difficulty.

Jane's 56-year-old widowed mother was providing for her family by manufacturing maple sugar and drying fish for winter. The Ojibwas' ancestral lands offered less and less game and even the best hunters brought in little meat. Jane could no longer offer her mother close moral support, and Henry was more and more insistent that she rely exclusively on his advice and counsel. He was becoming more and more involved in white politics and organizations as he sought to advance his standing in society. More than once, he admonished Jane to cling to him and the Christian god, not her Ojibwa family. He had undergone a religious conversion, and his letters were lectures on her lack of Christian piety and her failure to consider her husband her only true "guide, philosopher and friend." Jane's social skills, at which he had marveled in earlier years, now seemed lacking the refinement needed to deal with a "broad & mixed circle of society."

Though she seemed never to satisfy her husband, people who read Jane's poetry and prose sought her out, making the difficult journey to the edge of the wilderness to talk with her.

English author Anna Brownwell Jameson, whom the Schoolcrafts provided a room during her 1837 visit on Mackinac, found her visit with Jane delayed until she was strong enough to see guests. Jameson noted the "touching expression of her countenance, (which) told too painfully of resigned and habitual suffering." She noted "the exceeding delicacy of her health and the trials to which it is exposed." Jameson considered Jane's choice of language to be "pure and remarkably elegant" during their first hour-long conversation, was won over by Jane's charm and vowed to be her friend.

In 1838, Reverend Peter Dougherty found Jane "feeble" when he drew her out of her room which she had not left "for some time." Her visitors may not have known that in 1836 Jane was stricken with whooping cough. Her treatment was the standard prescription of laudanum. In the next two years her correspondence to her husband and brother-in-law included requests for more of the narcotic. Yet Jameson found her "genuine," refined, with an "enthusiastic and enlightened interest" in her people. She also noted her loving relationship with her two children. Reverend Dougherty described Jane as "all frankness and kindness," with "a highly cultivated mind."

During these years the family retired to Detroit for the winter, where the children attended school in 1836-37. Henry was increasingly absorbed with establishing the Michigan Historical Society, the Algic (derived from Algonquin) Society, and the *Michigan Journal of Education*. He successfully campaigned to be appointed superintendent of Indian Affairs as well as Ojibwa agent and his work load increased. For months at a time, the weakened Jane was left to cope with the household and children while he traveled on official duties, cultivated political friendships and visited his publishers. ". . .day after day I drag out a wretched miserable existence . . .," Jane wrote Henry, ". . .debilitated & worn down as I am—wanting all the little nameless kind attentions, so necessary to the comfort of a nervous invalid. . . . ." Her husband, more and more self-absorbed, was seldom there to answer her needs.

On November 18, 1838, Henry ushered his children and a reluctant Jane onto a steamship bound for New York City. Their mission filled Jane with dread. Henry hoped to find medical help for his ailing wife, but he also intended to leave his two children in Eastern schools. Although he had long decried sending Indian children off to boarding school, he enrolled eleven-year-old Janee in a private school in Philadelphia and left nine-year-old John at an academy in Princeton. Jane had once shared the tale of an Ojibwa mother whose Sioux husband took their children back to his people, leaving the mother bereft and inconsolable. That woman had been her great-grandmother. As Jane parted from her children and turned toward home, she penned a poem about her feelings. Usually her heart was eager to be home; this time it is still

With my sweet, lovely daughter and bonny boy dear.
And Oh! What's the joy that a home can impart
Removed from the dear ones who cling to my heart.

Once home, she tried to temper her grief by forming a Maternal Association of mothers who prayed for their absent children. Over the years, the children's letters were her major comfort, although John, who adjusted poorly to the change, wore out his welcome in school after school.

Her ambitious husband continued to publish, bringing out a two-volume set of Ojibwa legends, *Algic Researches,* in 1839. It opens with five and one-half pages of "General Considerations," then nine and one-half pages of "Preliminary Observations." On page 26 a note offers the information that the enclosed tales were "interpreted by various individuals, among whom it is deemed important to name: Mrs. Henry Schoolcraft . . ." and ten other people, including the Johnston family.

In 1841, political enemies combined with his own errors of judgment resulted in Henry's dismissal from his positions as agent and Indian superintendent for Michigan. That September, he moved the family to New York City, where the children enrolled in school. He wanted to seek a publisher in Europe, and in early May 1842, he sailed from New York City. The children were boarded out with a teacher in Albany and Jane went to visit her younger sister, Charlotte, who lived with her husband, Archdeacon William McMurray, at Dundas in Ontario. During Henry's many absences, Jane had often expressed the doubt that she would live to see him again. This time she did not. Perhaps her physical ailments and the mental anguish of trying to maintain her place in two worlds exhausted her strength at last. She died in Dundas on May 22, at the age of forty-two. Henry erected a gravestone for her there when he returned from Europe.

When Johnston and Janee finished school, Henry brought them to live with him in New York City. Five years after Jane's death, he married an intelligent but aggressively unpleasant Southern woman named Mary Howard, a champion of slavery. She wrote a thinly-disguised novel of Henry's life, in which she claimed Jane's continuing illness was drug addiction. One can only weigh *The Black Gauntlet*, published with Henry Rowe Schoolcraft's knowledge in 1860 as he lay partially paralyzed, dependent on his wife to relay his thoughts, against Jane's devout belief in her Christian duty and the lack of any indications that her visitors from the outside world found her anything but clearheaded.

Henry went on to publish his compilation of Ojibwa history and vocabulary in which Jane played so central a role, as part of his *Historical and Statistical Information Respecting the History, Condition and Prospects of the Indian tribes of the United States* in six volumes from 1851 through 1857. No place does he give Jane or the Johnston family credit for their contributions. Only in *A Personal Memoir of a Residence of Thirty Years with the Indian Tribes of the American Frontier*, which was published in 1851, did he describe his love for and debt to Jane and the Johnston family. Increasingly paralyzed, he died in 1864 at age seventy-one.

Of Jane's children, John Johnston Schoolcraft lived a troubled life and died of Civil War trauma in 1865. Janee advanced in her schooling and married the half-brother of Mary Howard Schoolcraft, who opposed the marriage. Mary deplored the contamination Janee's "hateful" Indian blood brought to the Howard line, and neither Janee nor her brother were friendly with their stepmother. Jane Howard Schoolcraft became a well-loved teacher and church member in her community of Charleston, South Carolina, but none of her children survived infancy.

The Ojibwa people and their lifestyle in the beauty of the Lake Superior country did not become well known to the American public through the scholarly writings of Henry Schoolcraft, though even today they remain a valued source on the tribe. It was in 1856, when poet Henry Wadsworth Longfellow published a small book containing *The Song of Hiawatha,* that the Ojibwa/Chippewa entered the American imagination. Longfellow studied Schoolcraft's research for three years and created the epic story of the hunter Hiawatha, born "On the shores of Gitche Gumee/By the shining Big-Sea-Water," of his love for Minnehaha, of the heaviness of the white man's footsteps, and the leader's eventual retreat westward "To the land of the Hereafter!" The printing presses could not keep up with the demand for the book.

Jane Johnston Schoolcraft's influence led her husband to his prolonged study of the Indian way of life. Her contributions are today a respected source of Ojibwa history and culture. The Johnston home in Sault Ste. Marie, Michigan, is a National

Historic Site, and Elmwood , where Jane and Henry spent both their happiest and saddest years, is scheduled for restoration. The Michigan State University Press reprinted *The Literary Voyager or Muzzeniegun* in 1962, and Jane's work is the subject of study in college courses.

Jane Johnston Schoolcraft Bibliography

Books

Brenner, Richard G. *Indian Agent and Wilderness Scholar: The Life of Henry Rowe Schoolcraft,* Clark History Library, Central Michigan University, 1987.

Osborn, Chase S. and Stellanova Osborn. *Schoolcraft – Longfellow – Hiawatha,* Jacques Cattell Press, 1942.

Schoolcraft, Henry Rowe. *Algic Researches,* 1839. (Reprint, Menton L. Williams, editor, Michigan State University Press, 1956.)

-----. *Archives of Aboriginal Knowledge,* Six volumes, J. B. Lippincott & Co., 1860.

-----. *Narrative Journal of Travels Through the Northwestern Regions of the United States,* 1834. (Reprint, Mentor L. Williams, ed., Michigan State College Press, 1953.)

-----.*Personal Memoirs of a Residence of Thirty Years with the Indian Tribes of the American Frontier.* Lippincott, Grambo and Co.,1851.

-----.and Jane Schoolcraft. *The Literary Voyager or Muzzeniegun,* 1826-1827 (Reprint, Phillip P. Mason, ed., Michigan State University Press, 1962.)

Articles

Buffalohead, Priscilla. "The Sault Ste. Marie Ojibwa and Henry Rowe Schoolcraft," www. famousamericanindians4homestead.com/thehenryschoolcraftstory, 2004.

Jameson, Anna Bromwell. *Winter Studies and Summer Rambles in Canada,* Excerpt reprinted in *Michigan History Magazine,* v. 8, (1924):140-69.

Mason, Philip P. ed. "Introduction," *Schoolcraft's Expedition to Lake Itasca,* Michigan State University Press, 1958.

Parins, James W. "Jane Johnston Schoolcraft," *Dictionary of Literary Biography, Native American Writers of the United States,* v. 175, Bruccol: Clark Layman Gale Group, 1997.

-----."Jane Johnston Schoolcraft (Ojibwa), (1800-1841)," *The Heath Anthology of American Literature,* Paul Lauer, ed., Fourth Edition, Houghton Mifflin Co., 1998.

Ruoff, LaVonne Brown. "Jane Johnston Schoolcraft (Obahbahmwawagezbegoqua) (1800-May22, 1841)," *Dictionary of Native American Literature,* Garland, 1994.

Severud, Timm. "Jane Johnston Schoolcraft (Obahbahmwawageezhagoquay) Biography," *Canku Ota,, A Newsletter Celebrating Native America,"* Issue 85,(2003).

Timeline of New York History, 2005.

Helen P. Clarke

Montana Historical Society

Chapter Two

WHY WOULD ANYONE BE ASHAMED?

Helen P. Clarke, 1843-1923
Blackfoot – English

When 3-year-old Helen Piotopowaka Clarke left Fort Benton, the primitive adobe fur post on the upper Missouri River, about 1849, she was scarcely cognizant that the parents she bid a tearful goodbye had been brought together by the soft pelts that made her small dress.

A few missionaries in black robes had come seeking souls, and Helen was one of those they had baptized. But the only treasures most white men recognized in the vast expanse of high plains, rivers and mountains frequented by the Blackfeet people were soft, gleaming furs.

Helen's mother, Cothcocoma, was a Pikuni (also known as Piegan) of the Blackfeet nation, daughter of a tribal leader. But her father, Malcolm Clarke, was a Scottish-American, from an educated, military family. Clarke insisted his children by Cothcocoma receive good educations. There was no school at the fur post so Helen Clarke was being sent east to the town developing around Malcolm's boyhood home of Fort Snelling, Minnesota Territory. She would grow up in the home of Malcolm's sister, Charlotte Van Cleve, in the town that would become Minneapolis. She and her brothers were soon enrolled in convent schools.

For years, Helen saw her fur trader father only once a year. He arrived, she remembered later, a compelling presence who "flashed on us like meteors, bright, beautiful and brilliant." He had West Point training, experience in the Texas fight for independence, and courage and skill that had awed even the Blackfeet. On first coming to know him in his twenties, they had named him for the white lodge pole which was the center of attention in the sacred tipi. The Pikuni often searched long and hard for a timber perfect enough to fulfil this role, and such a pole was revered as strong medicine. Later they had renamed him Four Bears after he killed thirty grizzlies in a month's time, four before breakfast one morning. It was a name no Blackfeet had ever earned.

The bearded trader had a gift for oratory and could hold an audience spellbound; his children reveled in the tales he told of narrow scrapes with the Indians. Helen loved to hear the tale about the time some Arickara attacked Fort Benton when she, a baby, was outside the walls under the care of a young Indian boy. A fellow trapper had snatched her from a Ree's grasp as her father raced through zinging arrows to carry the Indian boy to safety.

Malcolm Clarke traveled up and down the upper Missouri, from Fort Union to Fort Benton, befriending, cajoling, advising and intimidating as needed to get the Blackfeet's valued furs. His marriage to Cothcocoma was his entry into tribal councils and he treated her with the respect she deserved. After Helen was born, Cothcocoma gave him two sons, Horace and Nathan, and a daughter named Isabel. During these years he also married a mixed-blood wife named Good Singing who added another daughter, Judith, to the family.

The Blackfeet had had little tolerance for whites since the incursion of Meriwether Lewis four decades before. Subsequent epidemics of small pox had reinforced their hostile stance. But Four Bears thrived on the challenge of keeping their goodwill. He told his children about the time he had been invited into a council where Chief Calf Shirt admonished him for not paying enough for their furs. Yet, he complained, his people continued to sell to Four Bears under the spell of "that silvery tongue of yours." Puzzling, the chief said, "There is something about you which steals away our hearts against our inclinations."He added, "I say to you I hate the white man, but I hate you less than any white man I ever knew." Clarke attributed his persuasive powers to his special "medicine," but he had the good sense to acknowledge the chief's warning and pledged with several puffs on the passing pipe to heed their concern. His willingness to listen and learn kept the difficult relationship alive.

By the time Helen returned from school in the mid-1860s, that remote and primitive world she left as a child was totally changed. Her father had left the fur trade in 1864 to homestead a ranch about ninety miles southwest of Fort Benton, and he wanted his family together once more. Helen, "Nellie," to her family, and just over 20 years old, had grown into a tall, graceful woman with upswept hair and deep-set black eyes; she had absorbed social skills along with the classics.

The mountains and valleys upstream from Fort Benton were caught in the throes of rampaging growth. Prospectors moving east from the Idaho mountains first picked up nuggets of gold from Alder Gulch, 200 miles southwest of the fur post in1863; Virginia City sprang into being and became capital of what was soon named Montana Territory. Then word racing like a grassfire before a Montana wind ignited hopes for new strikes in Last Chance Gulch in a town that became Helena, 100 miles closer to Fort Benton.

All manner of prospectors, dreamers and schemers were rushing into the gold fields; settlers were hurrying to claim land under the 1862 Homestead Act; merchants were throwing up buildings and unpacking crates to supply the new population. The docks of the Clarke's old Fort Benton home sagged with the weight of scores of steamboat loads of miners and machinery, followed by merchants, gamblers, saloon keepers, farmers, ranchers, and all their paraphernalia. Thirty-one boats forced their way up the Missouri to the old post in 1866. By then the town had turned from housing fur traders to serving as head of navigation on the newly important river. Suddenly there was need for roads, for stagecoaches, for freighting wagons, for crime-bashing vigilante committees – for government.

Malcolm had chosen the Little Prickly Pear Valley for his cattle ranch. The creek emptied into the Missouri from the west, seventy-five miles south of Fort Benton, and Malcolm settled in the southern end of the canyon. His experience and reputation earned him a seat on the new Edgerton County Board of Commissioners.

The Clarke ranch home had several rooms; one was set aside as Malcolm's office. As Helen settled into life on the ranch with her brothers and little sisters, Isabel and Judith, she had new opportunities to appreciate her father's strength and wisdom. And she became reacquainted with her mother, her childhood feelings of love and warmth growing to adult affection and respect as she observed Cothcocoma's generosity and devotion to her husband.

Helen had been conditioned from childhood to admire and value the Blackfeet culture, and she eagerly accepted their continual presence at the ranch as they brought their problems to Four Bears and he counseled with them in his office. But it was a relationship as prickly as the cactus that studded their pastures. As more and more settlers and miners poured into the countryside, and the army built Fort Shaw and Fort Ellis to protect them, the fragile relationship was strained to the breaking point. Helen knew Blackfeet were being attacked by settlers without cause and she could understand their striking back in return.

In the spring of 1867, a cousin of Cothcocoma's visited the Clarke ranch with his family. In keeping with Indian culture, the ranch was always open to visits from family; whatever they had was willingly shared. Helen remarked later that they had been happy to welcome Netuscheo and his family. But before the week was out, all the horses, Clarke's and Netuscheo's alike, were stolen from the corral. Tracking the herd, it became obvious the thieves were white men. Embarrassing as this was, the deed took on darker tones when, late in the day, the Clarke's horses were evidently released to wander home. Only Netuscheo's remained missing. There was nothing dearer to an Indian than his horses, and that his white host could not keep his herd safe from white men was the severest breech of hospitality. In the early morning hours, the angry brave crept away, taking Clarke's horses, and the family's valued spy glass with him.

The next day, Malcolm (Four Bears) and his son, Horace, rode to the Pikuni village to demand restitution. One of the first things they saw was Netuscheo riding Horace's favorite mount. The impulsive young rancher rushed him and struck the thief a sharp blow with his riding crop. Hot words flew and Horace was quickly surrounded by furious young braves promising death to Horace. Malcolm, still strong and virile despite his white head of hair, reflexively reached for his gun. But surrounded as they were, he knew firing would start a bloodbath. He stood in helpless fury. Luckily tribal elders rushed to the scene and pushed the young warriors away. A shaken Horace was free to leave camp with his father. But the angry Four Bears took time to publicly shame Netuscheo by calling him "an old woman."

Malcolm visited the village that next winter and tried to smooth things over. Netuscheo apparently forgave Four Bears, but he said his heart was still sore toward Horace. Mountain Chief, a long-time friend of Clarke's, told the rancher how the Blackfeet had hardened toward the whites. "I despise the whites," he said. "they have encroached on our territory; they are killing our buffalo, which will soon pass away; they have treated my nation like dogs. . . ." Only because Four Bears had married into the nation and had children, "we suffer you among us." On that slender thread of confidence, the relationship continued.

But animosities grew steadily, and during the summer of 1869, the antagonists traded atrocities. A wagon train out of Fort Benton was attacked and a man killed. Before it was proved the attackers were Crows, not Blackfeet, Mountain Chief's brother and his teenage companion were maliciously shot down on the streets of Benton. Within a month, raids on ranches had killed several settlers and more than 800 horses were stolen, including Clarke's. But ranchers in the territory were accustomed to risk, and as dusk gathered on August 17, Helen and her 52-year-old father sat engrossed in a game of backgammon. Their concentration was interrupted about nine o'clock when visitors knocked at the door.

Netuscheo and three braves, one Mountain Chief's son, another named Owl Child, were invited in and greeted Cothcocoma and her aunt, Black Bear, and the rest of the family, including Horace, whom Netuscheo embraced. The Indians asked about Helen's 17-year-old brother, Nathan, who was away hunting the horses, and both groups expressed regret that he would miss the Indians' visit. The family emphasized the sorrow and regret they felt about the two Blackfeet killed in Fort Benton, and Helen's little sister, 8-year-old Isabel, chattered about the love Eastern-educated Helen felt for the Blackfeet people until Netuscheo told her to hush. The men shared a pipe and supper with the family. Also present was a young Blackfeet boy, Malcolm, who Helen's father intended to educate. As the meal settled and the men smoked again, the visitors said they had come to return Clarke's horses stolen three years before by Blood Indians, and also to invite the rancher to again serve as their trader. It was an invitation Clarke had been working for, one which would provide the family with needed extra income.

The family was cheered by the double dose of good news. Helen felt a bit uneasy about the way Netuscheo kept his hands under his cloak, and the restless pacing of Mountain Chief's son as he roamed the room handling family possessions. But when Owl Child asked Horace to go out with him to identify the family horses and her brother hesitated to search for his gun, she urged him not to bother with his weapon. "What's the use of a fire arm? You are with a friend," she counseled. Malcolm Clarke echoed Helen's advice, and the two men went out the door. Clarke continued a conversation he had begun with Netuscheo, and in a moment the two men stepped outside to speak in private.

It seemed to Helen, "the door had scarcely closed," when she heard the sound of a gunshot. Young Isabel tried to rush outside but Netuscheo pushed her back in, claiming the shot was only a little target practice by the boys. Then another shot sounded. Helen's mellow mood drained into terrible fear, and weak-kneed, she hurried toward the back of the house, where she found the room empty, the door wide open. Outside, horses with Indian riders galloped wildly across her astonished view. There seemed to be dozens—hundreds—riding like demons. She breathed a quick prayer for mercy.

Just then Horace cried out from the distant darkness. "Father, I am shot!"

There was no answer from her father. Helen had a terrible feeling that he would never answer again. As she started to run toward the sound of Horace's voice, she called to Isabel to check on their father. She found Horace, blood streaming from a head wound, a few hundred feet from the house. Her great-aunt Black Bear was at her heels and as the two women dragged Horace toward the house, Helen beseeched Horace to tell her who had shot him. "It was not the Indian who went with you that shot you! On, no," she cried desperately, wanting the villain to be anyone but Blackfeet. "It was a Penned d'Oreille was it not?"

"No, Nellie," Horace managed. It was the Blackfeet.

Still unable to believe their own relatives had attacked them, she asked again. But Horace had no reassurance to offer. Their own family had violated their trust. He asked for his father. "Gone," Helen answered with dreadful certainty.

Finally at the house, the two women pulled and lifted Horace over the threshold and gathered blankets to make him a bed on the floor of Malcolm's office. His pulse grew weaker as blood continued to gush from a bullet that had gouged a course through his face from his right nostril to his left ear. He had played dead for Indians searching his body, and Helen was afraid that soon would be reality if the bleeding continued. At last she remembered tobacco could staunch bleeding and grabbed up a bucket to fill at the stream. Then Isabel bravely said she would go. The child returned shaken but unharmed after an encounter with Mountain Chief's son. The Blackfeet were still nearby; soon they would return for plunder. While Helen worked over Horace's wound, fashioning a poultice of tobacco, Isabel again ventured out to search and found their father's body a few feet from the house. Helen, Cothcocoma and Black Bear pulled him inside. As they lay him in his room, the little girls began to cry and the two Indian women to wail their grief.

Helen, close to breaking down herself, turned on them and snapped, "It is no time for crying. It must be stopped. Pray!"

"Yes, Nellie, pray!" the wounded man muttered.

The elderly aunt slipped out to try to reason with their attackers or find help, and Helen and Cothcocoma were suddenly aware that the doors still stood open. Hurrying to close and barricade the lockless doors with furniture, Cothcocoma passed a window. A bullet pieced the pane but it missed its target. Seeking safety where there was none, the women decided to move Horace from Malcolm's office—familiar ground for the Blackfeet—into Helen's adjoining room, which they had never entered. Grabbing up the bedding, tobacco, water, a hatchet and a knife, they hurried through the door and Cothcocoma nailed it shut.

For an hour they sat in rigid silence. Then the attackers returned. The women and children listened as they broke open trunks, shattered mirrors, broke furniture and talked of who would be killed, who taken prisoner. In Helen's room breathing all but ceased. There was Netuscheo's voice, and that was Mountain Chief's son, that one Bear Chief, and finally they heard Great Aunt Black Bear. By then, they were on the other side of Helen's door. "Horace is alive. . . and he is in that room." It was Netuscheo's voice, his weight against the door panel. As it creaked, Horace rose shakily and raised the hatchet.

"Oh, no." It was Black Bear's voice. "He is dead. The Four Bears is dead. Have pity!" She begged them to go, then dared to say more. "The man murdered tonight was your best friend. You have committed a deed so dark, so terrible that the trees will whisper it." Before daylight, she told them, a hundred men would come to avenge the rancher.

After a moment, Bear Chief agreed. There was enough blood shed. He had no desire to war on women and children. All agreed but Netuscheo, who left reluctantly, calling back his promise to return and finish off the family huddled inside. They listened as the men gathered up some family possessions —sugar, flour, clothing—destroyed others and left, herding the ranch's cattle before them. They also took Black Bear, whom Netuscheo whipped for crying.

Again they sat in the dark until about one in the morning when Horace suddenly vomited blood. Panicked, Helen thought his end was near. She dared to light a candle to tend him, but moments later a noise frightened them and they blew it out. Wrapped in sorrow and exhaustion, they endured another three hours. Helen sat holding Judith as Isabel leaned against her on one side and the young Indian boy clung to the other. She had never been so weary. Yet, she could not rest. Now and again she used her spare hand to help Horace apply tobacco and water to his wound. Every moment she expected the attackers to return. She quailed when she thought how easily they could fire the ranch house.

When at last the sky lightened about five o'clock, she and Isabel hesitantly opened the front door and started for help. A sudden motion brought their hearts to their throats, but it proved to be only their dog, Jack, whom they'd thought dead, who came barking and whining to jump on them and lick their hands. But they had to go three-quarters of a mile to reach an outbuilding where a ranch hand should have been available to help. Nerves taut, they walked a narrow path between bushes and hedges, Helen aware of every trembling leaf, imagining an attacker around every bend. Finally they reached the house, found the employee still had a horse, told their tale of terror and sent him first to Horace and then to Helena for a doctor. She and Isabel continued walking to the next ranch house, hoping the women there could come with them and dress Horace's wounds. But when the women heard about the killing, they were too frightened; they refused to accompany Helen and Isabel back home. Feeling terribly alone, the sisters returned to the home that could never again seem a haven.

Soon it was midday and her younger brother Nathan was still out there somewhere. She was afraid to think why he had not returned. Half-heartedly, Helen tried to straighten the mess, but there was so little left she soon gave up the effort. It was another three hours before the doctor and an army major arrived to provide help. At least the news about Horace's wound was good; his facial bones were not fractured and recovery seemed probable. Nathan arrived shortly after, and Helen walked to meet the teen at the corral to prepare him for what he would find in the house. The shocked young man looked long and hard at his dead father and vowed vengeance. Soon after, the house filled with friends and food, light and warmth.

For her part, Helen did not blame the Pikunis. She knew the majority of the tribe wished Malcolm Clarke no harm. Many of them grieved with Cothcocoma and his children. The family buried their husband and father on August 19, 1869, at the edge of Little Prickly Pear Canyon.

But the populations of Helena and Fort Benton were not so forgiving. Terrified at what might happen next, they demanded the military find and punish those guilty. Sixteen months later Major Eugene M. Baker left Fort Ellis, south of Helena near Bozeman, with four companies of the Second Cavalry intent on punishing the Blackfeet. The force, augmented by infantry from Fort Shaw, marched through temperatures forty degrees below zero and came upon a Pikuni village on the upper Marias River at dawn, January 23. Despite the fact that a chief ran out waving papers identifying him as a friend of the whites, they attacked and killed 173 Blackfeet, fifty-three of them women and children. Some of the survivors, suffering smallpox, were left without lodges, food, clothing, weapons or horses to sustain them through the winter. It was only later the army learned this was not Netuscheo's band; this village was not involved in Clarke's murder. Horace, bearing the scar of his wound, and Nathan, who had vowed vengeance, were part of the attacking force.

Just over three years after her father's murder, Helen learned of Nathan's death in a drunken fight with another half blood. He was stabbed and died without saying a word. The letter stated baldly that Nathan was the aggressor and his opponent acted in self-defense.

By then Helen and her sisters had moved back East, where they lived with her Aunt Mary Lincoln in Cincinnati. Trying to turn her back on her Indian heritage, Helen decided to attend a New York school of drama. She was a handsome woman, with large, expressive, if somewhat haunted, black eyes. In later years a friend would address her as "Woman With the Shadow Eyes." She was also blessed with a "deep, thrilling voice" that could carry to the back rows of a theater. With a persona a friend later described as "intense (and) vivid," she soon was appearing on New York stages, and in the next few years she accumulated a scrapbook of clippings describing her performances in London, Paris and Berlin. She loved Shakespeare, and the German Kaiser was impressed enough by her performance of Lady Macbeth to send her a complimentary letter. Another performance was commended by the Queen of the Netherlands. Helen worked on the same stage as the famous Sarah Bernhardt, and knew other theater luminaries such as Maude Adams. But after the first rush of success, her career in the limelight began to pall. "I was too much of the self to become great," she explained later. "I could not forget that I was Helen Clarke and become the new being of imagination."

Her Blackfeet name, Piotopowaka, meant "Bird That Comes Home," and in 1875 she returned to her family at Fort Benton and began teaching school.

In April 1876 she moved to Helena to teach. With a population of about 4,000, the booming town was now the territorial capital. As placer mining produced diminishing returns, Helena miners turned to the silver and gold imbedded in quartz and the huge equipment necessary to extract the ore. With fire in the wooden jumble of original buildings along the gulch a recurring threat, people began to build more substantial stone homes on higher ground. The town had organized a library, and theatrical troops occasionally visited the Wood Street Theater.

Helen was hired by attorney Wilbur Fiske Sanders, who had been active on the Vigilante Committee ten years earlier. He was now president of the Montana Historical Society, active in politics and on the Helena School Board. He became a lifelong friend. Helen was to live in the Sanders' family Italianate-style mansion on North Ewing Street for many of the next twenty years. A warm, bright woman described as "independent in thought and character," she was elected superintendent of schools for Lewis and Clark County in 1882. Reorganized under a new name, it was the same county her father had served as a commissioner. Helen Clarke was the first woman elected to public office in Montana Territory. Reelected in 1884, she continued to work for good schools, contributed greatly to the Montana Historical Society, was a devout Catholic and a leader of the community.

Through these years she maintained close contact with her mother and brother, Horace, who were living in Highwood, near Great Falls. Cothcocoma had never recovered from the shock of losing her husband, but Horace had married and was raising a family. The Blackfeet living on the reservation itself were finding life increasingly hard. Each year there were fewer buffalo to supplement their annuity rations, yet the government failed to increase those rations. Winters in the early 1880s were brutal, and as many as a quarter of the Blackfeet, weakened by starvation diets, died of disease and hunger. The people whom her father had respected and feared, who had been the scourge of the northern plains, were pushed north of the Missouri River and against the eastern slope of the Rockies, a threat to no one but themselves.

Throughout these years Helen remained single, despite suitors attracted by her beauty and vitality. One wrote her a passionate letter from San Francisco in 1884, referring to their daily correspondence and his impending visit to Helena. He closed "Goodbye my darling Piotopowaka, I love you and will love you always." What happened to that relationship is unknown, but Helen had difficulty believing she could be loved and accepted for who she was. She was convinced no man could accept her Indian ancestry without feeling he was her superior, a condition she would never tolerate. She chose to remain "Miss Nellie."

With the passage of the Indian Allotment Act in February 1887, Helen's life turned a new direction. Montana—indeed, the whole West—was entering a new era. The Great Northern Railway connected Helena with the East that year, after it swallowed more sections of Blackfeet land, and steamboats traveling the Missouri began to disappear. Montana miners now dug for silver and copper, rather than gold, and mining magnates and town fathers built substantial, two- and three-story stone or brick homes. The county commissioners of Lewis and Clark County began erecting a huge, multi-story, stone building topped by a landmark clock tower, where the territorial legislature met until statehood was granted in 1889.

The mind set of the United States Government—and many educators and missionaries who worked among the Indians—was that the Native Americans would best survive if they forsook their own lifestyles and took on all attributes of the white culture. So altered, they could be absorbed into the white world. The reservation, the tribe, the group, the band were to be broken up and individuals given their own land to farm and make their living. Some Indians sincerely believed it would free their people from arbitrary, heedless, hurtful decisions by the bureaucracy. Others saw the policy as destroying their last sanctuary.

On October 3, 1890, President Benjamin Harrison appointed Helen Piotopowaka Clarke a special agent to help the Indians chose their individual allotments. She was assigned to work with five different tribes attached to the Ponca Agency in Oklahoma Territory. The forty-three-year-old teacher had to support herself, and she saw the assignment as a way to help the Indian people. Helen's mother was now making her home on the Blackfeet Reservation, and Helen left Montana for Oklahoma and the Ponca Agency to see what she could do there. Commissioner of Indian Affairs Thomas Morgan had recommended her, believing that her "being identified with the Indian race" would give her influence other agents could not exert. Morgan knew she would need something special, as both the Otoes and the Poncas were nearly unanimous in violently opposing allotment. They "refuse to even listen to any argument advanced" in allotments' favor, Morgan had written the summer before.

Helen commenced her work with the more agreeable Tonkawa tribe on May 19, 1891, and was finished by the end of June. Her approach is illustrated in a letter she sent the Pawnees:

"I was sent here," she wrote, "because Congress has made a law. This law requires you all to take your allotment—every man, woman and child in the tribe. Turn whichever way you may, there is no path that leads around this law. You must do as it tells you. . . ." She tried to use illustrations with which they could identify. "You may say that you won't do it but that will do no good. It would do just as much good for you to tell the sun to stop shining at this moment. If you told the sun to stop shining it would shine on just the same as if you had said nothing. Just so, this law will go on and do its work."

It was a hard message to deliver to people who once had the sweeping prairie to wander almost at will, who had fed themselves from its bounty, who had enjoyed the closeness with their kin of all ages in their villages, whose hands shaped themselves to the stock of a rifle, not the handle of a plow. They had seen their land whittled and slashed away to fragments of what they had first been promised. Now they were to be tied to 160 acres per family man, with lesser amounts to single persons and children. Even that portion came with strings. They could not sell it for twenty-five years, could not lease it without government permission. Those clauses were put in to protect their holdings, but the restrictions meant government agents still had the final say over their lives.

Helen next moved on to face the Otoes, knowing their outspoken opposition influenced the other tribes. The Otoes told her to leave their reservation. Instead, she proceeded to survey the lands. They threatened to kill anyone who dared take the first allotment. They threw away the stones left to mark plot boundaries. It was a long, hot July, but by August she could identify the three men most responsible for the resistance. Agent D. J. M. Wood ended the destruction of survey markers with threats of punishment, and Helen continued to cajole, pressure and persuade the reluctant Otoes. She found it "a very unsatisfactory and discouraging business," but by September 7 she had made 108 allotments.

She was the only woman employed as allotment agent in Oklahoma Territory, and now a local Interior Department supervisor openly questioned the wisdom of giving the assignment to any woman. Indian leaders seized on the possibility that her work was not authorized and demanded a male agent. Others were against accepting allotments no matter who filled the role of agent. She moved among them, clad in the high collared, puff-sleeved long dresses of the time, often living in a tent, working from daylight to dark for eight dollars a day and travel expenses. It was her job to pacify and persuade the reluctant members. She tried to be their friend. She promised to talk with each one of them as she went about the reservation, to respect their manhood, to help them make the best of an inevitable situation. But there were endless difficulties and complications. One correspondent wrote her of his heartbreak when the wife with whom he had taken land decided she wanted to marry another man. Since she was an Omaha, and their system was matriarchal, he was afraid she could take the land. "I call on you to help me," he pleaded.

Helen's days were filled with distressed Indians who looked to her for answers she could not give. A contemporary newspaper article praised her as a "remarkable native genius" whose success "is valuable as an indication of the latent capacities of her race." But she found it hard to stay positive in the face of so much despair.

She worked among the Otoes until November 23, having satisfied 122 recipients who had chosen their plots and assigning lands to sixty-five elderly and orphans. About 100 men insisted on waiting the four years the law allowed before surplus land would be sold to non-Indians. Another eighty educated men adamantly maintained they wanted no land. Deciding she had done all she could, she moved on to the Pawnees. "The work of allotment must necessarily be slow," she advised her supervisors. She was willing to spend the necessary time. She tried to keep everything ready so that when an Indian was finally ready to accept allotment she could "clinch the nail on the head." Months turned into years. By August 1894, she was writing, "I am working among a people whose very soul abominates anything tending toward civilization, and they are bright enough to see that allotments mean civilization." But bitter as the people were, she believed, "I have in a great degree overcome this feeling so that they now listen to me when I talk and go among them."

But other agents did not have her endless patience, and even she admitted that "the sooner the Indian selects his land or has it assigned, the better for him and for his race." On August 31, the Commissioner of Indian Affairs ordered her to complete her work by the end of December, assigning lands to all remaining Indians. By then 375 Indians were land holders of record—a record they continued to protest.

Helen returned to Montana, and in the next two years she buried her mother and helped the Blackfeet negotiate a treaty that sold a portion of the spectacular mountainous western side of their reserve for what would become Glacier National Park. Two years later she was once again working with the Otoes. They were still resisting, still protesting. "We can live like white men without cutting up our land. . . ." a spokesman insisted; it was their right to hold the land in common.

Helen was glad to be working again, but she faced her duties "with a heavy heart," knowing persuasion would never move the Otoes. However, in late April 1899, she reported 440 allotments had been made. The Otoes' case was considered closed, and she applied for further work with other Indians, describing herself as "a struggling woman without fortune," who needed the job. "Therefore I beg you sincerely not to let me remain idle." Hoping for work on the Wichita Reservation, she secured endorsements from powerful Montana citizens, but to no avail. The Wichita situation was considered too "difficult, if not dangerous for a woman." Helen was ordered to return home.

For the first two years of the twentieth century, she lived in San Francisco, supporting herself as a teacher of elocution. Readily accepted at first, she then found herself shunned. Eventually, she learned that a Helena correspondent of the *San Francisco Chronicle* had submitted a story declaring Helen was ashamed of her Indian ancestry. The correspondent claimed she had left Helena because she was being ostracized by local gentry. The article described her as living in "dire poverty," barely eking out a living. Once Helen knew the source of the slander, she was able to refute it and gradually rebuild her damaged business, but when she visited Helena in September 1903, the untruth still upset her. She gave a lengthy interview to the *Montana Daily Record*, telling all its readers just how she felt about her father and her Indian mother.

"Now, as a matter of fact, I am far from being ashamed of my origin. . .," she told the reporter, describing her father's place as an early settler. Of Cothcocoma, she said, "she was a good woman, a good wife and a loving mother, and why anyone should be ashamed of her is more than I can comprehend."

Helen also forthrightly refuted the description of her poverty. "I have always managed to make an honest living," she said, and have always "numbered the very best people of Helena among my friends." She was, in fact, visiting friends in Helena on the way to the Blackfeet Reservation, where she was already engaged in the cattle business. She had registered a brand in 1895 and perhaps payment she received in June 1902 for damages done by the Pikunis in 1869 helped build her herd. She had moved to the reservation and lived with her brother Horace in Midvale since that time.

Helen settled into ranch life, reveling in the beauty of the mountain scenery and always keeping the latchstring out to her many visiting friends, writers, artists, musicians and historians. They gathered often to enrich themselves with her warm hospitality, bright mind, wide knowledge and large library. She enrolled in the Blackfeet tribe in 1909 and her people frequented the large frame Clarke bungalow to get help with a problem or share a story. She and Horace helped Helen Fitzgerald Sanders compile the Blackfeet legends for *The White Quiver*, published in 1913. Sanders dedicated the book to the two of them and said of Helen: "To her the Indians turn in time of trouble and perplexity; in hunger, sickness and distress knowing that in her they have a wise counselor, an unfailing friend and an intellect of which their nation may be proud."

Helen had not always experienced this appreciation of her intellect; she knew she had been disdained as a half-breed both on and off the reservation. But she tried to attribute the prejudice to ignorance and take pride in her individuality. She lived at Midvale (later East Glacier Park), content at the foot of the "grand old Rockies" until she died of pneumonia at age 76 on March 5, 1923. In his eulogy, a Catholic priest described her as "the friend the soul is ever seeking, the friend that understands, the friend that sympathizes, the friend that knows our weakness and still loves us, the friend that sees only the best in us." A mountain peak in the Two Medicine Valley at Upper Two Medicine Lake is named for her, its thousands of appreciative viewers mostly unaware of the talented, courageous woman it honors.

Helen Clarke Bibliography

Archival Collections

Helen P. Clarke Papers; SC 1153, Montana Historical Society
Application for enrollment on the Blackfeet Census.
Clarke, Helen, Letter to Pawnees, n.d.
Crazy Arrow, David. Letter to Helen Clarke, July 6, 1892.
Halligan, Rev. Father. "Eulogy for Helen P. Clarke," March 7, 1923.
Wells, Toni. "Interview with Helen Clarke," MS n,d.

Miscellaneous correspondence.
Clarke, Helen P. Certificate of Death, Montana Bureau of Vital Statistics.
Sanders, Helen Fitzgerald, "Introduction,"*The White Quiver,* Duffield, 1913.
6685, Record of Brand, General Recorder of Brands and Marks, State of Montana, Dec. 28, 1895.
Turvey, Joyce Clarke, "My Clarke Connection," MS, April 4, 1976, Montana Historical Society.
-----."Helen Piotopowaka Clarke," and "Clarke History," MS
Conversations with Joyce Turvey Clark, John L. Clarke Western Art Gallery & Memorial Museum, East Glacier Park, Montana.

Books

Chapman, Berlin B. *The Otoes and Missourias; A Study of Indian Removal and the Legal Aftermath,* Times Journal Publishing Company, 1965.
Malone, Michael B., Richard Roeder and William L. Lang. *Montana, A History of Two Centuries,* Revised edition, University of Washington Press, 1991.
Shirley, Gayle. *"Helen P. Clarke,"* More Than Petticoats; Remarkable Montana Women, Two Dot Press, 1995.
Schultz, James Willard. *Blackfeet and Buffalo,* University of Oklahoma Press, 1962.
Toole, K. Ross. *Montana, An Uncommon Land,* University of Oklahoma Press, 1959.

Articles

"Claim Allowed At Last," *Choteau Montanian & Chronicle*, (June 27, 1902).
Clarke, Helen P. "Sketch of Malcolm Clarke," *Montana Historical Society Contributions,* v. 2, (1896):255-268
"Color No Barrier; Brains Count Against the Handicap of Dusky Skin," Montana Historical Society clipping, n.p,, n.d., circa 1889.
"Death of Helen Clarke Recalls Tragedy of the Murder Of Malcolm Clarke By the Blackfeet Fifty Years Ago," Montana Newspaper Association Inserts, *Grass Range Review,* (Mar. 23, 1923).
"Helen Clarke Dies At Glacier Park," *Helena Independent,* (Mar.6, 1923).
Hoffman, Jack. "Helen Clarke always returned to Montana and her Blackfeet people," *Glacier Country History,* 1994.
Lange, Minna N. H., "Helen P. Clarke," *Inter-Mountain Educator,* v. 18, n. 10, (1923).
"Malcolm Clark's Daughter Was Treasure State Heroine," Montana Newspaper Association, (Dec.11, 1939).
"Maligned by a Newspaper," *The Montana Daily Record,* (Sept. 26, 1903).
Rowell, Agnes Sherburne. "Malcom Clark, Fur Trader, Was a Power Among Blackfeet Indians," *Great Falls Tribune,* (May 15, 1932).
Swallow, Joan. Photograph, *The Women by the Editors of Time-Life Books,* Time-Life Books, 1978.

HELEN P. CLARKE

Turvey, Joyce Clarke, "Helen Piotopowaka Clarke," "Horace John Clarke," "Major Malcolm Clarke," *History of Glacier County,* Glacier County Historical Society, 1984.

"Walking Tour of Helena's Historic Courthouse Square and Central Neighborhood," Montana Historical Society pamphlet, n.d.

Nebraska State Historical Society

Susette LaFlesche Tibbles

Chapter Three

BRIGHT EYES SPEAKS OUT

Susette LaFlesche Tibbles, 1854-1903
Omaha – French-American

Susette LaFlesche, born into the Omaha nation in 1854, may have had dim memories of being welcomed into the fellowship of her people as she passed from babyhood and took on her own, unique personality. The tribe had embraced each child with this rite as long as anyone could remember. The people faced a future that looked to be a drastic change from their past years on the west side of the Missouri River in country the whites had named Nebraska Territory. But the old ways were their anchor in a vastly confusing world.

It would have been in the greening spring, after the meadow larks had begun to sing, that children who had reached the age of three or four years came with their parents to the Sacred Tent where the priest waited. Introduced at the wide tent door by her mother, barefoot and carrying her new moccasins, Susette would have been led in alone to the central fire, where the priest sang an invocation to the winds and lifted her so that she stood on a stone, the symbol for long life on earth. Turning her to face each of the four directions, he sang of the strength she would gain by facing the varied winds of life, strength that would enable her to live long and well. Then, as he placed the new moccasins on her small feet, he announced to the hills, grasses, trees, creeping things and assembled people that this child had thrown away her baby name. From now on she would be known as Inshta Theamba, the words describing the shining, black Bright Eyes with which she observed the world. None present could have dreamed this small girl's name would someday be known throughout the United States.

With their home ground immediately beside the Missouri, the favored route west for trappers and traders nearly fifty years before, the Omahas were long accustomed to the white man's presence. Inshta Theamba herself had white ancestry from both her mother's and father's heritage. Her mother, Mary Gale, was the child of Doctor John Gale and an Omaha/Iowa woman, Nicomi. Her father, known as both Iron Eye and Joseph LaFlesche, was the child of French trader Joseph LaFlesche and a Ponca woman. Joseph had lived for some time in St. Louis with his father, spoke fluent French, and had seen enough of white civilization to decide the Omahas had no choice but to embrace the new ways white settlement was thrusting upon them. Joseph was one of the two principal chiefs of the Omahas, and was instrumental in the tribe's agreeing in 1854 to move onto a small reservation several miles north of the village where Inshta Theamba was born.

The Omahas, like other Missouri River tribes, including their close relatives, the Ponca, had long lived in permanent villages made up of substantial earthen lodges. In the villages, they could winter, then plant crops on river bottom land before ranging out to hunt buffalo.

But when they moved onto the tree-topped bluffs that made up their reservation lands, Joseph had led his followers in the construction of frame houses like the white man's. He built a large, two-story residence, using the first floor for a trading store and housing his family on the second. He and the others, known as the "young man's party," bore the derision of more tradition-minded men, who called their dozen houses ranged along a road Joseph laid out just south of the Presbyterian Mission, "the Village of the 'Make-Believe' White Men." The traditionals organized themselves into two villages north of the mission.

Yet, Joseph never wavered in his conviction that his people must choose the white road. With a steamboat landing at the foot of the bluff, a sawmill, gristmill, blacksmith shop and other Indian agency buildings nearby, and the new town the whites called Omaha a day's ride down the river, he could see no other future. He fenced off 100 acres of bottomland, divided it into garden spaces, and planted crops. The people continued to get much of their sustenance from buffalo, which they brought back from semiannual hunts. However, this resource, which had seemed inexhaustible, was shrinking fast. Joseph fulfilled his obligations to become tribal chief, which required considerable skill, effort and sacrifice. But when it came time to give the marks of honor he had earned to his children, he refused. His sons were not to have pierced ears; his daughter Inshta Theamba and those who came after her were not to be tattooed—marked with a hollow, blue four-pointed circle on the throat and a red dot on the forehead. Convinced his children would someday have to mingle with white people, he said, "I determined that they should not have any mark put upon them that might be detrimental in their future surroundings."

Inshta Theamba walked to the three-story, stone mission to begin classes when she was 8 years old. Even though it was but a short walk to her father's house, she was required to live in the school with twenty-six boys and fourteen girls. They slept on the upper floors, went to class on the lower.

At the school, her dress was cloth, long and full, covering her all over and held together by buttons. She could not talk like her family talked, could speak only English. If she did not know the right word, she must say nothing or risk being punished. They learned how to speak, read and write; they learned how to work with numbers. When she could, she stole a little time to draw—a newly discovered talent. But the girls devoted time to sewing, cooking, cleaning and other chores of the home. The boys spent much of the day learning to use farming, carpentering and smithing tools. Saturday was the only day in the week could she be at home with the family, dress in her own clothes and eat familiar food. The next day it was back to the mission school to spend the day learning about the white god.

Joseph was a Christian, but he had five children with Mary and three with his second wife, Tainne. In that, he was not too different from the Mormon men who lived nearby. He insisted all his children attend school and learn to read, write and speak English, even though he could not.

Susette, as she was known in school, proved to be a bright student and she eagerly absorbed all that was offered until the school closed when she was 14. Too old to attend the government day school which replaced it, she resorted to learning what she could by reading from the small library of missionary William Hamilton. He had a Bible, of course, and a volume of Shakespeare; she read church history, and in desperation, newspapers that had been used to wrap mission parcels.

Luckily, by 1872, one of the mission school's former teachers had become headmistress of the Elizabeth Institute for Young Ladies in Elizabeth, New Jersey. Remembering Susette's intense desire to learn, she raised funds among her friends to offer the girl a scholarship.

New Jersey was a world away; she would be the first of her people to go so far for learning. The 18-year-old girl traveled by train to the small city just across the water from the docks of New York City. She was shy by nature, and there must have been lonely days in the next three years so far from home and family, but she excelled in her studies and graduated with honors in 1875.

Suzette was 21 and eager to put her knowledge to work back on the reservation. But the Omaha agent rejected her application to teach in the Omaha school. Frustrated, bored and feeling out of place in the family she had so longed to see, she realized she was no longer quite an Omaha, yet certainly not a white person.

Needing to contribute to the family income as well as use her mind, she researched laws governing the reservations and discovered a statute she could employ. Thus armed with white man's law, she countered, going over the agent's head with a letter to the commissioner of Indian affairs. She reminded him that the agent could not legally refuse her, because reservation rules required that qualified Indians be given preference over white applicants. With no effort to mince words, she told him it was a "farce" to educate and supposedly civilize Indians if they were then denied positions where they could use their knowledge. She closed with a threat to take her story to the public by means of the press. "They might listen," she warned.

It took persistence, and an unauthorized, illegal trip off the reservation to get a Nebraska teaching certificate, but in 1877 she was hired as a teacher at what was now a day school. The $20 salary was only half that of the white teachers, but it was a start. She also began a Sunday school and bought an organ with her own funds so the children could be exposed to music. For the next two years, she was absorbed with her classes, but she was also aware that the buffalo hunt attempted in 1876 was a frightening failure, and the once prosperous people were poor, hungry and ever more dependent on what their land could produce.

Larger events were soon to pull her from her classroom and give new direction to her life. In late May of 1876, Susette and her father traveled west to bid their relatives, the Poncas, goodbye. They had been counseling with Susette's uncle, White Swan, Chief Standing Bear, and his brother, Big Snake, for months. They were trying to get the government to reverse a ruling ordering all the Poncas to leave their homes and farms on their reservation just above the Niobrara River, near the Nebraska/Dakota Territory border. A peaceful people who had never resisted white encroachment, the 700 Poncas had developed successful farms, built 236 frame houses and were transforming their culture as the Indian Bureau desired. But a mistake by government negotiators had given their land to the Sioux, and despite their protests, the army was escorting them by force south to Indian Territory.

When Susette and Joseph found the caravan, they listened as their relatives poured out their despair at leaving everything they had built, their anger at the injustice, their worry for their young, elderly and ill who were being trailed through cold spring rains, bottomless mud and swollen streams. Two already had died and Prairie Flower, the young daughter of Standing Bear, lay shaken with coughs in her father's wagon. But the Omahas could offer only sympathy; the troops' bayonets prodded the Poncas on south.

For the next two years, Susette tended to her students. The school was housed in a rickety old building that leaked rain and snow. Her requests for books and supplies went unanswered. A deep slough, which students had to wade in warm weather and cross perilously on ice in winter, lay between them and the school building. Requests for a bridge were ignored. Day after day she faced a roomful of shivering children, often with feet raw and bloody from the walk to school. Yet the students continued to come.

Reservation officials turned an indifferent eye on other Omaha problems. More and more often, she was asked to write letters to the president or Interior Department officials, cataloging the wrongs and injustices Omahas experienced every day. Soldiers took their women and dishonored them, white men stole their horses with impunity, and tribal money was spent foolishly or disappeared into white pockets. Distrusting the agent, the people would call Susette out to a spot on the prairie, where they could compose the message without fear of interference, then carry it to a nearby town to mail.

Through it all, the welfare of the Poncas in the south was never far from her mind. The hot, barren territory was known for its many paths to death. And the Omahas had their own fears that a similar arbitrary action might well strip their own lands away and send them to Indian Territory, which they called "The Land Toward the Heat." On March 4, 1879, they learned just how bad that could be.

Susette entered her father's house to find several families of exhausted Poncas, fearful, famished but almost too weary to eat the food Joseph's wives immediately prepared. Standing Bear's wife, his only living daughter and his two orphaned grandchildren were among the thirty refugees who were seeking shelter with Joseph. The 60-year-old chief told how they had lost so many in the hot country it was difficult to count—almost one in four met death. Little Prairie Flower had died before they even reached the hot land, and once there hunger had weakened the disheartened people and malaria easily carried them away. When Standing Bear's last living son lay dying, he had asked his father to take him home to the Niobrara country so that his bones could rest with their ancestors. The promise given, the grieving chief had put his body in a box, hitched up his wagon and, joined by a few other families in two additional wagons left the reservation the night of January 2, 1879. More than half the group were women and children. In a few days, their small supply of rations and $20 cash had run out; the frigid weeks plodding north since had turned them into desperate scavengers and beggars. Several were too ill to stand. Would the Omahas shelter them until they could go on to the Niobrara?

Joseph did better than that. With the time for sowing crops upon them, he gave the Poncas land, seed and tools to grow food so they could sustain themselves, promising to accompany them to the Niobrara after the weather warmed.

On March 23, Standing Bear was in the field sowing wheat when the soldiers came. Their agent had reported their absence from Indian Territory. They were arrested for leaving without permission. Ignoring Standing Bear's protests that they had harmed no one and broken no laws, despite the pleas of Joseph and Susette that the Omahas welcomed their relatives to their land, the troopers bound one man who refused to move on his own and herded the wailing group together for the march to Fort Omaha. They would be kept there until they could be shipped back to Indian Territory. The Omahas signed a petition offering to give part of their land to the Poncas, but government officials remained adamant that they must return south. The Poncas' case seemed hopeless.

Susette and her family heard that some whites were speaking up for the Poncas. An article in a newspaper, the *Omaha Herald,* called their imprisonment "criminal cruelty." A group of Omaha ministers petitioned Secretary of Interior Carl Schurz to free them. When Schurz did not respond, the group filed suit in the United States District Court of Nebraska against the army and General George Crook, commander of the Platte District, charging that the government was depriving the Poncas of their rights.

That Indians *had* rights was a revolutionary idea, and Susette soon heard from the reporter who had instigated the protest. The tribe received a letter from a Mr. T. H. Tibbles, asking that someone write a statement in the Poncas' behalf. He had enlisted two lawyers who were volunteering their time to argue that the Poncas had rights under the Fourteenth Amendment not to be imprisoned or detained without due process of law. The lawyers needed information to build their case. Susette was asked to write what she knew about their situation.

On April 29, Susette picked up her pen. What she knew about their unjust treatment, hardships and suffering would have filled scores of pages, but she concentrated on the salient facts. She explained briefly, unemotionally, that the Poncas were the Omahas' relatives, that she and her father had visited them on their journey south, and heard Standing Bear and other chiefs deny they had ever agreed to go to Indian

Territory. For the most part she let the Poncas speak for themselves. She enclosed a statement, signed by seven chiefs, that she had helped them write two years earlier after they had visited Indian Territory and witnessed the shocking illness and poverty of people there. They had written in good faith to the president of the United States because they had been unwilling to believe the government would allow a peaceful people to be driven from their homes and forced to live in a hot country without resources. She also included a telegram sent by the chiefs to the president at that time. "Please answer, as we are in trouble," they had said in their wire, ". . . with heart and spirit broken and sad."

They had waited for months; their answer had come at the end of bayonets. Two years later, the Poncas were still appealing for justice.

Yet now there seemed to be hope. On May 1, 1879, Susette, her father, and Willie Hamilton, son of the missionary, were in Omaha for the Poncas' trial. For two days they listened as lawyers argued whether the Poncas must do the government's bidding or whether they were people with the right to go where and when they pleased. She would long remember the lengthy, excited arguments of the lawyers, the reasonable, dignified stance of Standing Bear as he asserted he was a child of God, driven from his homeland to a place his people could not survive. He said he was only a man who had done no white man harm, trying to take his dead son home for burial. This son was the one Standing Bear had sent to school to learn English, the one chosen to help their people find their place in the new future. That hope was gone now, but he wanted to save what remained of his family.

They had all waited ten days for Judge Elmer Dundy's decision. When it came, it was revolutionary: Indians were persons before the law; they could not be forced back to Indian Territory because they had chosen to separate themselves from their tribe and live as white men lived. It was a victory heavy with irony. To achieve their freedom they had to deny their heritage.

By then Susette had met Thomas H. Tibbles, some fifteen years her senior, and been engulfed by his passion, energy and pervasive self-confidence. A sometime preacher, the leonine crusader with a bronze complexion and long, thick black hair, had fought for the rights and welfare of slaves, of blacks, of starving settlers. He was currently serving as assistant editor of the *Omaha Herald.* He was busily publicizing the Poncas' plight with dispatches to newspapers in the East and enlisting the support of community leaders. And he asked Susette's father to take the young teacher down to Indian Territory to ascertain the welfare of the other Poncas still there.

Visiting the Poncas in the south, Susette was shocked that six shacks and a few scattered tents had replaced more than 200 houses. The Poncas' twenty-five yoke of oxen were all dead. Only 100 scrawny horses were still alive out of a herd of 700. A people once rich with household furniture, farming equipment and tools now had none. Most disheartening of all was the sight of grave after grave after grave.

Returning with Chief White Eagle's eloquent request for help, written in her firm hand, Susette found Tibbles was trying to organize a lecture tour of eastern cities to raise funds to help the Poncas fight the government and buy land to live on. Later that summer, the Omaha Ponca Relief Committee asked her to come tell about the Poncas' troubles at a large Omaha church.

Horrified by the thought at first, she was gradually convinced she must talk before this large meeting of white people. When she stood trembling before them, it was a long moment before she could make her voice work. But when she began to speak, her voice gained strength and the words began to flow. As she told of Standing Bear's suffering, the tremor in her voice was not fear, but emotion. The audience absorbed every word, then erupted in applause and cheers. Women wept. Men shouted their support. Tibbles, ready to leave with Standing Bear to spread the Poncas' story, had a new idea. He said he must take Bright Eyes with him to interpret the words the chief spoke to eastern audiences.

She quailed at the thought of facing any more audiences and was desperate to refuse. But the Omahas felt their position in nearly as much jeopardy as the Poncas. The Indian Commissioner had said the Omahas must go south. A bill had been introduced in Congress to move the Omahas from their reservation to Indian Territory. Closer to home, the Nebraska Legislature had long promoted the removal of all Indians from the state. Now, lawyers the tribe consulted warned them the certificates of land ownership given to them after their treaty was signed had no legal standing. Her father reluctantly agreed that she must go. With grave misgivings, led by Tibbles, chaperoned by her 22-year-old-brother Francis (Frank), she set out with Standing Bear in October to tell of the Poncas' desperate plight.

Traveling by train, first to Chicago, then to Boston, the three spoke in churches, meeting houses and private homes. They shook hundreds of hands at receptions and were honored guests at luncheons and banquets. Gradually Susette learned to at least partially control her trembling, to project her low but compelling voice to the back rows. Susette wore simple black dresses, a white collar framing her attractive face, often wearing a bonnet. She stood in marked contrast to the six-foot-two-inch chief, draped in his ceremonial garb of red-and-blue blanket, with a necklace of grizzly bear claws draped across his blue shirtfront. It was a costume he wore only on the platform; audiences preferred the picturesque image. In addition to interpreting for Standing Bear, Susette discovered she had her own story to tell. At each meeting she delivered a speech she had written. Reporters took down long segments of her speeches, and newspapers were soon describing Susette's refined, intelligent, sweet but passionate presentations. Their story began to reach people who had not heard them in person.

Early on, the papers chose the Indian name she had been given in the Turning the Child ceremony so many years before. Readers heard about Bright Eyes, sometimes even Inshta Theamba, not Susette LaFlesche. Frank was referred to by his Omaha name of Woodworker.

In Boston, they were welcomed by the mayor, city council, and other prominent citizens. Standing Bear, speaking for his people in his own language, was an articulate man, and Susette sometimes had to search for the words to accurately portray his deep feelings. In the midst of the great city, looking into the street from her hotel, Susette was enthralled by the flow of people up and down the street, going where and when they liked. Knowing she and Frank were even then subject to arrest for being off their reservation, she marveled that these people could go anywhere—even to Europe if they pleased—without fear. It was because they were recognized and protected by the law, she concluded with new insight.

After the warm welcome, buoyed by new hope, both Standing Bear and Tibbles received stunning news. Standing Bear's brother, Big Snake, had been killed by troops as he resisted arrest out in Indian Territory, and Tibbles learned that back in Nebraska, Amelia, his wife of eighteen years, had died. The men bore their sorrows privately and continued scheduled appearances. The city was aroused and they found supporters in editorial offices and pulpits.

At one of their many receptions with leading citizens, Susette met a woman whose intense blue eyes dominated a face topped by a high brow line and anchored by a prominent chin. Well known for her skills with a pen, writer Helen Hunt Jackson heard the Poncas' story, met the odd foursome that made up the Ponca delegation, and quickly took up their cause. She began writing in the Indians' behalf, a labor she would continue until her death five years later. She traveled with the group, pressured newspaper editors to attend their talks and publish her accounts of their activities, and developed a deep friendship with Susette. Another new friend of import, white-haired poet Henry Wadsworth Longfellow, declared Susette his Minnehaha and praised her "simplicity, fluency and force" of speech. Another woman, anthropologist Alice C. Fletcher, was drawn to the group, struck up a friendship with Frank, and began absorbing his wealth of knowledge about Omaha culture.

After a month, during which Susette had become the first woman ever to speak at famed Faneuil Hall, they left Boston. They had raised substantial money and won important friends; Boston leaders had organized a Boston Indian Citizenship Committee to press Congress for action. Tibbles, under the pseudonym "Zyliff," had collected all the documents from the Standing Bear case to be published in a short book titled *The Ponca Chiefs*. The book came out as Tibbles' party began appearances in New York City. In the book's introduction, Susette wrote that her people asked of the nation only a little thing, a simple thing, but a thing "endless in its consequences. They ask for their liberty, and law is liberty." It was the concept she had formulated her first day in Boston. She signed the introduction "Inshtatheamba."

In December and January 1880, New York and New Jersey newspapers were filled with favorable accounts of the delegation, as well as some attacks on their integrity. During an immensely satisfying appearance at Elizabeth, Susette spent time with Marguerite and Susan, her two younger sisters now attending her alma mater, and gratefully absorbed the pride her teachers felt at her accomplishments. She needed that boost in her spirits, because the almost-daily appearances, the stress of being continually in the limelight, the burden of knowing the importance of every word she spoke, and the drain of constant travel were sapping her strength. She endured as their itinerary took them on to Pittsburgh and Philadelphia, yet her most important appearance lay ahead.

On February 10, 1880, the four were in Washington, D.C., where they had to counter the testimony of Secretary Schurz, Commissioner Hayt, and other officials before a special Senate committee investigating the Ponca problem. Her testimony on February 13 was contested by the Omaha agent, who called her a liar; Tibbles was accused of misuse of funds and immoral conduct. But an evening with President Rutherford B. Hayes, sympathetic Senator Henry L. Dawes and their wives was encouraging, and Dawes' introduction of a bill returning the Poncas to their Dakota reservation brought hope. They continued the exhausting round of travel and speeches through the spring. On May 31, 1880, the Senate committee unanimously recommended that the government redress the wrongs done to the Poncas. The fugitives were assigned a piece of land near the mouth of the Niobrara.

Back on the reservation for the summer, Susette looked around her and realized how fast their old world was disappearing. She revived her abilities with the sketch pad and began recreating familiar childhood scenes. With the encouragement of Helen Hunt Jackson, she wrote a children's story, "Newadi," about her great-grandmother and Omaha life, which was accepted by *St. Nicholas* magazine.

Collaborating with the son of an Omaha minister, William Justin Harsa, Tibbles and Susette worked on a novel titled *Ploughed Under, the Story of an Indian Chief*. Susette wrote an introduction which put forth what she believed was the answer to all Indian problems. "Allow an Indian to suggest that the solution of the vexed 'Indian Question' is citizenship with all its attending duties and responsibilities, as well as the privileges of protection under the law," she wrote. "The huge plow of the 'Indian system' has run for a hundred years, beam down, turning down into the darkness of the earth every hope and aspiration which we have cherished. . . . What sort of harvest will it yield to the nation whose hand has guided the plow?"

It was the "Indian system" she fought, not the general white population. She loved the missionaries and her teachers, and she had made deep friendships with some white people. Yet she felt troubling ambivalence at times, when bitter memories of the Omahas' treatment came flooding back. Little children stripped of their identity—clothes, language, even their name – when they entered school, traditional leaders such as her father unilaterally dispossessed of their power, men cheated out of their horses and crops, tribal monies spent on worthless materials while real needs went unanswered. The numbing knowledge that their protests, if heard, often brought punishment instead of redress. Sometimes frustration overwhelmed her and she wondered if anything she did could make a difference. Yet, she had to try.

By fall, she and Tibbles were back on the lecture circuit and in March of 1881, Congress passed legislation providing 160 acres for every Ponca, either on their old reservation or in Indian Territory. After four discouraging years, some Poncas in Indian Territory had given up hope of returning home and signed away their Niobrara lands, believing a return home was "impossible, impossible, impossible."

The book Jackson had researched when they were together had come out that January. *A Century of Dishonor* was a seething indictment of the Indian Service and the government's continual betrayal of treaty after treaty, tribe after tribe. It caused a sensation and cries for the government to undo the wrongs perpetrated against Indians. Perhaps their work was done. Susette longed to return to the reservation and a quiet life with her family, time for study, to absorb new knowledge and serve her people. Yet the Omahas' title to their land was still not secure, and she remembered how discontented she had been on her return from school, wondered if she could really adjust to reservation life.

Widower Thomas Tibbles solved her dilemma by proposing marriage. With the exception of her brother, Frank, who distrusted the crusader, her family accepted the union. He was a hero to the Omahas and Poncas. If Susette had doubts, she put them aside; the two were married on July 23, 1881.

That fall, ethnologist Alice C. Fletcher, who had befriended them in Boston, arrived for a stay on the Omaha reservation and a six-week camping tour of nearby reservations. The newlyweds had been living in Omaha, in the house Tibbles had shared with his first wife. His two adolescent daughters were home from school in the East, their resentment of their new stepmother palpable. A move to a house on the reservation gradually eased the strain, as Susette's sisters and mother welcomed them and eased them into the family. Susette began to write more stories.

In a year's time, with Alice Fletcher's persistent pressure, Congress passed an allotment act that gave the Omahas their land in severalty. Fletcher returned in May 1883 with Frank LaFlesche, who was now working in the Department of Indian Affairs in Washington, and they began to apportion the land. Accepted as a friend and counselor, Fletcher urged the Omahas to choose better farming ground north of their current agency in the Logan Valley. Susette and her extended family moved there, near the new town of Bancroft. They broke the land to farm, with limited success.

When the final allotments were signed in June 1884, Susette felt they were safe at last. No white man could send them away to Indian Territory. Her husband, whom the family called "T. H.,"disagreed, holding that citizenship was the only answer. It was a source of conflict within the family, which was finding T. H. increasingly overbearing.

The Tibbles made several trips east to lecture. At times she was left at home with his teenagers as they struggled to understand each other. T. H. was not at heart a farmer and food was often scarce. After 1885, with the daughters in school in Lincoln, Susette accompanied her husband more often to work for Indian rights.

With the passage of the Dawes Act of Severalty in February 1887, which assigned 160 acres to the heads of families in all the tribes, the major threat seemed to be gone. The Tibbles were in Boston and joined in the celebration. Susette was more than ready to leave the stage, but T. H. received an offer for them to lecture on Indian culture in England and Scotland. After a troubled start when their theatrical agent resigned, Bright Eyes was invited to break a precedent against women speakers and address the congregation of a Presbyterian Church in London. Raised by a new agent to the status of princess, she vehemently objected to what she considered a repulsive title, but the British had no such aversion to royalty. Often, a whole roomful of people stood when she entered, and she did not know whether to laugh or cry at the contrast to the United States. For most of a year, up to five times a week, in London, Birmingham, Edinburgh, Glasgow and other cities, Bright Eyes talked about her people, their history and their future.

They returned in 1888 to a state inundated with grasshoppers. The plague was more than enough excuse for T. H. to lease their farm and take a position on the editorial staff of the *Omaha World-Herald*. They moved to Omaha, where Susette was no longer a princess, only a half-breed. The next year her father died and her youngest sister, Susan LaFlesche, became the first Indian woman to graduate from medical school. The world of her father, the world of her childhood had vanished. To the north, at Pine Ridge in Dakota Territory, the Sioux dreamed they could bring that old world back.

Late in 1889, the *Omaha World-Herald* asked T. H. to cover what excited editors across the country were terming a war. While the Omahas were feeling secure in their established homes, the Sioux in Dakota were starving. Their land was marginal farm ground at best, much of it craggy badlands on which even experienced farmers could grow nothing. They had no agricultural skills, little equipment and no interest in farming. They wanted to live by the hunt as they always had. With failed crops and reduced government rations, the desperate people looked for help. It came from the West: word of a savior, a messiah, who would come from the skies to create a new earth, green with grass, rich with buffalo and free of white men. They would be reunited with their dead loved ones. The Sioux were dancing a Ghost Dance to make it happen.

Frightened government employees and nearby residents, certain an uprising was in the making, called for help. Troops were gathering. T. H. was told to cover this new Indian war. He took Bright Eyes, as he always called her, with him. Accompanied by her sister, Marguerite's husband, Sioux-speaking Charles Picotte, the two talked with Sioux they had met on a visit to Rosebud nine years earlier. They were invited to stay in a Sioux home.

Certainly, there was unrest on the reservation, but the Tibbles could see no real danger. They felt pity, not fear, for the Sioux involved in the Ghost Dance religion. Witnessing the wistful religious dance, Susette could feel only sadness. When T. H.'s dispatches to the *World-Herald* portrayed a nonthreatening scene, the paper terminated his expense money and ordered him home. However, the couple decided to stay on, hoping there was a way they could help defuse the situation. But events quickly escalated beyond anyone's control.

With the atmosphere increasingly tense, Susette celebrated a somber Christmas in the Episcopal mission at Pine Ridge. Four days later, T. H. was following the trail of a large force of troops toward Wounded Knee Creek. After talking to the officers and assessing the situation, T. H. foresaw no trouble ahead in the troops' objective of taking Chief Big Foot and his people on into Pine Ridge, where they were already headed. He turned back to Pine Ridge to send his dispatch. He was still close enough to hear the firing—first a single rifle shot, then volleys, then blasts of artillery that rocked the hills for perhaps 20 minutes. Wanting to be the first with news of a fight, he hurried on through increasingly bitter weather toward the agency. Gathering what news he could there, he sent the first dispatch about the battle.

Fear drove the turmoil that roiled through Pine Ridge as news of a disastrous fight became known. A Sioux brave rode down the main road shouting a warning: the agency was going to be attacked. Frantic people tried to decide whether to flee, where to hide. They turned toward the agency for haven. But the agency was the target. Bullets could easily pierce buildings made of boards. As rifle fire began pinging into the grounds, Susette grabbed a box to stand on, and with her hostess interpreting, called to the women again and again to go to their log houses, which would be much safer. Shots continued to rain in most of the afternoon, but the warriors made no attempt to take the agency.

After the early dark of December 29, the wagon loads of wounded began to arrive. With the hospital full of army wounded, the injured Sioux had no place for shelter. They were left shivering in wagons until discovered by the Episcopal minister. He quickly ordered the chapel emptied of pews and the floor spread with hay. Susette, hurrying there with her hostess, was horrified to find forty-nine bloody patients, most of them women and children, in two long rows on the floor of the makeshift infirmary. Until early morning, working with Sioux doctor Charles Eastman, Reverend Thomas Cook and his wife, teacher Elaine Goodale, and some Indian women, Susette did what she could to help the suffering people. They were strangely silent, expecting the soldiers would soon come to finish them all. Eventually, when they understood they were to be helped instead of killed, the moaning and groans and cries added another layer of horror to the gruesome scene. Finally, an army doctor was free to help repair what mangled bodies they could.

It spite of their efforts, many of their patients died. The fight, now known as the Massacre at Wounded Knee, would be the final tragic interaction between troopers and the Plains Indians.

With Indian issues nominally settled, T. H. Tibbles' crusading mind looked for new causes to champion, and he focused on the hard life of the Western farmer. The Populist Party was organized in Omaha the next spring and T. H. quickly took up the cause of the oppressed farmer.

During the 1890s, Susette and T. H. lived for a time in Washington, D.C., to report on Congressional activities for a chain of newspapers, and after 1894, in Lincoln, Nebraska, where he was editor of the *Weekly Independent.* Her step-daughters were now grown and married and their relationships had warmed. She served as a writer for her husband's paper, as well as others, and wrote in support of Free Silver and Populist issues. These were not Indian issues, but the Omahas were never far from her mind, and in her Lincoln parlor a display of quill embroideries, bead work and a buffalo robe held equal place with souvenirs of her travels in the East and abroad.

She enjoyed time to sketch and paint, and in 1898, she collaborated with writer Fannie Reed Griffin on a book titled *Oo-mah-ha Ta-wa-tha,* or Omaha City. While she contributed material for many stories about the Omaha people and her family, she became particularly absorbed in illustrating the volume. There were two pages of full color, and each chapter began and ended with black-and-white sketches of Indian life. When the ninety-page book was published, it identified her work as "the first artistic work by an American Indian ever published."

Susette had never had a strong constitution and with her health increasingly fragile, they moved back to the reservation in 1902 and continued to write from there. She was happier there, close to her sisters. Susan was doctor for the reservation, and Marguerite was a teacher and former-field matron. Her family's tolerance for T. H. was always strained. Susette thought more and more often of the world her people had lost.

Watching them now, she knew many of them either leased or had sold off the allotments she and others had worked so hard to obtain. Many were sunk in alcohol and apathy. She wondered if walking the white man's road had gained them anything worth having. A once-prosperous people was impoverished and degraded. She was glad her father was not there to see it.

On the day she had received her name, the priest had tried to prepare her to face the varied winds of life; they had blown inconceivably strong, from alien directions. She had done what she could. It had seemed right at the time.

Yet, she remembered a young Omaha lawyer who had recently told her she had inspired him to get a law degree and work for their people. She thought of Frank, absorbed in his research with Alice Fletcher to prepare a comprehensive Omaha history that would preserve the rituals that seemed more and more important. She thought of the bright, inquiring minds of her nieces and nephews, and of the many young people now in school. Although there would be many hard years to come, she was leaving the heritage of her people in capable, caring hands.

She died on May 26, 1903, at age 49.

Susette's crusade for her people had brought her national celebrity which offered only fleeting satisfaction, but she had helped awaken the conscience of a wider world and set in motion reforms designed to help all Indian people.

Susette LaFlesche Tibbles Bibliography

Archival Collections

LaFlesche Family Papers, Manuscript Collections, Nebraska State Historical Society.

Books

Fletcher, Alice C. and Francis LaFlesche. *The Omaha Tribe,* 1911. (Reprint, University of Nebraska Press, 1972.)

Green, Norma, *Iron Eyes' Family.* Nebraska State Historical Society Foundation, 1969.

Griffen, Fannie, *Oo-ma-ha Ta-wa-tha.* Privately published, 1898.

Harsha, William. *Ploughed Under,* Fords, Howard and Hulbert, 1881.

Mathes, Valerie Sherer, ed., *The Indian Reform Letters of Helen Hunt Jackson, 1879-1885,* University of Oklahoma Press, 1998.

Odell, Ruth, *Helen Hunt Jackson,* D. Appleton-Century Co.,1939.

Sheldon, Addison. *Nebraska: The Land and the People,* Lewis Publishing Co., v. 1, 1931: 111.

Tibbles, Thomas H., *Buckskin and Blanket Days,* 1905. (Reprint, University of Nebraska Press, 1975.)

-----.*The Ponca Chiefs,* 1880. (Reprint, University of Nebraska Press, 1972.)

Wilson, Dorothy Clarke, *Bright Eyes,* McGraw-Hill Book Co., 1974.

Articles

Bataille, Gretchen M. and Laurie Lisa, ed.."Susette LaFlesche Tibbles" *Native American Women, A Biographical Dictionary,* Garland, 1993:182-83.

Clark, Jerry C., and Martha Ellen Webb. "Susette and Susan LaFlesche: Reformer and Missionary," *Being and Becoming Indian: Biographical Studies of North American Frontiers,* Dorsey Press, 1989): 147-59.

Diffendal, Anne P. "The LaFlesche Sisters," *Perspectives: Women in Nebraska History,* Nebraska Dept. of Education, 1984.

-----."The LaFlesche Sisters: Victorian Reformers in the Omaha Tribe, "*Journal of the West,* v. 33, n. 1, (1994): 37-44.

DiFrance, Charles O. "Some Recollections of Thomas H. Tibbles," *Nebraska History,* v. 13.n. 4, (1932): 238-247.

Green, Norma, "Four Sisters: Daughters of Joseph LaFlesche," *Nebraska History,* v. 45, n. 2, (1964): 165-176.

-----."LaFlesche Sisters Write to St. Nicholas Magazine," *Nebraska History,* v. 62, no. 4, (1981).

-----."Susette LaFlesche Tibbles," *Notable American Women,* Howard University Press, 1971:182-83.

Hardy, Gayle J., "Susette LaFlesche Tibbles,"*American Women Civil Rights Activists: Bibliographies of 68 Leaders, 1825-1992,* McFarland, 1993: 247-9.

King, James T. "A Better Way: General George Crook and the Ponta Indians," *Nebraska History,* v. 50, n. 3, (1969): 239-56.

Lake, James H. "Standing Bear! Who?" *Nebraska Law Review,* v. 60, n.3, (1981): 451-503.

Mathes, Valerie Sherer, "Iron Eye's Daughters: Susette and Susan LaFlesche, Nineteenth-Century Indian Reformers," *By Grit and Grace,* Fulcrum, 1997:135-52.

Omaha Daily Herald: Accounts of Standing Bear's Trial, May 3, 4, 6, 7, 13, (1879).

Susan Bordeaux Bettelyoun

Nebraska State Historical Society

Josephine Waggoner

Nebraska State Historical Society

Chapter Four

Telling Their People's Story

Susan Bordeaux Bettelyoun - 1857-1945
Brule Sioux - French-American

Josephine Waggoner, 1882-1942
Hunkpapa Sioux - Irish-American

Susan Bordeaux Bettelyoun

Susan Bordeaux Bettelyoun remembered the gripping sight all her life. When she was seventy-eight-years-old, living in a room of the Old Soldiers' State Home in Hot Springs, South Dakota, she could vividly describe the three twisting bodies she had stared at when she was eight. Two were Lakota Sioux, as was her mother. One was a Cheyenne named Four Antelope. He had hung there the longest, accused of stealing horses from the emigrants that thronged the trail passing Fort Laramie in the spring of 1865. They were accused, sentenced and hanged in short order. There was no appeal of Army justice. A ball and chain, and the leg to which it had been manacled until decay finally freed it, lay in a heap beneath the body.

On May 26, 1865, a second scaffold had been raised beside Four Antelope's. Two Oglala leaders, Two Face and Black Foot, were led up the hill. They had been accused of abusing a white woman who had been captured along the Little Blue River the summer before. Thinking to collect a ransom for returning the woman and her baby boy to her people, they instead were charged, sentenced and hanged with but a brief time to sing their death songs.

The hill drew the Indian and mixed-blood children who lived near the fort like a macabre side show. Susan remembered how a silver Mexican medallion that hung from a black scarf around Four Antelope's neck caught the sun as the wind swayed the bodies. It flashed "bright and glistening like a looking glass against the sun," she remembered later. The children could never get too close, as a sentry marched there daily, a rifle on his shoulder. Relatives of Two Face and Black Foot were also denied access to the bodies. The corpses were left as a warning and example for the Indians, as a feast for magpies and crows.

Even as a child she knew it was a shameful business. To die in such an ignoble manner was indescribably repugnant; to be left dangling as a show of power was a willful, aggressive insult. The incident was the beginning of a chain of events that would end Susan's carefree life on the Laramie plain. In later years, trying to tell the Lakota side of this and similar conflicts would become her obsession.

Susan's father, French-American fur trader James Bordeaux, had been an interpreter at Fort Laramie, and she had actually been born within the fort's complex of large white buildings. When she was born in 1857, Bordeaux was operating a trading post and ranch eight miles east of the fort beside the North Platte River, and her mother's Brulé family were constant visitors to his post. They were leaders of their band, the Tisaoti, who were recognized by the red-painted tops on their lodges.

Huntkalutawin, known as Red Cormorant Woman, had been a woman honored by her own people even before she married Bordeaux in 1841. She was a member of the Hunka order, the only honor society open to women. Her grandfather, parents and brothers were leaders of the Brulé.

With the trapping era all but over, Susan was living in a time of transition. A middle child of eight, she enjoyed their busy family life even as endless wagons filled with white people rumbled past along the Platte. They would stop in for a drink from the post's excellent spring, to buy supplies (after a strenuous argument about the cost) and perhaps to trade off a lame ox or a mare about to foal. Her father, whose rounded front was usually covered in a proper shirt, vest and jacket, reminded them you couldn't expect to buy at Independence prices goods he had freighted 600 miles. He gladly took worn cows, pigs, mules—whatever was too exhausted to go farther —off their hands.

But that was only in the summer months. After the weather cooled and the dust settled, Susan loved to listen to her grandmother, Gray Buffalo Woman, tell stories of her family's lives. She told of running frantically from cholera that spread death along the Platte River Road. They fled northeast toward the Paha Sapa, where the slopes were so dark with timber that the whites called them the Black Hills. A few in their band died each day, until by the time they reached the Niobrara River only she and her brother were left. When he felt the illness envelope him, he told her she would find other Brulés farther north on the White River. Then he dressed in his finest clothes and shot himself. Gray Buffalo Woman had struggled on through the snow until she found another band, including Lone Dog, the man she later married. A child who listened instead of talking, Susan took note of those around her, storing away tales she heard around the fire until sometimes she felt she had been there herself.

Bordeaux still bought furs from—and often housed, in one of his several buildings—trappers who worked the nearby mountain streams. Susan was in awe of their fur-clad presences, their unkempt hair hanging below their shoulders, and their beards so bushy she could see only their blue eyes peering out of wind-burned faces. She thought they looked like animals themselves, and she beat a "hasty retreat," if one stared at her too long.

Though her father was often gone on long trips east to sell furs and buy trade goods, when blizzards swept the prairie he was at home. Secure within the old but sturdy structure of cedar logs, he told stories, too, of his early years as a trapper, boating up the Missouri to Fort Union, and of a perilous trip carrying mail south to the post that would become Fort Laramie. Attacking Arickara Indians besieged the two men and killed his partner, but Bordeaux finally escaped and arrived safely.

He had later forsaken the trapping life for that of a prairie storekeeper. His closely trimmed black hair and mustache, and the gold watch chain swagged across his vest were more emblematic of a St. Louis businessman than a fabled mountain man, but Susan had no trouble imagining his adventures as a young man.

The story about carrying the mail was a family favorite and Susan soon knew it by heart, familiar with its smallest details. She had a gift of putting herself into such a situation, living it through her father's words. When she was an old woman and first saw the butte where her father had suffered through thirst, hunger and fear, and finally buried his young companion seventy-five years before, she was moved to sudden tears.

Bordeaux was only one of several French-American trappers settled in the area. Many had married Indian women and the families gathered often for social evenings. Usually someone brought out a fiddle and everybody danced. There could be a dance every week. Sometimes soldiers joined the fun, both as fiddlers and dancers, and Susan recalled in later years how "a number of half-breed girls, all dressed up in bright calico with ribbons in their hair and on their waists," could "fly around in a quadrille as well as anybody, stepping to the music in their moccasined feet." Little ones were not barred from the floor and Susan danced, licked stick candy and ate ginger snaps with many other youngsters while music and laughter brightened the night.

Far from living an isolated existence, Susan was exposed to people of many cultures. An intelligent, energetic German blacksmith named Jacob Herman worked for the army at the fort. He repaired everything from machinery to clocks, raised a huge garden, preserved and pickled much of what he raised, and cooked with skill. An educated man from Nebraska named Sam Smith worked as her father's clerk and also frequently interpreted for the army.

Two ranchers and freighters, brothers from Pennsylvania by the name of Bettelyoun, lived nearby. They were of Dutch heritage. A New York state man, Enoch Raymond, stayed nearby after his army stint ended to raise fancy cattle. All of these men had married Indian women, and their large families frequented Bordeaux's post. The Jesuit missionary Father DeSmet occasionally stopped by to say a mass and urge that children such as Susan be sent east for an education. He knew the world they would have to deal with as adults would be far different from their life on the wild prairie.

The cooperative atmosphere of coexistence along the Platte was quickly eroding. With the white's Civil War over, more and more immigrants surged west and hundreds of troops were freed to protect them from an Indian population increasingly desperate about the intrusion of whites on their lands. These newer troops had meager knowledge of the Indians and little interest in their welfare. Fewer soldiers made any effort to differentiate between friendly and hostile Indians. Indian hunting parties discovered they could be attacked without provocation; hunters went out never to return, and Indian scouts saw scalps in troopers' hands.

As distrust deepened, some Indians refused to eat any food the army distributed, believing it might be poisoned. The Lakota began to shoot first when they encountered a patrol. The previous year had seen multiple attacks, mostly by harried

Cheyenne, responding to a brutal slaughter of their people, peacefully encamped on a little stream called Sand Creek, south of Fort Laramie in Colorado Territory. Settlers and travelers along the trails paid a bitter price for the military's grievous error.

At times, Susan looked out over a valley dotted with white; circles of lodges housing resident Lakota families, as well as wary visitors from outlying bands, and a jumble of wagon tops and tents of emigrant trains. But there also were more neat rows of white tents filled with soldiers. The bodies of Four Antelope, Two Face and Black Foot were visible evidence of their hostility. Susan may well have listened to angry talk among her uncles about the insulting manner of the soldiers —the willful disregard of Lakota feelings and customs—but she had no knowledge that the depth of their discontent was about to put her family in a dangerous no-man's land.

Two weeks after the hangings, the valley was alive with movement. But the mass of people was heading not west, but east along the Platte. And most of those making up the crowd were moving only under duress. Army command, ignorant of the sacrifice inherent in what they decreed, had decided it was easier to move the Lakota to their annual annuity rations than to bring the supplies to them at Laramie. If the Indians wanted the goods promised them in treaties in exchange for their land, they would have to move to the Missouri River. That was the territory of their enemies, the Pawnees. They would be giving up a high, dry prairie replete with game for a hot, muggy climate where natural resources were already depleted by a growing white population. Most of all, it was not home.

On Monday, June 12, 1865, the Bordeaux family was herded from their home with whatever they could load in their wagons and joined the procession with 1,500 other Sioux who had left Fort Laramie the day before. It was exciting to fall into line after the small cavalry force that led the way east down the south bank of the Platte. Susan had seen the soldier chief who was called Captain Fouts before. She knew his bleary-eyed, red face and gruff manner from his visits to her family's home, when she and her siblings had to play elsewhere while the captain slept off too many drinks. In addition to about 135 troopers, army wagons loaded with tents and supplies rolled through the dust. One wagon contained a Lakota prisoner in irons; three other relatives of Two Face and Black Foot walked beside him, their chains clanking. Another wagon contained Captain Fouts' wife, his two daughters, and the woman who had been turned in by Two Face and Black Foot with her baby son.

The mixed-blood families, about fifteen in number, were second in the line of march, their ox-drawn wagons rumbling along at a stolid pace. Young boys raced about, urging their families' herds of horses and cattle along the trail, with the accompanying din of animals protesting the move, and dozens of irrepressible dogs. Last in the procession came Indians of all ages, lodge- pole travois piled high with tipi skins and parfleches filled with belongings, some carrying elderly or babies. Nearly all added horses, until their herd numbered in the hundreds.

Susan saw her uncle, Swift Bear, who was leader of her mother's band, and his children. A 28-year-old cousin, White Thunder, rode strong and straight astride his horse. Brulé Chief Spotted Tail's face was less familiar, as his people kept their distance from Laramie except for an occasional visit. And there were hundreds of wilder Sioux, who had come to the Platte only to obtain their annuity ration.

The river beside them raced bankfull and turbulent, chilled by snow melt from the mountains they were leaving behind.

The second night out of Bordeaux's, when they reached the confluence of Horse Creek and the Platte, the Army and the trappers' families crossed the creek, the troopers camping a mile father east. The mixed bloods pulled up a short distance west of the troops, but the Indians chose to erect their lodges farther back on the stream's west side. In the warm dusk, Susan and other children playing along the creek between the camps saw braves on horseback riding into the Platte and pushing saplings they had cut and sharpened into the river bed in an angled path to the north bank. She noticed that the water was often over the horses' backs, and sometimes forced the animals to swim, but she gave it little thought and they settled in for the night.

They were all up and about early the morning of June 13. Susan's father and brothers had their wagon hitched and ready as the troops started down the trail. But there seemed to be delay in the Indians' camp. Suddenly rifles cracked in the still morning air. The next thing Susan knew, bullets were whizzing over their heads as mounted warriors galloped toward them, firing through them into the soldiers' camp.

Caught between the two forces, Bordeaux whipped up his team and raced for the protection of the soldiers, who were now pulling into a defensive position. Wagons careened wildly, throwing dust into the air, as they skidded in to form the west side of a ragged square. Warriors galloping just yards behind veered off as troopers began returning fire from hastily dug rifle pits, but the braves kept up a peppering fire.

In the chaos, Susan saw her teen-aged brother, Louis, grab a rifle from the wagon and fire at the braves racing toward the wagons. His first shot bored into their cousin White Thunder's foot; then his father snatched the rifle away. Susan watched transfixed as a mixed-blood woman in a bright red calico dress ran a gauntlet from the wild camp to the wagons. Arrows spurted dust all around her, but she made it to safety. Three others raced to a different safety; the prisoners who wore balls and chains had complained of the difficulty of walking and been allowed horses. Already mounted, they kicked their mounts to a gallop at the first shots and disappeared toward the Lakota camp.

With the soldiers outnumbered about three to one, how safe the families were was in question. Word spread that Captain

Fouts and his escort were dead, shot down in the first flurry when they had tried to push the Sioux onto the trail. Second-in-command, Captain John Wilcox, saw to defenses, herding the mixed-blood families into a trench. Then he led a squad out far enough to recover the body of Fouts and the three privates killed with him. Wilson saw that the Indians were hurriedly swimming their ponies across the Platte on the ford they had marked and disappearing to the north. But more than enough furious warriors remained to chase the troopers back to their corral in a headlong retreat. The braves kept up a steady fire, keeping the soldiers caged and taunting them to come out. Enraged and humiliated, the soldiers dragged the one remaining prisoner out of the wagon. His leg, swollen from the manacles, had been too lame for him to escape with the others. He was pulled from the wagon, killed and scalped.

Mrs. Fouts and her daughters were wild with grief, screaming over the captain's mutilated body. She implored the troopers to kill any full-blooded Sioux among the trappers' families. Susan's mother and the other wives were in sudden jeopardy. Angry soldiers muttered that "squaw men" weren't any better and probably knew of the escape plan. Red Cormorant Woman's brother, Swift Bear, had been prominent in the escape and his family was gone with the rest. As the tension escalated, an old man named Green Plum stepped forward with his four orphaned grandchildren. He was full-blood, he said, if the whites wanted to kill people they could start with him and the children. Chastened, Mrs. Fouts relented and said they should be spared. Emotions cooled and the troopers aimed their guns back outside the corral.

The Indians, who could have overrun the soldiers' position, seemed unwilling to pay the price. They were content to drive off the horse herd and push back any contingent that tried to leave the corral. By the time reinforcements arrived from nearby Camp Mitchell, it was too late—and the water too dangerous—to try to cross the Platte and follow the Lakota.

The trappers' families were escorted on to the small, palisaded rectangle that was Camp Mitchell, where they waited an uneasy ten days to find out where they should go. Finally, they were escorted back to their homes near Laramie where, in August, Susan joined a procession led by Father DeSmet as he gave the still-hanging remains of Two Face, Black Foot and Four Antelope a Christian burial. She spent her last winter in the warm fellowship of family and friends. Decades later she could remember how dear the Laramie country was to the Lakota who roamed between the Platte Valley and the Black Hills. "The waving grass, the sparkling streams, the wooded hills were filled with life-giving foods that the red man appreciated more than gold," she wrote. "But the arrival of the gold-crazed emigrants . . . came like a living avalanche sweeping before it all that the Indian prized."

As the Indians struggled to hold on to what they could, Bordeaux decided it was time to move his family to safer territory. He sent Susan and her mother to a settlement begun by French traders in the far southwestern corner of Iowa. Her sister, Louise, and her husband, Clement Lamareaux, were already there, as were her two brothers, sent earlier to attend school. Bordeaux paid additional tuition for Susan and bought a spacious house with landscaped grounds.

Susan was suddenly living a life far removed from trading posts, Indian lodges and cavalry troops. The small town was soon incorporated as Hamburg, and the Bordeaux youngsters were the only Indians in a school of about 100 children. When her mother returned to Laramie the next year, Susan lived in her sister's home. She wrote nothing of this experience, beyond that it lasted four years. One can only imagine the shock of displacement, the drastic change in the society with which she had to come to terms. But she did learn to communicate in the white world and she would put her skills to great use in the years to come.

In 1870, Susan re-crossed the Missouri to live in her parents' new home in Wheeler, Dakota Territory, near the Whetstone Agency. In 1868, while Susan was at Hamburg, the Lakota had signed a treaty which limited their territory to land which lay roughly above the Platte and between the Big Horn Mountains and the Missouri River. They were now to live only on this land reserved for them and restricted for whites. They were to receive an annual payment in annuity goods.

Whetstone Agency was a sizeable collection of log buildings that included a trader's store, dispensary, blacksmith shop, sawmill, storehouses for annuity goods and piles of farming machinery the sanguine government hoped would soon be tilling the bottomland as the Lakota turned into farmers. Her father turned from ranching to farming and he also suppled nearby army posts with hay and wood.

Some of the Lakota set up their lodges near the agency, but Spotted Tail kept his camp far removed from the whites. Still it proved to be an unfortunate home for the Brulé.

Now 13, and literate, Susan was quickly enlisted to help in the first school built for Spotted Tail's people. Neither of the other teachers, Indian Agent D. C. Poole's two daughters, could speak the Indians' language, so Susan was hired to interpret. It must have been a strenuous task, as children of all ages came and went as they pleased. However, Pool had the Lakotas' welfare at heart, and he was supportive, making sure the log school building was well supplied with fuel for the stove and plenty of coffee and bread for dinner. Some days there might be a dozen students, other days only two or three. However, a few mothers cared enough about their children's learning to spend the day waiting outside the building until dismissal time.

The Missouri teemed with white traffic. The agency was just across the river from white settlers and before long liquor was being smuggled to the Indians. The quiet of the night was continually disrupted by drunken song and angry shouts and gunfire as fights erupted. Many fights resulted in deaths, and sometimes such turmoil lasted into the day, making it impossible to keep the students' attention. The school became a haven for frightened women who gathered for the safety of the group, the warmth of the fire and a meal of bread and strong black coffee.

With alcohol so easily available and raising havoc among his people, Spotted Tail asked that the agency be moved back west. This time they were settled at Beaver Creek in northwest Nebraska. In the next eight years, the agency was moved six times to sites in northwestern Nebraska and southern Dakota Territory. Susan went with the people she considered her own. She seems never to have thought of doing otherwise. Although she loved and admired her father, the white world held no appeal. In 1874, when she was seventeen, she married a prominent, well-educated mixed blood named Charles Tackett, four years her senior, who had been born near Horse Creek in Wyoming.

The Lakota were now a divided people. The hostiles, determined not to accept reservation life, spent the summer of 1876 battling the Army. Sitting Bull's Hunkpapa and Crazy Horse's Oglala took part in the triumphant destruction of Custer and his command in June 1876. But Spotted Tail's Brulé and Red Cloud's band of Oglala believed resistance was hopeless and cooperation was the only road they could walk. They were trying to adjust to agency life, and Susan was thankful for a new school established by Episcopalian missionaries.

During these years of continual forced movements for the friendly Lakota, Tackett spent some time as an interpreter and scout at Fort Robinson and Susan went with him. It was a tumultuous period, with continual clashes between the hostiles and the army. Indians, such as those from Crazy Horse's band, were constantly slipping in and out of the area, keeping contact with those on the agencies. Couriers carried the news from camp to camp. In this atmosphere, on October 5, 1876, the couple had a baby girl they named Marie, the English name of Susan's mother. She was baptized on Christmas Day at the fort. Later that winter, Susan's husband went out with a peace envoy to persuade Crazy Horse and his Oglala band to surrender.

As warming days began to melt the winter snows, they heard that while Sitting Bull had led his followers up into Canada to avoid the army, Crazy Horse was coming in to surrender. In May he arrived at the nearby Red Cloud agency with some 1,000 worn and weary followers whom the army had chased until they were gaunt and exhausted. Susan learned that Crazy Horse had smoked the peace pipe, and she knew that this sacred ritual meant he would fight no more. She saw the fabled warrior that summer in the store at the fort and was impressed with his good looks and presence, but she heard it said that Spotted Tail and Red Cloud were both jealous of the young Oglala's fame.

Four months later Crazy Horse was dead, murdered in a struggle at the fort when he refused to enter the guardhouse. Both his fellow Lakota and army troopers took part in his slaying and there was hot talk decrying such a betrayal. Susan's brother, Louis, sat with the wounded leader and his elderly parents until he died. Days later, the friendly Lakota were forced to move back east to the Ponca Agency on the Missouri to get that year's annuities. Crazy Horse's grieving parents and his body went with them, until he was buried somewhere along the way. The Lakotas knew the Poncas had been removed to Indian Territory and they had long feared the government had similar plans to force them down to that hot, unhealthy climate. Despite protests and a refusal to march that ended only because they were starved into motion, 12,000 Lakota were herded east for another long winter.

Again Spotted Tail and Red Cloud put pressure on the government to move back west, a move they believed they had been promised, and in the spring of 1878 the Brulé were finally settled at a new agency at Rosebud which would become their permanent home. The government hurriedly threw up a few frame buildings and the Indians scattered their lodges and huts nearby among the sandy hills. It might have looked barren and forbidding to eastern eyes, but to the Lakota it was familiar and comfortable. Red Cloud's Oglalas were established at Pine Ridge, ninety miles west. Both agencies were in Dakota Territory, southeast of the Black Hills.

Spotted Tail had a strong personality and definite ideas about what he wanted. Perhaps his daughter, Red Road, had an equally compelling personality; perhaps serving as son-in-law to this powerful figure had its appeal. For whatever reason, sometime during these moves, Charles Tackett "put away" his wife, Susan, and took Red Road as his partner.

Susan and Charles had been married in the church, and Charles' reversion to tribal ways must have been devastating. She never wrote of her feelings about this upheaval in her life. But years later it was still so painful that she falsely reported that Tackett had died leaving her and her two-year-old daughter alone. Within months of the breakup, Spotted Tail sent Tackett east to Carlisle Indian School with his new wife, charged with watching over the chief's children who were in school.

Susan's Christian faith had always been important to her, and she had been grateful for Episcopalian missionaries who had worked among the Brulé the past three years. She admired their dedication to her people, and she appreciated a school and mission house they built at Rosebud. When her father developed pneumonia and died that October, she must have found solace in their ministering to her family. He had secured a government contract to supply the Rosebud agency, and according to one report had recently sworn off alcohol after years of overindulgence. He was a prudent man, always interested in keeping the peace, some thought to the point of cowardice. But, unlike other trappers who had sired Indian families and deserted them, he had always been loyal to his Indian family and worked hard to care for them. She considered him an excellent manager who earned the respect of whites and Indians alike. Like him, Susan was proud of his French heritage. Her memories of her father were good ones.

Six years later, in July 1884, Susan's mother died at the age of 63. Susan made sure that she was interred in the church burial ground at Rosebud. She was conscious that her mother's choice in life—to marry a white man—had been a powerful influence on her band to try to cooperate with the whites rather than fight them.

That year, Susan took her daughter, Marie, now eight, to Anoka, Minnesota, so she could begin her education at St. Anne's Catholic School. She, herself, had begun school under nuns tutorage at Hamburg when she was little older than Marie, and unlike some people of Lakota heritage, she was grateful for the learning she attained. She found work there as a matron of the girls' dormitory for four years before choosing to return to Rosebud, where her brother's family and her grandmother, Gray Buffalo Woman, made their homes.

Marie remained in school in Anoka, returning to the reservation in 1891, where her mother was working for the Indian Service as a matron. However, the reunion was brief as that fateful year the 15-year-old girl died. Susan mourned her only child. She had had visions of Marie completing a master's degree in education and coming back to teach their people. It was heartbreaking to face the end of that dream. However, she evidently found comfort in the company of the college-educated Isaac P. Bettelyoun, a mixed-blood whose family had lived near the Bordeaux Ranch on the Platte. Nearly a dozen years younger than Susan, he had been educated at an Episcopalian mission and then attended college. He worked as an interpreter and guide for the army, and as a clerk and farmer for the Rosebud Agency. As field matron, Susan taught homemaking skills to the Brulé women, while Isaac's job as farmer involved educating the Indians about growing crops.

After marrying, the couple resigned from the agency to concentrate on their own farming and ranching efforts. In 1909 they moved to Winner, South Dakota, and invested in a bank, which ultimately failed. They returned to the reservation, where they still had land, and remained there until ill health forced a final move to the Old Soldiers' Home in Hot Springs, South Dakota, in 1933. Isaac died the next year, but it was then that Susan developed a friendship with another mixed-blood woman and a purpose which would dominate the rest of her life.

As she aged, Susan Bettelyoun had become increasingly angry when she read accounts by white historians that purported to tell the story of the Lakota, especially the Brulé and Oglala she knew so intimately. Nothing that she read "entirely reflected the facts as I know them from my own observations and from statements made to me by my parents and other relatives," she said. She deeply felt the "lack of understanding of the Plains Indians" these authors exhibited. She longed to tell the Lakota side of the story. Josephine Waggoner was to become her partner in that effort.

Josephine Waggoner - 1882-1942

Born fifteen years after Susan Bordeaux Bettelyoun, Josephine Waggoner had known only reservation life. The daughter of Irish-immigrant Charles A. McCarthy and the Hunkpapa woman Wind Woman, 5-year-old Josephine's exposure to education at a Catholic day school on the Standing Rock Reservation was an ordeal. Abruptly separated from her mother, she was allowed only what glimpses she could snatch through cracks in the timber stockade that surrounded the school. The enforced separation from her mother continued when, at age nine, she was sent east to Hampton Normal and Agricultural Institute in Virginia. However, she found learning English surprisingly easy and stayed at Hampton for six years, with a one-year break spent back on the reservation.

Josephine remained grateful all her life for the education she gained at Hampton. It remained in her thoughts as a place where everything "is pure, good, and holy." Yet, when her schooling was completed in 1888, she returned to Standing Rock. She worked for a time as an interpreter for Episcopal missionaries, and as nurse and interpreter at a Congregational mission. There she met a white soldier, John Franklin Waggoner, whom she married in 1889, just after she turned 17. She and Waggoner had nine children, whom they raised on a ranch near Keldron, in northern South Dakota.

Josephine had a creative nature, finding time to paint and write history and poetry despite the strenuous life of ranching and caring for her large family. She researched and wrote a long, detailed account of the first white man to whom her mother had been married, Benjamin Connor Arnold, and his life in the West. Her material was included in *Rekindling Camp Fires: The Exploits of Ben Arnold (Connor)* which the South Dakota Historical Society published in 1926, with only nominal recognition of Josephine's work. She saw to it that all of her children received advanced education and later spent several years caring for grandchildren.

Through it all she was always driven to write the history of the Lakota people. As a young woman she translated letters for Sitting Bull, experienced the Ghost Dance turmoil, and helped lay the great chief's body out after he was killed when an attempt to arrest him erupted in violence. She was conscious that the people who actually lived these and other events were rapidly dying and their voices were being lost. Before 1930, she was seeking out those who could give her first-hand accounts of events in Lakota history. After long days fulfilling her obligations to her family, she sat far into the night at the kitchen table recording what she learned. In later years she was plagued by diabetes and money was often short. She had been collecting stories from elders on the Standing Rock Reservation, and when illness forced a move to the South

Dakota Old Soldiers' State Home in 1932, she added Rosebud and Pine Ridge agencies to her search for people with stories to tell.

She was generous in sharing what she learned with white historians. In 1933, she wrote one scholar: "I am always glad to help if I can to those who are interested in Indian history. I have been corresponding with several writers who have been wanting to know historical facts. There has (sic) been so much fictitious and misleading stories written about the Indians. I am always anxious to see the truth about these stories brought before the public." A few historians, such as Walter S. Campbell (Stanley Vestal) made extensive use of her knowledge, seeking her answer to specific questions and sending her questionnaires to complete. The compensation offered was usually meager and slow to arrive.

However, her primary intent was to create a written history for the Lakota. "My work is for the Indians," she said. She plumbed the memories of her mother and grandmother to record tribal traditions, collected eyewitness accounts, and compiled a history of the Lakota nation and their chiefs, which she tried repeatedly to get published during the 1930s. Despite her connections with white historians, the work remained unpublished.

Susan Bordeaux Bettelyoun and Josephine McCarthy Waggoner began their collaboration in June 1934. Bettelyoun provided the voice, Waggoner the hand, as Susan's was too crippled with rheumatism to spend days at a desk. Waggoner first wrote to the superintendent of the Nebraska State Historical Society, Addison E. Sheldon, informing him of their intent and asking help with some dates that Bettelyoun could not supply. He supplied the dates, encouraged their work and offered to provide a typescript and help with publication when the time came. Waggoner described how she sat with pad ready and "wrote the words just as they were spoken," recording Bettelyoun's memories. But this was not a typical memoir; both women focused on recreating the history of the Lakota people. They worked to tell about the conflict between the white and Indian cultures and its aftermath; their personal stories were of import only as they provided access to events, individuals, and tribal customs.

Bettelyoun described several events as she remembered living them. Others that happened before she was born, she recreated from accounts she had heard. Sometimes the stories were so familiar that she must have made herself believe that she was there. She related them as if she had been a participant. As sections of the manuscript were completed, Waggoner sent them to Sheldon for corrections and typing. For several years the material went back and forth, with Bettelyoun and Waggoner answering detailed questionnaires from historian Sheldon, who was trying to accommodate conflicting statements in different parts of the manuscript. Sheldon showed the work to Nebraska writer and historian Mari Sandoz and submitted it to editors at *The Atlantic Monthly*. In 1937 and 1938, all regretfully came to the same conclusion. It contained valuable, new historical information, but its lack of continuity, its many contradictions, and some errors of fact made it unpublishable without extensive editing.

Susan's memory did not operate in a lineal fashion. She would begin the story of an incident or a person, such as her mother, then veer off into related details, such as how her people captured wild horses and dug caches to store food.

Still, Sheldon persevered. He let the Depression-era Federal Writers Project workers have a free hand at editing. Susan's fresh and vital voice disappeared. He proposed that the Nebraska State Historical Society publish it, and in 1939 asked the Nebraska Legislature for the necessary funds. Through these years Bettelyoun and Waggoner were writing to Sheldon, asking when they could expect publication of their 376-page manuscript. His answers were slow in arriving and their frustration is obvious in their correspondence. In fragile health, both feared they might die before they saw results of their work. Perhaps lack of money, perhaps Sheldon's ill health, perhaps an academic point of view that could not be surmounted, possibly the country's entry into World War II, probably a combination of these issues combined to prevent publication. Waggoner died on February 14, 1943, and Bettelyoun on December 17, 1945, without ever seeing their work in print.

The Bordeaux family's drive to preserve Lakota history carried down to succeeding generations. Susan's nephew, William J. Bordeaux, authored a book and two booklets dealing with Crazy Horse and Sitting Bull. Self-published in limited numbers, they are today rare and sought by collectors.

Josephine Waggoner's own manuscript, titled *My Land, My People, My Story,* was published in a limited edition by her family in 1994. It is rarely found today. Ben Arnold's story was reprinted by the University of Oklahoma in 1999 as *The Exploits of Ben Arnold.* In his foreword, historian Paul. L. Hedren gives notable credit to Josephine's fourteen notebooks of stories as told to her by Ben Arnold. Her role in preserving the story is at last recognized.

For years, the manuscript Susan and Josephine compiled continued to be accessed by historians doing research; numerous bibliographies give credit to Susan Bordeaux Bettelyoun. Mari Sandoz was still seeking a way to publish the work in 1960, but white historians' attitude toward oral history—and toward women's history—would have to change before that finally happened. In the late 1980s, with attitudes changing about the acceptability and proper treatment of authentic Native American accounts, scholar Emily Lavine undertook another preparation of the Bettelyoun manuscript. In a ten-year labor, she extensively researched the background of each name, place and event that Bettelyoun mentioned, then prepared explanatory footnotes. With a newly imposed order, and a minimum of changes and corrections, the Nebraska Historical Society published *With My Own Eyes; A Lakota Woman Tells*

Her People's Story in 1998. Fifty-three years after her death, the voice of Susan Bordeaux Bettelyoun began speaking out, telling the truth as she knew it to be.

Susan Bordeaux Bettelyoun Bibliography

Archival Collections

Bettelyoun, Susan Bordeaux. "Autobiography," MS185, Nebraska State Historical Society.
Correspondence, Josephine Waggoner, MS.
U.S. Congress, 39th, 2nd Session. Senate Report 156, March 3, 1865, "Statement of Mrs. Eubanks."

Books

Bettelyoun, Susan Bordeaux. *With My Own Eyes, A Dakota Woman Tells Her People's Story,* Emily Levine, ed., University of Nebraska Press, 1998.
Crawford, Lewis F. *The Exploits of Ben Arnold,* foreword by Paul L. Hedren, University of Oklahoma Press, 1999.
Eastman, Elaine Goodale. *Sister to the Sioux,* University of Nebraska Press, 1978.
Hafen, Leroy. *Fort Laramie and the Pageant of the West,* University of Nebraska Press, 1938.
Hyde, George. *Spotted Tail's Folk,* University of Oklahoma Press,1961.
Nadeaux, Remi. *Fort Laramie and the Sioux,* 1967. (Reprint, Crest Publishers, 1997.)
Poole, Capt. D. C.. *Among the Sioux of Dakota,* D. Van Nostrand, 1881.

Articles

Anderson, Harry. "Fur Traders as Fathers; The Origin of the Mixed-blooded Community Among the Rosebud Sioux,*" South Dakota History,* v.3, n.3, (1973):233-70.
Goddard, Carol Case. "Mrs. Susan Bordeaux Gives Interesting Interview," Pioneer Daughters Collection, South Dakota Historical Society, n.d.
Hagerty, Leroy W., "Indian Raids Along the Platte and Little Blue Rivers, *Nebraska History,* v. 28, n. 4, (1947):176-86.
Nelson, Grace."Time, Arthritis Slow Fingers of Artist,"*Rapid City Daily Journal,* Pioneer Daughters Collection, South Dakota Historical Society, n.d.
Pattison, John J. "With the U.S. Army Along the Oregon Trail, 1863-66," *Nebraska History,* v. 15, n. 2, (1934):79-86.
South Dakota Historical Collections, v.17, 1934; v.24, 1949; v.33, 1966; v.36, 1972.

E. Pauline Johnson

Chapter Five

THE PEOPLE'S POET

E. Pauline Johnson, 1861-1913
English – Mohawk

On July 30, 1907, when the Chautauqua audience in Boulder, Colorado, gave warm applause to the performer headlined as Tekahionwake, the Indian Poetress, they had no idea what grit and stamina her small buckskin-clad figure contained. She had possessed remarkable beauty when she was younger; even now, with a fuller form and rounder face, hers was a striking, commanding presence on the stage. And, as her rich, melodious voice reached even those seated at the back of the large wooden auditorium, they would have been surprised it had not its usual strength.

For the past nine days she had scarcely spoken because of a severe chill caught in a wet, steamy Chautauqua tent during a Missouri thunderstorm the week before. It was a catastrophic event for a woman who made her living with her voice. E. Pauline Johnson was still not completely well, but she could not afford to miss another performance and she gave the Colorado crowd all the vibrancy she could summon.

The annual Boulder Chautauqua was nearing the end of its ambitious six-week schedule. The series of educational and cultural performances was both an intellectual and social highlight of each year, as it was in 400 or more communities across the country. The Boulder Chautauqua Assembly was unusually strong, and members were proud their performers had appeared in a substantial two-story building for nine years now. In 1907, Boulder crowds watched magicians, listened to bell ringers, marveled at the balance of a young man called an equilibrist, and listened to professorial addresses on Matthew Arnold and Sir Walter Scott. But what Pauline Johnson offered was unique.

She was a gifted writer and the poems she recited were her own, celebrating her Mohawk heritage and decrying the damage that had been visited on native peoples. Tired near to death as she was, feeling every one of her 46 years and the toil of a month on the Chautauqua circuit, with two performances many days, riding the train every day to a different town, she had to reach deep inside to find the fire to ignite her words with feeling.

Evidently she was successful. The *Boulder Daily Camera* described her performance as "the very embodiment of the passion and fire of the Red Man." The reviewer said, "Her figure sets off to advantage the Indian trappings of her rich buckskin garments." When the reviewer went on to say that while she "is cultivated and brilliant," the "dramatic vigor of her work has a barbaric swing of primeval emotion," he neatly evoked the dual nature of the poet's character.

It had not been difficult to unleash her emotions fifteen years before, the first time she stepped onto a Toronto stage and began to recite "A Cry from an Indian Wife." Told from the unprecedented viewpoint not only of an Indian, but of an Indian woman, the poem was an angry indictment of European suppression that had given the Indians nothing but "war and graves." But the poem acknowledged that "a pale-faced maiden" also grieved when she lost her mate to battle with those who "by right, by birth" owned Western lands. The poet could identify with both races because she had the blood of both in her veins. Her bold gestures, her voice—now ringing, now soft—gave outward expression to the turmoil she had known since she was old enough to realize that having an English mother and an Iroquois chief for a father set her apart.

E. Pauline Johnson's parents had angered and alienated both sets of their parents when they married in 1853 and settled on the Six Nations Reserve in what would become Ontario, fifty miles west of Niagara Falls. Although George Johnson dressed European style, spoke perfect English, was a devout Anglican and was a hereditary chief with a maternal pedigree in the Mohawk nation almost as long as some English kings, none of Emily Howell's family attended her wedding. For his part, George Johnson, whose surname honored an Irish lord who had championed the Mohawk people, whose father loved and fought for the English, found his family horrified that he would betray his heritage by marrying outside the clan, giving up the title his sons should inherit. But the couple would not be dissuaded, and the marriage had been a close and happy union in a mansion George built and named Chiefswood. The union produced two boys and two girls, the youngest being Pauline, who was born on March 10, 1861.

Pauline was schooled at home to her demanding mother's English standards, and she developed both perfect manners and, from the time she learned to speak, a love of poetry. Often alone in the schoolroom of the square two-story house, she absorbed romantic English poets, such as Keats, Byron and Browning. Paid by the government to interpret for the Six Nations and by the Nations to enforce their rules, George Johnson was wealthy enough that they lived in a home staffed with two or three servants. The family always dressed for dinner, eating it in a dining room adorned with Queen Victoria's portrait. Pauline was aware of her father's importance as an interpreter, a government forest warden and a ranking member of the tribal council. He graciously received emissaries from the British government and often traveled to Ottawa to speak to Parliament for Indian causes.

Her mother believed fervently that the children should be well informed about both their parents' cultures. She and George strove to prove the two races could live in peaceful harmony. Pauline and her siblings often listened as George counseled with tribal members, and while they could not understand the Mohawk language, they were entirely familiar with the beat of their drums and loved to watch their dances and ceremonies. Pauline also found pleasure in memorizing long stanzas of Longfellow's epic, "Song of Hiawatha," and became fascinated with Indian culture. She spent long hours with her grandfather, John "Smoke" Johnson, walking the banks of the gentle Grand River that fronted their home while he related Iroquois legends.

As soon as she grew old enough to sit safely still, her father passed on his family's skills of canoeing. Traveling by river was often the easiest path in the Canadian wilderness, one the native people took as a matter of choice and practicality. People on Six Nations Reserve had traditionally used the dugout canoe, but by the time Pauline was a girl, most had switched to a newer bentwood canoe manufactured in nearby Peterboro. She took to it immediately, increasing her skills until she became expert at maneuvering the small craft. As she moved into her teens, hours on the river in the canoe she'd christened "Wild Cat" became her joy. She was small, only five-feet-two inches, but agile and strong, and she delighted in challenging rough water, admitting, "My brain goes aflame when I see the distant whitecaps. . . ."

When she was fourteen, Pauline's parents had sent her to a public school in nearby Brantford called Central Collegiate. She and her brother, Allen, were the only children from the reserve at the school. Shy and miserable at first, forced by distance to spend week nights away from home, she gradually relaxed enough to enjoy the company of other girls her age. Before she graduated two years later, she was a lively presence at the school who loved making her classmates laugh. She starred in school plays, established a circle of white girlfriends and reveled in the social life of the small manufacturing town. Her mother had always insisted on proper dress, but now Pauline joined the town girls in studying fashion magazines and shopping for fabric with which she could create the latest styles.

She was aware of the widening difference between the rural, old-style life on the reserve and the bustling town's reach for prosperity. Indians were no longer partners but wards of a state intent on assimilation. In 1877 she returned to Chiefswood, where she became increasingly restless in the quiet farming community. When she couldn't finagle a visit to the home of a friend in one of the nearby small towns, she spent long dreamy hours on the river. One thing she dreamed of was being a writer; increasingly she wrote poetry.

But her idyllic, if too quiet, life at Chiefswood came to a sudden end when George Johnson died. He had long crusaded against liquor being smuggled onto the reserve. Unscrupulous European settlers induced the Indians to illegally cut valuable hardwood on reserve lands and paid them in rotgut whiskey. George often traveled the woods, patrolling for the bootleggers, and one of Pauline's earliest memories was of her father's bloody face when he staggered home after being attacked on the trail in 1865. It had taken long weeks of Emily's dedicated nursing to bring him back to health, but Emily and George had tried to put the bad experience behind them. His children were unaware, but he continued to harass the bootleggers, and in 1873 he had been beaten with clubs, shot and left for dead. He'd managed to crawl to help and again Emily had devoted all her skills to his recovery, which was never complete. Although he continued to suffer attacks of neuralgia and had recurring infections of erysipelas, he stubbornly searched the forest for signs of cut timber and spoke out at council meetings against the liquor trade. In 1878, walking home from a council meeting, he was assaulted by one of his own people who wanted the whiskey trade to continue. With both his body and his spirit broken, he was easy prey when he developed pneumonia in early1884. Pauline stood at his bedside with her mother and sister when he died a week later at age 68. Haunting cries of grief spread the news along the river that the Mohawks had lost their vaunted chief.

His loss wreaked both emotional and financial havoc on the family. Without his salary, they could no longer afford to live at Chiefswood. They rented out the farm and a few months later Pauline moved with her sister, Evelyn, and her mother into a brick duplex in Brantford. Evelyn found a clerical job to pay expenses and Pauline helped her grieving mother with the housework. She had had a few verses published locally and she attracted notice with poems written for two local ceremonies. Now 26, she was profiled in a Toronto paper, placed more verses, flirted with a long line of suitors (her sister said she knew of eight proposals) and produced sensuous, erotic poetry about canoeing which seemed to focus on one particular young man. But he was a preacher's son, five years her junior, and intent on an academic career. In 1887 he left for college in England, where he later married, and Pauline was left to publish poems about unrequited love. In an age of coquetries and shrinking violets, she wrote openly and frankly about a woman's passion.

But she still had writing and canoeing, a sport that was rising to prominence on the social scene. It boasted canoeing clubs, races and excursions. Pauline was eager to show off her skills and prided herself that the local men considered her equal to "one of the boys." She and her friends traveled about Ontario lakes and the grandeur of the scenery evoked a strong emotional response she expressed in verse. One poem, titled "Shadow River," led to editors' demands for more and she was soon publishing poetry and prose in a widening ring of publications, including the New York magazine *Outing,* the *Detroit Free Press*, and an anthology of Canadian poetry, *Songs of the Great Dominion,* pubished in 1889. She was contributing a little—if very little—to the family coffers. However, she was already dreaming of a book all her own and was determined to reach "the heights of literature."

She was more and more aware that her educational background was scant compared to her competitors, and as her thirtieth birthday passed she knew some looked on her as an old maid. Discouraged, she asked aging American poet John Greenleaf Whittier's opinion of a few of her poems, and his encouraging letter might well have been written in gold, it touched her so deeply. She was to treasure it all her life. He especially admired her poems dealing with her Indian heritage, and with a new faith in her talent she renewed her efforts to improve her work and to make the connections that seemed so important for the literary life. One contact which would loom more important than she could imagine was a friendship developed with a witty American actress named Rosina Voke, who annually toured Toronto. Although her mother detested the theatrical world, Pauline attended each nightly performance as a guest, and she observed closely how the vivacious performer captured and controlled her audience. Members of the tour critiqued Pauline's delivery of some of her poetry and she felt new ambitions stirring.

She got the chance to exercise them in 1892, when a fellow writer, Frank Yeigh, a friend from childhood, asked her to be part of an evening devoted to Canadian authors. On January 16, 1892, she stepped on stage for the first time. Perhaps she was lucky that the performers who preceded her were long-winded politicians and poets who stood like statues and read woodenly from a page. But she could see the audience was restless and bored and she knew how to get its attention. Becomingly attired in a stylish long gown, she swept onto the stage, struck a pose staring at the rafters and waited for silence. When she had it, she began reciting "A Cry From an Indian Wife" from memory, rasing her voice in rage at the Indians' losses, dropping it to almost whisper tragic passages that her audience leaned forward to hear. Suddenly she would thrust her arm in the air and thunder phrases deeply imbued with emotion. But every word was enunciated, every phrase projected to an audience enthralled. She finished to silence, then thunderous applause. The crowd demanded an encore, which she graciously gave them. She loved every moment of it. It was a night that set the path for her future.

She knew now that in the crowded world of performers and writers she had something unique to offer. Whittier had been right; her Mohawk heritage was her strength.

Just over a month later, Yeigh arranged another appearance and this time Pauline, described as "the Indian Poetess," was the featured attraction. A poem about bloody revenge between Indian warriors joined the cry of the Indian wife. Then she launched herself into an account of canoeing. "The Song My Paddle Sings" was to become her most famous poem, but in this first performance her memory failed her and she fell silent. For a moment, Yeigh and the audience squirmed, then Pauline quietly admitted she had forgotten what came next and asked to continue with another work. Another Indian poem followed and later, when she returned to recite "The Song My Paddle Sings" with faultless rhythm and feeling, the audience responded with cheers; she had made them a part of her triumph. "Miss Johnson is sure of a hearty welcome whenever she may visit Toronto," *Saturday Night* magazine declared.

But she realized she could not continue as Miss Johnson, encased in a corset and draped in a ball gown. To proclaim the Indian cause, she needed to look like an Indian. She knew audiences familiar with Buffalo Bill's Wild West Show, which had performed in Toronto in 1885, expected Indians to be dressed in buckskin and feathers. And she would need moccasins, beaded or quilled, probably a sash of some kind. But the Iroquois had long worn European clothing, perhaps woven leggings and a tunic, not buckskin. She wrote to the Hudson's Bay Company in Winnipeg. The two-piece outfit which arrived was buckskin, but painfully plain. With her sister's help she remodeled the sleeves, added ermine tails, her grandmothers silver trade brooches, her father's hunting knife and a Huron scalp from her Grandfather Smoke. An acquaintance in Ottawa promised to search for a bear-claw necklace, and when she added family wampum belts of beads made from shells around her waist she was transformed from Miss Johnson to a "wild Indian." Or at least what audiences thought a wild Indian should look like.

Under Yeigh's management the next winter she gave 125 recitals in fifty different cities, in churches, schoolhouses, and private homes. After her melodramatic Indian poems and costume, the refined Miss Johnson would reappear on stage in a stylish gown and read lyrical verses about Canada's natural beauty. Audiences were fascinated. She appeared in the capital city of Ottawa, in Newark, New Jersey, in Boston, for historical societies in New York and Connecticut. Then Yeigh teamed her up with a young English entertainer named Owen Alexander Smily, whose dialogs and piano tunes lightened the evenings. He helped her learn to disarm hostile or restless crowds with humor, and she began to enjoy the repartee. To add an exotic note, she began the Indian portion of the program with an off-stage war whoop. They were to perform together for six years.

Yet Pauline was increasingly dismayed that she was leaving the literary world behind to become an entertainer. She could make the money they needed on the stage, but what of the "literary heights" she had aspired to? She still wanted her book of poetry and, perhaps because the first poetry she had loved was English, because her parents loved all things British, she believed it would gain cachet if it were published in England. By April 1894, she had managed to save enough to pay one steamship passage. She would have to cross the Atlantic alone to Liverpool, then take the train to London. The hometown folks gave her a grand sendoff, but she was still wobbly from seasickness when she alighted from the Liverpool train in

London. Alone, unknown, she prepared to knock on London society's doors.

She had carefully prepared her strategy. She knew she had to establish a reputation in London before she could approach a publisher, and that meant performing. After a discouraging week or more in her small flat, she used letters of introduction to call on Canadian officials. One had heard her perform in Ottawa, and he got her an introduction to an important Mayfair society matron who, after meeting Pauline, asked her to perform at a dinner party. Drawing on her mother's teaching and her own observations of "society manners," she made an excellent impression. That invitation led to others, but she soon realized bored socialites were easily entertained. She needed entry to what she called "thinking London," and aware of her meager education she recoiled at the thought. "I feel like a worm, a veritable nothing in the critic's den or the author's library," she wrote a friend. A letter from a Toronto friend achieved an invitation to appear in a well-known author's drawing room and her poetry challenged the attendees' notions of what a native might accomplish. Other literati took her in tow and on June 13 she was delighted to read a flattering profile of Tekahionwake in a London weekly.

Increasingly aware of London's fascination with her "Red Indian" image, Pauline had stressed her fraternal Mohawk lineage and used her great-grandfather's name as her own. It was an unprecedented move—one to which she had no right —and a step into Mohawk identity she had never taken before. The name signified a double life, a person who would survive a fatal attack to live again. Perhaps she identified with its link to determined perseverance, a trait she would have to summon again and again. Questioned about a scalping knife, she refused to apologize for Indians' savage behavior and smartly reminded the newspaper reporter that had the Iroquois helped the French instead of the British in early colonial wars, their New World Dominion might never have come to be. With not one but two accompanying photos, that article led to another and doors began opening.

Toward the end of June she visited with noted—and dreaded—critic Clement Scott and charmed him into recommending her to a prominent, free-thinking publisher, John Lane at Bodley Head. In a few weeks thirty-six of her poems were chosen, edited, proofed and designed into a volume to be titled *The White Wampum*. In her introduction, Pauline likened a poet's poems to a cherished Mohawk wampum belt and the book's design emphasized her Indian heritage. After nearly two months in the capital, she had achieved her goals to a remarkable degree. Both her money and her tolerance for urban crowds and snobbish cliques were running short. With a promise her book would soon see print, she left for home on July 9, 1894.

To the distress of her mother, who had expected her to leave the platform when she had a published book, and her sister, who felt more and more imposed upon by Pauline's continual absences, she spent only a few days at home before embarking on another tour with Smily. This one would take the pair 3,000 miles across southern Canada on the luxurious Canadian Pacific Railway. Although Pauline had invested in several elaborate gowns from one of London's stylish stores, she usually appeared in Indian costume, and her feelings for her father's people had solidified. And now she told a writing friend, "Never let anyone call me a white woman! There are those who think they pay me a compliment in saying that I am just like a white woman. My aim, my joy, my pride is to sing the glories of my own people."

As she sped west across the high plains, she loved being surrounded by polished brass, sparkling mirrors and mahogany fittings, but she discovered there was another car for "colonists," crowded with families of immigrants who made their own wooden bunks and cooked on an iron stove. The contrast was marked, but even more noticeable were the Ojibwa camps along the tracks, the copper-skinned families garbed in blankets, the women drying fish between the tipis. Pauline felt ashamed that her olive Mohawk skin had been "thinned by European blood." After eleven performances in and around a thriving Winnipeg, well received despite the boom town's intolerance for native populations, long segments of train travel stretched between small settlements on the great plains, and Pauline began seeing Indians quite different from her European-leaning ancestors.

While the Blackfoot, Cree and Lakota people were struggling to maintain their traditional way of life on shrinking reserves, those who lived within traveling distance of the tracks had concocted "Wild West" entertainments, and often posed for photos to coax dollars out of train tourists. But she saw that often those dollars went for alcohol, which combined with disease and dishonor, was decimating the population. One Sioux she glimpsed beside his tipi inspired her to write of ". . . eyes that lost their fire long ago," looking toward an empty West to see "the never-coming buffalo."

Her distress at the degradation of her people was lightened by the glories of the scenery she was passing through. "This trip is a revelation to me," she wrote. "I cannot tell you . . . how infinitely dearer my native soil is to me since I started on this long trip." She was writing continuously, letters to her mother and friends, travels articles for newspapers, poetry when something moved her strongly.

The last two weeks of touring were shadowed with grief after she learned her oldest brother had died at 40. But she performed because she had to, "with laughter on my face and tears in my heart." And, after only a week back in Brantford, she headed out for recitals in Ontario. She was one of many such entertainers, but she was the only poet reciting entirely her own work.

In the summer of 1895 her book finally appeared in print. While reviews were mixed—several criticized her Indian poetry as too melodramatic and partisan—*Canadian Magazine* described her as "the most popular (and prominent) figure in Canadian literature." She broadened her schedule to include towns in the American Midwest, and as her reputation grew, her earning power increased to more than $1,000 for a three-month tour. Half of that went for expenses, but what remained could have made substantial savings. However, Pauline subscribed to poet James Terry White's advice when facing a pantry containing only two loaves of bread: eat one loaf and sell the other to buy "hyacinths to feed thy soul." She scandalized her sister by buying fresh flowers in winter and gave generously to friends and acquaintances.

Again in 1896 and 1897 she spent months on the road. It was strenuous, changing costumes wherever she could, eating whatever the hotel had to offer, to rise every morning from a different bed and climb on another train. She was always short of money, dodging creditors, borrowing from friends; she could not afford to be idle. And she was aging. Seeking change, she moved from a society-bound Toronto west to the newer, more tolerant Winnipeg.

As 1897 drew to a close, it appeared an admirer named Charles Drayton might be a solution for all her life's problems. Eleven years younger than she, athletic, well bred but with a certain amount of daring, he courted the woman his family considered, "a half-breed, but such a nice one." Before events could proceed, Pauline's mother, Emily, died in Brantford, and Pauline fell ill with rheumatic fever. The wedding was postponed. Then Charles lost his own mother and the times the betrothed couple could spend together dwindled. Pauline had insisted from the first that marriage would not end her performing and, although she and Smily had ended their partnership, she set out to tour alone, wrestling with her own luggage, dealing with staging problems, finding somewhere to eat.

In the midst of a blizzard in early 1899, she took shelter in a Royal Canadian Mounty's home and discovered a new subject for her pen. Throughout the year's tour she celebrated the Mounties' heroism in verse. Charlie remained distant, and on the eve of the new century she released him to marry another, a more acceptable Toronto socialite. She had always been sought after, always imagined herself an acceptable mate for any man. Now both Charles and her illusions were gone.

In 1900 she performed in benefits to support Canadian troops in the Boer War. Yet she also wrote poems and stories protesting the damage boarding schools visited on young Indians as they were forbidden to use their own language and deliberately stripped of their family heritage. She had to tread carefully; her audiences would tolerate only a limited amount of scolding and the load of debt she carried was a constant reminder not to go too far.

A strange interlude in her life began that spring, when some contact in the theatrical community brought a new manager to her side. German-born Charles H. Wuerz took over her affairs with a new energy, printing up posters, designing new stationery that trumpeted a world tour that would include Australia. She borrowed future earning from the Chiefswood estate and pawned some of her jewelry to help finance the trip. In preparation, he sent her off on an extensive, exhausting tour of Canada's Maritime Provinces.

She had added plays in verse to her repertoire, playing each part herself, and she'd begun including sketches of her mishaps on the road. She could be a wicked mimic and reviewers were delighted with her sense of comedy. However, her relationship with Wuerz was a disaster financially and emotionally. He planned poorly and wasted money, but he was able to arouse in her passions she had thought were dead. Her poetry written that year celebrates their time together while seeming to anticipate a painful parting. There is no record of the circumstances, but when the break came in the fall of the year Pauline disappeared from public view for three months, saying later she had fallen into a "black pit of sunless hours."

Where she was is still a subject of conjecture. In the spring she wrote her old friend and manager Frank Yeigh, saying she had been "in a network of tragedy—too sad for human tongue to tell." She asked for a loan of $15, finished an unsuccessful tour in the East and returned to Ottawa on borrowed money.

There she teamed with a brash, 25-year-old actor named Walter McRaye. "Dink," as she came to call him, had no polished manners and their partnership distressed her friends. But he had the energy she lacked at 40 to deal with the hassles of constant travel. And he treated her like the royal personage her billing sometimes described. His talent was negligible; she was still a headliner. She had to help him with his elocution to improve his monologues and taught him some of the routines Smily had used. However, he insulated her from the nitty gritty of performing arrangements, and when she fell deathly ill with an attack of erysipelas the week before Christmas, he kept dedicated watch at her bedside. She had watched her father fight the same virulent infection, and she knew there was no medication to suppress it. Her face covered with bright red blistered patches, her temperature soaring, she lay unconscious. Doctors could only prescribe morphine and wait to see if she lived, warning that if she did she'd probably lose all her hair.

Gradually, her body defeated the infection. On February 7, 1902, she was still weak but she was back performing, a wig covering her naked scalp and heavy makeup disguising her scarred face. She had no choice; she needed the money. The wig sufficed for her Indian costume and she crowned her gowns with large hats. The pair headed west on the Canadian Pacific Railway to tour the rugged mountain mining towns in the Kootenay district. Branch lines threaded the mountain valleys, and miners who had spent the day grubbing silver, gold and lead from the earth, who seldom saw a woman—let alone a lady—were delighted to spend the evening engrossed in Pauline's poetry and laughing at McRaye's routines. She charmed the miners like the pro she had become. Writing poetry had taken a backseat to the stage, and when her second book *Canadian Born* came out in 1903, most critics expressed disappointment in its uneven quality. That year and the next two, the partners "hit the boards" across Canada and dipped down into the United States, working benefits, such as one in Ontario to buy a wooden leg for the town constable, and celebrations, such as the formation of provinces of Alberta and Saskatchewan in 1905.

That year she discovered a new source of income that would help sustain her the rest of her life. She wrote a short story for *Boys' World* magazine, published in Illinois, and the editor eagerly asked for more. She was paid six dollars per thousand words and for Pauline the words came easily. After four years of constant travel, she was near enough out of debt that she decided she and McRaye should go to London. She offered one of her wampum belts for sale and embarked, only to land in a country much changed since her successful 1894 visit.

With a new king, Edward VII, 1906 London streets were crowded with automobiles, electric lights glittered, a new tube railway swished to the heart of the city, and Indian performers were passé. Expatriate Canadians, one the financier of the Canadian Pacific Railway, now Lord Strothcona, another a popular author, came to her aid. With their contacts and support she and McRaye gave a recital which earned fair reviews. Pauline was invited to write for the *Daily Express* and produced four articles about the Canadian Indians that championed their integrity, their government and their religion. For the first time, she wrote prose from an Indian's viewpoint and the articles, especially one titled, "A Pagan in St. Paul's," were the talk of London. The pair had enough success to enjoy their summer in London, but it was an accidental meeting that would influence Pauline's path in future years.

A Canadian chief of the Squamish people who lived on the shores of the Pacific in British Columbia arrived in London on

August 6 seeking an audience with King Edward. Dignified, elderly Chief Joe Capilano led a delegation to protest the province's restrictions on Indian fishing and hunting rights. With the King away for a few days, a British minister asked Pauline if she would meet with the chiefs. She was quick to oblige and when she greeted the delegation in Chinook, a hybrid language in which she luckily knew a few words, she began a relationship with Chief Joe that would prove increasingly meaningful in her final years. With more requests for her prose writing and the knowledge that her London successes would lead to increased bookings in the United States, she headed back home in November, joy in her heart but nothing in her purse.

Within two weeks, the pair was back on tour. A fire in a Nova Scotia hotel Christmas week nearly destroyed all of Pauline's possessions—her family keepsakes, her stage costume, her gowns, her writing portfolio. Quickly she shouted an alarm and stuffed things in trunks and bags while Walter raced back and forth carrying them down two flights of stairs. They were exhausted and disheveled, but they saved their belongings. During the winter, Pauline turned out more magazine stories, adding *Mothers' Magazine,* published near Chicago, to her credits. She and McRaye had committed to a lucrative Chautauqua tour scheduled to begin July 1, 1907. In the meantime, she borrowed against her Indian artifacts to return to England for the spring, a visit she apparently used to recoup her strength as she wrote more stories for U.S. publications.

She had needed every bit of that strength for the strenuous Chautauqua tour that had silenced her voice, but now they were nearing the end of their commitment. The nine cancelled performances had cost them each $450. But Pauline was finally back at work and the Boulder paper also praised McRaye's humor. Reinvigorated, the pair headed back east to finish in Iowa. After another ten months of touring Canada, Pauline bid

Dink goodbye and rode the CPR clear to Vancouver to rest for a month and focus on magazine writing.

In 1908, the busy port was growing, maturing as a city, establishing a cultural life. She soon received a welcoming visit from Chief Joe Capilano with the invitation to visit his home. He lived in a village across the inlet, and when Pauline stepped into a canoe to go there she felt at home as she had not in years. Time with his family warmed her heart, and the loan of a canoe she could paddle around the shoreline soothed her spirit. She felt accepted by and identified more closely with the Squamish people than she ever had the Mohawks. She wrote fifteen adventure stories for Illinois—based *Boy's World* which described in fictional terms the upbringing of Indian boys. Another eight articles for *Mothers' Magazine,* which had a circulation of 600,000, focused on women's lives in the West, often portraying an Indian woman left alone, her love of her children and her stewardship of Indian traditions. Several stories describe tragic betrayal of an Indian woman by a white man who does not respect her culture. With that body of work accomplished, she left for what she had decided would be her final tour. Crossing Canada for the nineteenth and final time, she and McRaye gave their last performance in the small town of Kamloops, British Columbia, in July 1909.

Pauline had decided to make Vancouver her home. Returning there, she rented an apartment and made her first home since Brantford. Delighting in domestic skills she had never exercised, she quickly became acquainted and made friends with the progressive town's other women writers. She saw Chief Joe and his family often and began hearing the legends of the Squamish people. She listened almost reverently—she had always regretted not paying more heed to her Grandfather Smoke's stories. Sensitive about interrupting Chief Joe, she made the notes she needed to record his tales only after he left her apartment. Vancouver's *Daily Province Magazine* was delighted to publish the stories as a series.

She was writing every day, pouring out stories for her American editors, knowing she had to keep selling to pay expenses. Twenty-one stories for the *Daily Province,* a total of twenty-three for her American editors—she added up the wordage and figured how much she could count on if it was all accepted. It all was, often as the lead story for the issue. However, she was beginning to fight more than fatigue. Her right arm was often locked in pain. She was losing weight. She found a lump in her right breast that proved to be cancerous. Without telling even her best friend, she had the breast removed, with no real hope it would help.

On a cold, grey day in March 1910, Pauline stood in Chief Joe's home, helping his wife, Mary Agnes, greet guests after his funeral. The old man had died of tuberculosis, the scourge of native peoples. Pauline, already sunk in despair, listened as dirt thudded down on the coffin lid. She was taken back to her father's passing, when the death cry echoed along the Grand River. "I'm coming, I'm coming, I'm coming," she murmured.

Trying "to chase the glooms away," by walking, whatever the weather, she struggled to write. She needed the money. Chief Joe's son, Chief Matthias, visited often, carrying more legends. Her Vancouver editor began visiting and took her stories by dictation. She refused to acknowledge or discuss her illness with her friends. Those in the International Order of the Daughters of the Empire named their chapter after her. The Women's Press Club asked her to speak and she gave a few recitals. In growing financial straits, she was often shy the quarters needed to run the gas stove to keep her apartment warm.

In September 1911, her friends gave her the only help she could accept. Members of the Women's Press Club and the Women's Canadian Club met with her Vancouver editor and convinced him to published the Squamish legends in book form. Money from sales would go into a trust fund to support Pauline. She had wanted it titled *Legends of the Capilanos,* but *Legends of Vancouver* was deemed more saleable. The first edition of 1,000 sold out in four days at one dollar a copy. Another edition was ordered. After consulting Pauline, her old partner Walter McRaye wrote to friends of theirs all across Canada, offering autographed copies for two dollars each, which Pauline thought was a scandalous price. The publishers were swamped with orders.

Pauline was soon resting in a private hospital, receiving excellent care, her room bright with her colorful Mohawk keepsakes. She rallied enough in the summer of 1912 that neighbors occasionally saw her out walking her favorite route in Stanley Park. In September she received the new Governor General of Canada, King Edward's brother, Arthur, in her room, elegantly garbed in a blue and gold kimono provided by her fellow writers. They reminisced about his first visit to Canada, when the 8-year-old Pauline had watched her father and grandfather award the young Duke an honorary chieftainship in the Six Nations.

Thanks to her Vancouver friends, and the knowledge that her death was imminent, Pauline's work was suddenly in demand. By late 1912, the Squamish book was in its fifth printing. In December, the Musson Book Company brought out a collection of her poetry titled *Flint and Feather*. Christmas week she worked long hours into the night signing books, thoroughly sick of using a pen but knowing she was "getting paid for it." Her mind hazy with morphine to fight ever-increasing pain, she learned her magazine pieces from *Boy's World* were to be collected into a volume titled *The Shagganappi,* and those from *Mothers' Magazine* would become *The Moccasin Maker*. But she did not live to see them in print. She died on March 7, 1913, just short of her fifty-second birthday.

Obituaries in magazines and newspapers across Canada expressed their sorrow at her death and admiration for her talent. The *Vancouver Daily Province* celebrated her genius and generosity of spirit, ending, "It was always fine weather and good going on the trail when Pauline Johnson blazed the way."

With special permission, her ashes were buried in Stanley Park, near a rock important in Squamish legends, and in 1922 Canadian women erected a monument to her memory. She had expressly forbidden any such memorial, but when the Canadian government recognized the centenary of her birth by publishing a postage stamp in 1961, she surely would have been gratified at this validation of her work. She was the first author and the first Indian to receive such recognition. Probably she would have been just as pleased to know that generations of Canadian school children memorized her poetry, and that more than ninety years after her death, this turn-of-the-twentieth century poet could still be quoted by turn-of-the-twenty-first century Canadians. *Flint and Feather* was reprinted in 1972.

In the United States, her prose is given significant value. Her translation and preservation of Squamish legends from an oral culture, her theme of the painful rejection mixed-blood people—especially women—experienced, her portrayals of the lives of both Indian and white women on the frontier were among the first of their kind. The University of Arizona republished *The Moccasin Maker* in 1987. In championing and depicting her Indian heritage both at home and abroad, she opened minds to the possibility that an accomplished woman who would find welcome in any parlor could lift her chin and declare, "I'm a Red Indian and I feel very proud!"

E. Pauline Johnson Bibliography

Books

Gray, Charlotte. *Flint and Feather; The Life and Times of E. Pauline Johnson, Tekahionwake.* Harper Flamingo Canada, 2002.

Johnson, E. Pauline. *Legends of Vancouver,*1912. (Reprint, McClelland, Goodchild and Stewart, Ltd., 1961.)

-----.*The Mocassin Maker,* 1913. Reprint, University of Arizona Press, Introduction by A. LaVonne Brown Ruoff, 1987.

Articles

"Chautauqua Notes," *Boulder Daily Camera,* Aug. 1, (1907).

Dockstader, Frederick J. "Emily Pauline Johnson,"*Great North American Indians, Profiles in Life and Leadership,* Van Nostrand Reinhold Co., 1977: 125-6.

"E. Pauline Johnson," *Larousse Dictionary of Women,* Laurousse Kingfish Chambers, Inc., 1996.

Gray, Charlotte. *Flint and Feather: The Life and Times of E. Pauline Johnson, Tekahionwake,* Harper Flamingo , 2002.

Gray, Janet, ed. *She Wields a Pen, American Women Poets of the Nineteenth Century,* University of Iowa Press, 1977: 261-64.

Hogan, Linda. "The Nineteenth Century Native American Poets," *Wassaja/The Indian Historian* v.13, n. 4, (1980): 24-29.

"Indian Poetess and a Canadian Humorist, An," *Boulder Daily Camera,* July 30, (1907).

Ruoff, A. LaVonne Brown. "E. Pauline Johnson," *Dictionary of Native American Literature,* Garland Publishers, Inc., 1994: 239-42.

-----."E. Pauline Johnson," *Dictionary of Literary Biography: Native American Writers of the United States,* Bruccoli Clark Layman, 1997: 131-6.

Woolhead, Henry, ed.. "E. Pauline Johnson,"*The Woman's Way,* Time Life Books, 1995.

www.voices.cla.umn/edu/authors/Johnson. (*Voices from the Gaps,* Department of English, University of Minnesota, Minneapolis, MN, 2003).

www.humanities.mcmaster.ca/~pjohnson (*Pauline Johnson Archive,* McMaster University, Hamilton, Ontario, 2003).

www.nlc~bnc.ca (National Library of Canada).

Susan LaFlesche Picotte

Chapter Six

SHE TURNED VISIONS INTO REALITIES

Susan LaFlesche Picotte, 1865-1915
Omaha – French-American

She was a "lady of fashion," 21-year-old Susan LaFlesche wrote her sister in high humor, discovering what it was like to wear a bustle. She was piling her long black hair on top of her head now, because her fellow classmates liked it best that way.

Susan also wrote sister Rosalie back in Nebraska on the Omaha Reservation about dreaming of the young Sioux student who was sweet on her—he was "without exception the handsomest Indian I ever saw," and she found his interest in her both intriguing and disturbing. But she also wrote from Philadelphia on October 27, 1886, how she enjoyed the study of anatomy. "Everything on a bone, grooves, depressions, tubercles and even little holes in the bones have names," she reported. "Sometimes you see a little tiny hole in a bone, well you have to tell what nerves and arteries pass through it." She found it all fascinating, but she worried about learning it all fast enough to pass the anatomy quiz. They were names she had to learn, because she was intent on becoming a doctor of medicine. It was a rare goal among American women of her time, an almost inconceivable goal for women of her race.

Susan's start in life had been markedly different from the traditional rites that greeted her older sister, Susette, eleven years earlier. Susan was reservation-born, and her first memories were of her father's two-story wooden house, which was the only home she had ever known. Books and learning had been part of her life from the beginning, and the white man had named her homeland Nebraska when she was only two.

Her Indian mother, Mary, and grandmother, Nicomi, were major influences in her home, and their Omaha customs and beliefs were ingrained in her being. But she and her siblings were also honoring their father, Joseph's, convictions that they must prepare themselves to step into the white man's world. It had been ten years now since there were any buffalo to hunt. White people, Joseph noted, had come "like blackbirds do, and spread over the country," until "We are strangers in the land where we were born." When the Indian looked to the future, her father said, he "sees his only chance is to become as the white man." Susan's feet were firmly planted on that path.

In some measure, Susan owed her presence in the lecture hall at the Women's Medical College of Pennsylvania to Susette's years of work as an advocate for the Poncas, and by extension the Omaha Indians, beginning in 1879. The Women's National Indian Association was organized that year as a result of the attention Susette, Ponca Chief Standing Bear, and T. H. Tibbles brought to the Indians' plight. The Connecticut Indian Association, an auxiliary of the national group, was financing Susan's medical education. Ethnologist Alice Fletcher, who had befriended Susette and Thomas H. Tibbles—the two were now married—had been instrumental in securing the scholarship for Susan.

Fletcher had visited the LaFlesche family for her research and become fond of them all. Susan's half-brother, Frank, was working with her to record Omaha history. The scientist had been impressed when Susan demonstrated tender skill in caring for her during an attack of inflammatory rheumatism she suffered while visiting the reservation in 1883. Susan had already completed two-and-one-half years at the Elizabeth Institute for Young Ladies in New Jersey, taught two years in the Omaha mission school and then graduated top in her class from Hampton Normal and Agricultural Institute in Virginia.

When Fletcher traveled to Hampton from Washington, D. C., for the 1886 Hampton graduation, she watched Susan give the opening address to the crowd of 1,000 with assurance and charm. Influenced by her salutatory message, "My Childhood and Womanhood," her clear voice and composure, and the medal Susan won for achieving the highest score in an examination, Fletcher was moved to approach Sarah Thomson Kinney, president of the Connecticut Indian Association and suggest Susan LaFlesche as a candidate for a medical scholarship.

If few women aspired to being physicians in 1886, the institutions which would admit them were practically non-existent. Women doctors were derisively called "doctoring ladies," and barred from internships, residencies and many state and county medical associations. The Philadelphia Quakers provided an exception when they founded the Woman's Medical College (WMC) in 1850. Persevering in their studies despite name calling, jeers, hisses—and even spitballs and stones—from their male counterparts at Jefferson Medical College, women had been earning medical degrees in Philadelphia since that time. One of those pioneering WMC graduates was Hampton Institute's resident physician, Doctor Martha Waldron, and she urged the school to accept Susan as a "beneficiary student." Hampton's principal, General Samuel Armstrong, endorsed the idea, saying Susan was "the finest, strongest Indian character we have had at the school. She is a level-headed, earnest, capable Christian woman."

Kinney quickly began soliciting donations from Connecticut women for the student she described as "gentle, refined and unselfish," and capable of ministering to both the physical needs and "deeper wants" of her people. The endorsements by Hampton professors and Susan's own carefully handwritten application won her a seat in the three-story brick college's lecture hall. With $167 the Office of Indian Affairs provided Indian boarding students, books and clothing supplied by the Connecticut women, and a room in the Philadelphia YWCA, the young Indian woman began her studies with students from many parts of the United States, Australia, India and Japan.

Accustomed to the military regimentation of Hampton Institute, Susan was puzzled to learn there were no requirements to attend class. But she soon realized students missed a lecture at their peril, because they faced weekly quizzes on material covered. Thrust into a demanding environment, wondering if she can keep pace with her classmates—all white—who are much more educated than she, her first letters speak of longing for home. Looking three years ahead to when she will finish her studies and return home seems like "paradise." How can knowledge compare "to my own dear family," she asks, "however poor we are it is enough that we are together."

Yet her professors had made a point of welcoming her, stressing how glad they were to have her there, how they respected her heritage. By November she was telling Rosalie and the family back home that she did not mind dissection "in any way whatever." They worked six students to one body, she explained, relaxed enough to "laugh and talk up there just as we do anywhere." Joking that she was wielding the knife— "not the scalping knife though," she described taking off little by little "first the skin, then the tissue—then one muscle is lifted showing arteries - veins and nerves etc.. . . . It is splendid," she wrote enthusiastically, promising several times to share her knowledge with Rosalie when she returned home. She reported gleefully in another letter that a boy from Jefferson Medical College had "keeled over" when they were all gathered around a Pennsylvania Hospital table to observe an operation. "I wasn't even thinking of fainting," she gloated. "I think no more of seeing an amputation now than I do to see a patient . . .who has a fever."

She wrote often of longing for home, praying that they were all well and picturing what the family was doing as she wrote. She offered medical advice to the 25-year-old Rosalie, married to Ed Farley and mother of four, who was again pregnant, and to her mother and father. Several times she remarked that Rosalie, whom she called her "Sister-Mother," would make a better doctor than she, and she anticipated the day they could sit together and study chemistry and treatment of burns, hemorrhages, poisons, colic and dyspepsia.

Addressed constantly as Miss LaFlesche, she longed to be called Susie and to romp with Rosalie's children. She was working so hard she was afraid she was getting "too quiet and dull," and she longed to sing and dance and cut up for the children. Having children was "a privilege denied to some women, " she remarked and it pleased her to think of Rosalie "so happy in your children."

It was a privilege she planned to deny herself. As 1887 opened she wrote an eleven-page letter pondering her relationship with Thomas Ikinicapi, the Sioux whom she knew from when she had tutored him at Hampton. Although he was less educated than she, he was thoughtful and kind, always a gentleman. He wrote to her often of his love and wanted to cement their relationship, but she did not believe she cared deeply enough for him to commit herself. Her college advisor admired noble qualities she saw in T. I., as they called him, but she was against the relationship, advising only a platonic friendship.

Susan evidently had promised her financial supporters not to marry. Her family also opposed the alliance and although she wrote Rosalie that she knew she was "cut out to be an old maid," she was obviously emotionally torn. Her 24-year-old sister, Marguerite, was attending Hampton and when Susan traveled south to visit her she observed Marguerite's developing relationship with a fellow student, Yankton Charles Diddock. She celebrated the pair's engagement, but as for her own relationship with T. I., she wrote Rosalie, "Friendship is all it can be. . . . I shall be the dear little old maid and come and see you all and doctor and dose you all. Won't that be fine?" But she wrote that she could still see the pain in Thomas' eyes when they parted. He continued to write to her through the spring but she did not weaken.

Her concern for Rosalie had been warranted. Her sister had all the work of a farmer's wife, the care of her husband, children and aging parents, and she constantly advised and interpreted for the Omahas, corresponded with aid organizations and kept track of donations from various groups. Rosalie had lost Joseph, one of twins from her second pregnancy, and in March her baby girl was stillborn. In a tender letter Susan reminded "Ro" her daughter is not lost, only gone for a little while to be with Joe until we go to them." Prayers for her family are a constant theme of her letters.

With the city's amenities available, Susan was absorbing more than medicine. She learned the street car system so well that she helped other classmates get around Philadelphia's winding streets. They visited the Academy of Fine Arts, attended the theater, where she enjoyed Lily Langtry's *Wife's Peril* and the opera, where she saw *The Mikado*. She was invited to tea in fine homes and heard Frances Willard lecture on temperance. Philadelphia had progressive attitudes toward Indians; it was the headquarters of the Indians Rights Association as well as the Women's National Indian Association. The Lincoln Institute and the Education Home provided homes for Indian boys and destitute children, and Susan made special efforts to visit both.

Although she found it uncomfortable at first, she spoke several times to interested groups about Indian policy reform, and on one occasion held a roomful of boys motionless as she described Indian life. She and a friend who had taught in an Indian school and planned to return there to practice when she received her M.D., celebrated doing well in an anatomy exam by traveling out of the city to Fairmont Park where they walked, collected pine cones and sat on a rock above the Schuylkill River. Money was always tight and she wrote that she expected a little pay for contributing a story of an Omaha buffalo hunt to a professor's book for children.

Lack of money kept her from going home that summer. Instead she taught at Hampton, where she was a recognized role model—a popular figure, she was often held up to the young people there as an example of what they could achieve.

As her course of medical studies resumed, she was regularly at the Clinic Hall in the Women's Hospital for lectures. Seated in one of five steeply ascending rows in the operating amphitheater, the women could observe as patients were examined and treated. What Susan saw made her grateful for her family's health. She was surprised at the suffering women's diseases could bring, and she was relieved that she could sympathize without it affecting her objectivity. But she worried constantly about her family—Rosalie's pregnancies, her husband's fevers, her aging mother and father—and her medical advice to them constituted her initial contribution to the Omahas' welfare. A noted lung surgeon she observed welcomed her "again and again," praising her for being, "the first woman who is in the college to go back and practice among your own people."

She spent her summer recess that year trying vainly to help stem an epidemic of measles that was sweeping the Omaha Reservation. With nutrition and sanitation at appalling levels, she could only show the families how to take the medication the local physician offered and comfort the sick and bereaved —almost every family lost at least one child. As the epidemic waned, she took the place of her ailing parents, harnessing the horses, racking hay, measuring their land for a fence, cooking , sewing and nursing her own family members.

On March 14, 1889, she received her diploma—the leading student in a class of thirty-six and the first female Indian physician. Her medical professor praised her for "courage, constancy and ability." That ability showed in high scores on a competitive examination which earned her a four-month residency at the Women's Hospital—an opportunity given to only five other graduates. By August 5, she was gratefully back home, although that home must have seemed emptier without her grandmother, Nicomi, and especially the vital presence of her father, who had died the year before. She was appointed physician at the agency school, and by December she was in charge of the health of 1,244 Omahas of all ages. It was what she had wanted ever since she was a small girl, she had told Sarah Kinney three years earlier, "for even then I saw the needs of my people for a good physician."

The tall, 24-year-old doctor maintained an air of dignified authority but, able to speak the Omahas' language and aware of their attitudes and fears, she was soon caring for more than their bodies. Working from an office in the school, where Marguerite was now teaching, she dispensed advice on cleanliness, hygiene and housekeeping. About half the Omahas still lived in cabins with dirt floors, and many families were crowded into one or two rooms; modern hygiene standards seemed impossible to fulfill. She handed out advice about land issues, annuities and legal matters along with medications and inoculations. Her roomy office was often crowded with both adults and children who entertained themselves with games, books and magazines the Women's National Indian Association donated.

Faced with serving patients scattered over the 1,350 square mile reservation, she walked when she could and rented a team for greater distances. Traveling over dirt roads so inadequate it required two horses to make progress, she often drove out six miles in one direction before returning for lunch and spent the rest of the day visiting homes in another direction. For a time she rode horseback, but she broke so many bottles and thermometers that she had to give that up. That first winter she fought two epidemics of influenza—which she knew as la grippe—one of conjunctivitis, and chronic dysentery and tuberculosis among other ailments. Often she provided food as well as medication, sometimes cooking it herself when no member of the household was able. Over and over again, she saw how lack of hygiene contributed to illness.

The slender woman handled the reins herself even when temperatures plummeted to fifteen and twenty degrees below zero. Sometimes it was ten p.m. before she made her way back home. And when she was home she kept a lighted lamp by the window so that anyone needing her help could find her.

When Susan was just beginning medical school in 1886, Sarah Kinney had written a letter which expressed concern about Susan's health, praying "that her health and strength will prove sufficient for her work." Soon after Susan became tribal physician, the Women's National Indian Association asked her to also serve as their medical missionary to her people. Her Christian faith had always been important to her life, and she willingly added Sunday school and morning services, where she and Marguerite sang and interpreted, Sunday evening meetings for young people and Wednesday prayer meetings to her schedule. She urged the people to be legally married and to be buried as Christians.

Her correspondence enlarged to include a detailed annual report to the women's group. She took time in the summer of 1892 to travel to Hampton and give an inspirational address about her work, but in January of 1893 she collapsed and spent weeks in bed, suffering pain in her ears, neck and head. In October that year she resigned as government physician, citing her own health and her mother's critical illness.

To the surprise of all who knew her, the young doctor married Yankton Sioux Henry Picotte in the summer of 1894. Henry was the brother of Marguerite's husband, Charley, who had died of tuberculosis in the fourth year of their marriage. Nearing thirty, Susan must have felt her obligation to the Women's National Indian Association had been fulfilled. Perhaps the recent deaths of Charley and her first love, Thomas

Ikinicapi, of tuberculosis bought home the fragility of life. For whatever reason, she chose to take the 35-year-old Henry as her husband. The decision caused deep concern among her friends, who worried about both her own frail health and her choice of a mate, but she was not deterred. John G. Neihardt, who later became Nebraska Poet Laureate, knew both of them a few years later. He found Henry a handsome, personable storyteller possessing a good sense of fun, and puzzled not at all that Susan could fall in love with him. The couple settled on Susan's allotment and Henry began to farm. Their first son, Caryl, was born in 1895 and Pierre three years later.

With additional responsibilities as wife and mother, she continued to be immersed in her people's health problems. She devoted hours of care to Omahas who came to the Blackbird Hills Presbyterian Mission for help. The more people she saw the more concerned she became about the Omahas' overuse of alcohol. Her father, Joseph, had kept it in check on the reservation while he was chief, but after his death, liquor interests began to push in. As physician, Susan witnessed the deaths, beatings, accidents, illness and poverty resulting from drunkenness and was forced to deal with the aftereffects when whiskey was as plentiful as water. She fought back with lectures on temperance and efforts to get effective legislation passed. She wrote to the commissioner of Indian affairs describing the chaos liquor caused. "Men and women died from alcoholism, and little children were seen reeling on the streets of the town. Drunken brawls in which men were killed occurred and no person's life was considered safe." She saw a people she had considered "a fine specimen of manhood," being "demoralized mentally, morally and physically."

Within a year of her marriage Susan was again so ill that Rosalie wrote their brother Frank, "I had given up all hopes of her when she commenced to improve." Back on her feet again, she continued to practice medicine in Bancroft, caring for white people as well as Indians. But illness continued to plague her. In 1897 another bout of the degenerative disease that caused her intense ear, head and neck pain laid her so low that patients and friends joined family members in fearing for her life. The flood of food, fruit, flowers and good wishes that flowed to help her was overwhelming, and she later admitted that while she had often before felt unappreciated, she now knew that was not so.

As the twentieth century opened, Susan suffered multiple sorrows. Her sister Rosalie died March 9, 1900, at age 39, leaving eight surviving children ranging in age from 2 ½ to 19. Her loss shadowed the celebration that fall when Susan and Henry moved into their new house. It was small but it was their own.

A small pox epidemic kept her busy vaccinating children for some weeks and there was always croup and sometimes diphtheria to deal with. Her crusading sister Susette, who had moved back to the reservation to be near the family, died in 1903.

And through these years Susan was also watching her bright, much-loved husband succumb to the curse which was robbing so many Indians of their lives. Henry died of complications of alcoholism in 1905. Left to support herself, her invalid mother and her two small sons, in late 1906 she purchased a lot in the new town of Walthill, about ten miles northwest of Bancroft, and built a comfortable two-story modern house.

The railroad had carved Walthill from the reservation, and Susan led a delegation to Washington, D.C., that convinced the secretary of the interior to outlaw liquor sales in towns that were formerly reservation land. The epidemic of alcoholism was in some measure reduced. With Marguerite and her second husband, Walter Diddock, living just across the street the two women busied themselves developing a community. They became charter members of the Eastern Star and worked to organize a new Presbyterian Church.

Yet she also was immersed in problems unique to Indians. Again devastated by an illness she called neurasthenia in the spring of 1909, she required visits from specialists and six weeks of private nursing before she began to recover. She had to get better, she wrote her mentor and friend from medical school days, because "The Omahas depend on me. . . ."

The problem was a familiar one—government interference with Indian land rights. Although they had been granted allotments in 1882, the Omahas' land was held in trust by the government. This meant they had to get official approval from the agent before they could rent or lease any of their property. The cumbersome trust period was scheduled to end in 1910, but government officials arbitrarily decided it was to be continued for another ten years, maintaining the Indians were too uneducated and backward to take care of such legal matters. Omahas attempting to lease land or secure their share of tribal monies were forced to go before a competency commission. Some of them had to travel many miles to see officials. Sometimes they brought their papers to the doctor's office, begging her to write letters for them so they could get their funds. She witnessed a case where a tubercular woman died, still waiting for the bureaucracy to release her money. Susan was incensed. The Omahas had a higher literacy rate than many tribes and were "independent and self-reliant," she wrote an Omaha newspaper. "You can never push an Omaha down or pass a thing over his head; he will light on his feet facing you."

She scarcely had the strength to stand on her own feet, but she could not refuse when tribal members insisted they needed her to head a delegation to Washington. "I will just have to take care of myself until this fight is over," she wrote her friend. On February 7, 1910, she spoke before the secretary of the interior and the United States attorney general. Speaking with a passion that may have surprised the bureaucrats, she said: "We are not stones—we are not driftwood. We have feelings, thoughts, hopes, ambitions, aspirations." Protesting that people who were treated as incompetent wards had no chance to learn responsibility, she said, "We have suffered enough from your experiments—we have been practically robbed of our rights by the government—In the name of justice and humanity—we ask for a more liberal interpretation of the law,"so they could become a "self-reliant, independent, self-sustaining people." John Neihardt described her presentations as simple, but most effective for her way of "increasing the impact of a climactic sentence by withholding it in silence overlong." After tension had built in the audience, "her face grew lighter, and she seemed to vibrate with intensity of feeling. Then, in a low voice, she said it!" The appeal was successful; the Omahas gained release from the harmful restrictions, and the delegation returned to a rejoicing population.

That year she kept a diary, filling the lined pages of the brown leather book with neat inscriptions in ink. On September 20, her day began at seven a.m. Her first patient had a ruptured appendix and she put him on the train to Sioux City. Then she advised a mother who was having difficulty feeding her baby. Next she helped with a land application. After advising another ill patient, she helped with a trust fund query for money that would enable a girl to get ear treatment. It was a quest that must have touched her; her recurrent ear disease was making her increasingly deaf. She helped two more Omahas with financial problems. At nine p.m. she was just heading out to treat a girl with tonsilitis. Then she stopped to see a new baby she had delivered and called at the home of another woman with a baby. It was eleven p.m. when she returned home. Through the rest of the week, in addition to medical care, she helped a boy get clothes for school, served as an interpreter, wrote letters, checked out kinship interests in a legal matter, helped patients with wills, advised on teeth care, obtained crutches for one patient and sought a loan for another. She finished the week by putting up a mother and her three children because her husband's drunkenness made the woman afraid to go home.

However, life was not all dark. As Christmas neared, her workload was lighter and she donated a box of apples for the children's Christmas tree at church. The day itself was brightened by the presence of Marguerite and her children; Susan was a devoted aunt to her nieces and nephews. They opened gifts around their tree and after dinner attended both afternoon and evening church services. Four days later she was back at work, diagnosing a woman with trachoma and a girl with tuberculosis. Then she drove—by car this time—to an impoverished one-room home where the mother suffered both influenza and tuberculosis, one daughter TB, an ear infection and caries of the bones in her foot, and two other children badly infected eyes. Sanitation was almost impossible in the crowded conditions and Doctor Susan advised a larger living space. Then missionary Susan led the family in prayer. As the new year opened, she traveled to Lincoln on the train to take care of tribal business.

Although she was a woman and an Indian, Susan was respected by other physicians; she helped organize the Thurston County Medical Society and was a member of the Nebraska State Medical Society. She also chaired the state health committee of the Nebraska Federation of Women's Clubs which worked to push health measures through the Legislature. Achieving an appointment as medical missionary from the Presbyterian Board of Home Missions—the only Indian so accepted—provided her with a small income, and she began to work more and more in the field of public health.

She had written in her college days of the pleasure she found in being able to wash daily and keep herself neat and clean. She knew that level of cleanliness was difficult on the reservation and she was ever more aware of the problems that ensued. When she had begun medical training, she had envisioned helping Omaha women learn modern housekeeping techniques. One of her campaigns was against the community drinking cup that serviced everyone who had a thirst. She wrote articles for the local paper declaring its use an "evil" practice and the Legislature soon outlawed its use. Disposable cups became available in stores, and schools began installing drinking fountains. The Walthill drug store began to dispense ice cream with disposable bowls and spoons.

Even more villainous in the doctor's eyes was the housefly —"the filthiest of all vermin." She designed a graphic poster depicting flies eating from such things as corpses, garbage and the spittoon of a consumptive, and describing ways to keep flies out of the home and away from food. She announced, "War declared on the Fly: From Breeding Place to Feeding Place." She urged people to sprinkle lime or kerosene where flies tended to congregate and breed. She promoted the installation of window screens and screen doors and soon the local hardware store was stocking flytraps. One did not have to be Indian to receive her advice; it was widely circulated.

Another major concern was the toll tuberculosis took among the Indian population. She began an in-depth study of the disease and developed lectures to share what she learned about prevention. The common drinking cup played its part in spreading the disease, she stressed. Walthill observed National Tuberculosis Day and with local doctors invited to lecture in two churches, Susan stood for two hours in the cold to alert people to the lecture. She urged officials to examine students monthly for traces of infection, citing the case history of several who had brought the disease home from boarding schools. Soon she, herself, was testing the students.

She diagnosed an 18-year-old girl with a fever of 103 degrees and sent her to Arizona only to learn she died a short time later. Another girl came home infected and lived only six weeks, but it was long enough to infect both her mother and grandmother, who also died. "It is so terribly hard to see the people undergoing hardships from a civilization new to them," she wrote the commissioner of Indian affairs. She lectured in schools and campaigned continually, but wrote with despair that eternal vigilance is possible "only when you stand a trained nurse over them."

Her own sons were teenagers now, and she felt they needed the discipline that Hampton Institute had given her. Caryl and Pierre were growing up in a world in which all but a few aged Omaha men dressed in white men's clothes, where ninety percent of those under forty spoke English, where 95 percent of families traveled by carriage or buggy. Frame houses were ubiquitous, train travel a matter of course. The most successful men of the tribe were attorneys, stock men, real estate dealers and merchants. But too many others were lost in drink; her own nephew and brother-in-law had struggled against its power.

When she found her boys were too young for Hampton, she enrolled them in a private institution for boys in Lincoln, called the Nebraska Military Academy. It was a school designed for whites and focused on "individualization." In addition to academics, the boys would have exposure to athletics, manual training, military discipline, and Christian instruction. It was an expense her devotion to education and self-discipline deemed necessary.

In her two dozen years of caring for the Omahas, nothing had proved as devastating to their health and well-being as alcohol. In 1914, Susan again protested to the Indian commissioner about lax enforcement of laws against its disbursement. Desperate alcoholics would drink anything; even lemon extract was causing deaths. An old man had died at the hands of a drunken young man who later committed suicide and nothing was done to the seller. She enumerated deaths attributed to liquor in the preceding ten years and a month later she was testifying at an inquest of another victim of drink about the "physical degeneration of the Indian." The Omaha child was "a weak, puny specimen of humanity," she declared. She stressed that detectives who patrolled the reservation must be impartial and above receiving bribes. The "courage, constancy and ability" she had displayed at medical school had been tried past the point of exhaustion, but still she fought for her people.

Through the years, she also did her part to keep Omaha legends alive. While her brother, Frank, who was now working for the Bureau of American Ethnology, teamed with Alice Fletcher to compile a lengthy, detailed history of the Omaha people's culture, Susan also committed to paper a number of folk tales and descriptions of Omaha life. She wrote of childhood memories of an elderly blind storyteller who was pampered and coaxed onto a soft buffalo robe, plied with drink and kinnikinick, entreated to begin his tales. She remembered the center fire throwing shadows on listening faces who leaned forward eagerly to hear each word, of feeling totally safe and secure as, with dramatic gestures and significant pauses, the storyteller led the way into another world.

She wrote of subjects that ranged from early farming practices to "The Dance of the Turkey." She could not help contrasting the former child nestled contentedly with her father and mother to contemporary Omaha children congregating in pool halls. Some of her stories were published in the local paper. The Fletcher - LaFlesche collaboration resulted in a noted two-volume history, *The Omaha Tribe,* published in 1911.

For many years, Omahas who needed hospitalization were forced to travel to Omaha or Sioux City. Susan had long dreamed of a hospital close enough for prompt and proper care, and she began to wok to make the dream a reality. Finally the Home Mission Board of the Presbyterian Church granted the cause $8,000. The Quakers gave another $500. Marguerite and Walter donated land for the building. Several fund-raising events, including a concert in Pittsburgh, raised money and she appealed to other organizations and individuals for equipment and furnishings. She persevered through disappointments, renewed her efforts when faced with denials, refused to admit defeat, and on January 8, 1913, the hospital opened with ceremony and celebration.

A one-and-one-half story frame building, its welcoming entrance opened into a long screened porch where ambulatory patients could congregate. Having available two five-bed wards, one two-bed children's ward, and five private rooms, a fully equipped operating room, two bathrooms, a laundry, a kitchen and a reception room, it must have seemed miraculous to Susan. She could remember only too well hours and days of jouncing on a hard wagon seat or heaving herself into a saddle and riding through intense cold or muggy heat to tend distant patients. Now she and the three nurses the building housed had steam heat, electric lights and city water. At last she could achieve the hygienic standards so necessary for good health.

However, she had little time to enjoy the luxury. Her recurrent problem with her ears was finally diagnosed as "decay of the bone." Surgeons tried twice, once in February and again in March 1915, to eliminate the diseased bone, but by June they had told the family she had little time to live. Nursed by a niece and her sons, Caryl and Pierre, who were home from school, she lived until September 18.

A simple service was held in her home the day after her death, with her family and as many of her friends as could find space to stand gathered around the casket banked with flowers. It was a Sunday, and participating ministers represented the Walthill Presbyterian Church she had helped organize, the Presbyterian Board of Home Missions, which she had represented for many years, and the Blackbird Hills Mission of the Omaha Tribe, where she had spent so many hours helping her people. After the English service concluded, an aged Indian gave the final prayer in the Omaha language. She was buried in the Bancroft cemetery next to her husband.

On September 24, 1915, the shaken community poured out its grief, filling two-thirds of the front page of the *Walthill Times* to mark her passing. Harry L. Keefe, who worked closely enough with her to know "her charities among her patients far exceeded her earnings," wrote ". . .this woman's character stands out in gigantic profile upon the horizon of human greatness."

Reverend D. E. Jenkins of the Presbyterian Mission board noted, "Dr. Picotte gave herself unselfishly, passionately and often with what amounted to reckless disregard of herself to the task of relieving, helping and uplifting the Omaha Indians. By day and by night she dreamed dreams and saw visions of larger and better things yet to come for her beloved people."

Seven months later the Presbyterian Board of Home Missions named the hospital she had fought to create the "Dr. Picotte Indian (Medical) Mission. In its first two years of existence 356 patients, both Indian and white, had occupied beds there. In 1915, 418 patients received care in its seventeen beds. Renamed the "Dr. Susan LaFlesche Picotte Memorial Hospital," the facility continued to serve the Omaha people until after World War II. Now a National Historic Landmark, it is used as a museum and a community center which commemorates the doctor as a model student, servant, healer and leader.

Susan LaFlesche Picotte raised two fine sons, ministered to her extended family and turned her vision of help for her Omaha people into reality. She put her fifty years, three months and one day to the best possible use, working for the Omahas whom all her life she called, "my people."

Susan LaFlesche Picotte Bibliography

Archival Collections

LaFlesche Family Papers: Susan's letters to her sisters, 1885-88, Susan's Diary, Sep 20, 1910-Jan. 2, 1911; Rosalie's correspondence and diary, 1893-1900; Sarah T. Kinney letters to Rosalie; April 29, 1914; letter to Commissioner of Indian Affairs Cato Sells; Testimony on the death of Henry Warner; Report to State Federation of Women's Clubs.

Books

Bix, Amy Sue. Review of *A New and Untried Course: Woman's Medical College and Medical College of Pennsylvania, 1850-1998.* Rutgers University Press, 2000.

Fletcher, Alice C. and Francis LaFlesche. *The Omaha Tribe,* 1911. (Reprint University of Nebraska Press, 1972.)

Articles

Batille, Gretchen, and Laurie Lisa, Editors, "Susan LaFesche Picotte," *Native American Women: A Biographical Dictionary,* Garland, 1989.

Clark, Jerry E. and Martha Ellen Webb. "Susette and Susan La Flesche: Reformer and Missionary," *Being and Becoming Indian: Biographical Studies of North American Frontiers,* Dorsey Press, 1989:137-159.

Davidson, Martha. "Dr. Susan LaFlesche Picotte: A Physician among Her People," *Perspectives,* v. 4, n.1 (1999).

Diffendal, Anne P. "The LaFlesche Sisters: Susette, Rosalie, Marguerite, Lucy, Susan," *Perspectives: Women in Nebraska History,* Nebraska Department of Education and Nebraska State Council for the Social Studies, 1984.

"Dr. Picotte Discusses New Policy," *Walthill Times,* Dec. 31, (1909):1.

"Dr. Picotte's Appeal, " *Walthill Times,* March 4, (1910):1.

"Dr. Picotte – An Appreciation," "Funeral of Dr. Picotte Marked by Simplicity," "One of the Church's Missionary Heroes," "The Mystery of Her Genius," " *Walthill Times,* Sep. 24, (1915.):1

Emmerich, Lisa E. "Marguerite LaFlesche Diddock, Office of Indian Affairs Field Matron," *Great Plains Quarterly,* v. 13, (1993):172-86.

Green, Norma Kidd. "Four Sisters: Daughters of Joseph La Flesche," *Nebraska History,* v. 45, n. 2 (1964):165-176.

-----."Susan La Flesche Picotte," *Notable American Women,* A Biographical Dictionary, Howard University Press, 1971.

Hauptman, Laurence M. "Medicine Woman, Susan La Flesche, 1865-1915," *New York State Journal of Medicine,* Sept., (1978):1783-88.

Mathes, Valerie Sherer."Dr. Susan LaFlesche Picotte, The Reformed and the Reformer," *Indian Lives, Essays on Nineteenth and Twentieth Century Native American Leaders.* University of New Mexico Press, 1985: 61-90.

-----."Iron Eyes' Daughters: Susette and Susan LaFlesche, Nineteenth-Century Indian Reformers," *By Grit and Grace: Eleven Women Who Shaped the American West,* Fulcrum, 1997,143-152..

-----."The LaFlesche Sisters: Victorian Reformers in the Omaha Tribe," *Journal of the West,* v. 33, n. 1, (1944): 37-44.

-----."Susan LaFlesche Picotte: Nebraska's Indian Physician, 1865-1915," *Nebraska History,* v. 63, n. 4,(1982): 502-530.

-----."Susan LaFlesche Picotte, M.D., Nineteenth-Century Physician and Reformer," Great Plains Quarterly, v. 13, (1993):172-86.

Neihardt, John G. "Dr. Susan Picotte," *Patterns and Coincidences, A sequel to All Is but a Beginning,* University of Missouri Press, 1978.

"Picotte Memorial Hospital," www.cr.nps.gov/nr/feature/indian/2001/picotte.htm.

"Presbyterian Hospital Named for Dr. Picotte," *Walthill Times,* (1916): 1.

Annie Lowry

Nevada Historical Society

Chapter Seven

LIFE ON THE FRINGE

Annie Lowry, 1869-1943
Paiute – American

Annie Lowry spent her early teenage years hiding from the father who wanted to make her white.

Jerome Lowry did not abandon Annie as many other white fathers abandoned their half-blood children, but he was determined she leave behind the Paiute culture of her mother. When he decided to depart northwest Nevada in the mid-1880s for an Oregon ranch, he had no intention of letting the Northern Paiute—Paviotso—wife he called Susie share his new life.

When Annie discovered this mind-numbing fact by overhearing a conversation, she did not hesitate; she decided to cast her lot with the woman other Paviotso called Sautaunee, or Willow Blossom. Hiding out in the scrub brush meant difficult, hungry days and nights. Although Annie was just into her teen years, she was steadfast in her choice.

"I know I was right to choose the Indians for my people," she said in later years, "because I loved them more."

She knew her two younger brothers would go with their father, and that life as a white rancher's daughter promised plentiful food, warm clothes and continued education, but she refused to listen to Lowry's promises, even when they turned into threats. She would remain a Paviotso.

The tall, reddish-haired Lowry was an early emigrant into northwestern Nevada. He had joined the hordes of whites who rushed to the Great Basin upon the 1859 discovery that precious metals lay under the forbidding soil.

The California gold strike had provoked the first real influx of whites through the barren country ten years earlier. Gold seekers on the California Trail had surged through the Humboldt Valley like a flash flood. The river the Paviotso had known for centuries was now named after a German scientist, and thousands of emigrants used its course as their wagon road to hoped-for riches. The desert landscape was littered with their abandoned wagons, carts and household goods, the air putrefied by the stink of their dead stock. The Paiutes found their lives changed by that seasonal traffic. But it was the 1859 discovery of the Comstock Lode near Virginia City, Nevada, and the 1861 find in the Humboldt Range that sealed the Paviotso's fate. The miners swarming through the rocky hills that edged the valley's eastern side, and the settlers who supplied them, came to stay. Heedless and disdainful of a culture they called "the diggers," they took the land they wanted and stripped the Indians of their always-scanty resources.

The Great Basin natives had managed for generations to exist on what slender fare the alkali wastelands, small river valleys and ranges of bald peaks provided. With rainfall an undependable blessing—only six inches per year—they gathered seeds from wild rice and barley, dug bulbs and yucca roots and harvested the green shoots and green and brown heads of cattails growing in marshes. Their gleanings were boiled, roasted or steamed and turned into meal or bread. Wild sugar cane growing on the lake's edge was pounded to release its crystalized syrup which they collected in baskets. Spring brought cutthroat trout and suckers up the rivers and Canada geese, mud hens, robins and flickers on their way north.

The green waters of Pyramid Lake on the elevated western edge of the Paviotso's territory were a reliable source of fish.

Every few years piñon pines growing in the foothills of the Sierra Nevada Mountains produced a good crop of nuts which greatly enriched their diet. Occasionally a pronghorn, mountain sheep or jackrabbit came their way. More dependable were ground squirrels, cottontails, rats, gophers, caterpillars, locusts, ants, grasshoppers and crickets. The insects were eaten raw, cooked or ground with seeds into a flour paste they made into gruel. Each food source required extensive labor and there was little time for other activities.

The people sheltered themselves in temporary huts covered with mats made from the marshland bulrushes. Little clothing was needed in the brutal heat, but bark from scattered, dwarfed sagebrush was moistened, pounded and worked until it could be fashioned into sandals or moccasins to protect feet from the burning sands. Skirts of grass, supplemented with a few rabbit skins or a hide, served for colder weather.

The women wove plant fibers into intricate hats, baskets, sieves and conical vessels that they lined with pitch for cooking and carrying water. The small family groups they lived in were always on the move, looking for their next meal. They had to know when and where plants would be ready for harvest, when migrating birds would appear, how to snare and trap elusive prey. It was a perilous existence, but they were an energetic, innovative people who made use of what there was to survive.

By the time Annie Lowry was born about 1870 (census records indicate 1873, her obituary lists 1869), the influx of white settlers in the Humboldt Valley had destroyed nearly all these natural resources. The Central Pacific Railroad had laid its iron rails through the valley in 1868 and trains began running regularly in 1869. The trains brought all manner of people; even more drove their wagons back from California, rode horseback, trudged beside a mule, pushed a wheelbarrow. The mining companies were waiting to take advantage of the noisy trains, having already erected a huge precious-ore smelter in the new town of Oreana in 1868. Other towns, Lovelock,

Humboldt City, Unionville, and Star City sprouted almost overnight. The grass seeds that had fed the Paiutes went into the stomachs of white cattle herds. The sage and piñon pines were cut to stoke the fires of the smoke-belching smelter. The carp which whites introduced into the river killed the trout. What game existed was quickly killed. The Humboldt Valley and nearby hills, which had supported native peoples for thousands of years, could no longer provide them sustenance.

There had been a few, doomed efforts to resist, but the Paiutes were scattered and few in number. After one initial success, their attempt to band together and battle the whites was brutally put down. When a few desert Indians continued to attack isolated ranches and small groups, the U.S. Army established a few posts to protect the settlers. And the Paviotso were at heart a peaceful people, usually too busy surviving to carry on wars. They had little choice but to adapt.

Thirty-year-old Jerome Lowry had been living in Oreana and working as a stagecoach driver, but a lucky hand of cards turned him into a farmer. Lowry's friend, hotel-owner Louis N. Carpenter, evidently staked the teamster to a poker game at which they won a section of land in an area the Indians called Big Meadows. In the hundreds of miles of forbidding clay and alkali, sand and rock, the wide expanse of grassland on the flanks of the Humboldt offered a startling green oasis of easily watered, fertile soil. The two men became partners and developed their land, near Lovelock, about twelve miles southwest of Oreana, into a cattle ranch.

Lovelock had developed from a trading post English immigrant George Lovelock set up in 1862 to serve travelers on the California Trail. With the advent of the railroad and the hills full of miners needing supplies, it quickly grew into a town. The Big Meadows had centered the Paviotsos' lives, but that was of little import to the settlers. The leader of Sautaunee's band of Paviotso, a man they called Captain John, also settled near Lovelock and began selling wild hay to the whites. He had learned enough English to be a guide for white explorers and claimed a relationship with John C. Fremont. Captain John was a leader of the Paiutes and he espoused friendship with the settlers. A powerful, colorful figure, he often proclaimed his views about Paviotso matters in a loud voice that carried beyond his station into town.

As more businessmen arrived and the town's population grew to several hundred, the Paviotso began working for the settlers, who could provide them with a square meal. Men hired on as farm laborers and guides. Women cleaned white people's houses and washed and ironed their clothes. They lived in an area set aside for the Paviotso in southwest Lovelock, in the traditional dome-shaped huts they called karnees, each housing a small family. The karnees were framed with willow and sagebrush branches and covered with mats woven from swampland tules.

Two of Sautaunee's sisters were married to Captain John, and when her own Paviotso husband deserted her and their baby daughter, she became dependent on him. Captain John wanted to add Sautaunee to his stable of four wives, some of whom he rented out to white men, but the tiny young woman stubbornly resisted.

Sautaunee thought the huge, black-breathing Montezuma Smelting Works was more terrifying than the monsters of Paviotso legend, but she had to earn enough to feed herself and her daughter. The smelter paid the Indians to collect sage, which it burned for firewood. Sautaunee was gathering branches of the silver-gray shrub when Jerome Lowry came into her life.

Frustrated at her refusal to grant his wish, Captain John often beat Sautaunee, and it was during one of these beatings that Lowry stopped by the chief's meadow to stock up on supplies. As Annie remembered her mother's story, Lowry ordered Captain John to "Stop beating that squaw!" After he had completed his purchases, he looked at Sautaunee and said,

"I need a wife. Get your kid, little woman, and come along with me." She climbed into his wagon and after a year in the bustling mining town of Oreana, they settled on the Big Meadows ranch. Lowry built a roomy dugout where Annie and her two brothers were born.

From the beginning her father was determined Annie learn English and act like a white child. He saw to it that her first words were in English, and Paiute words brought scoldings. Sautaunee prepared food on a cookstove and they ate at a table and chairs. But when Annie was four or five, business took Lowry away for six weeks at a time, and the family quickly reverted to Indian living. Annie and her older half-sister, Toodles, loved running free over the fields and darting in and out of the gold-tipped rabbit brush. When wild berries were ripe, Sautaunee would carry the toddler, Robert, on her back and the family would gather the fruit to eat. She taught the girls which seeds to gather and taught them the laborious process of winnowing, drying and grinding the tiny seeds between rocks to make them into Indian meal.

Sometimes they walked for miles, and Sautaunee would begin telling legends from the old days, stories her mother had told her, and tales of how the people had lived before the white intruders. She described the big mudhen hunt in the fall, when many families gathered together and they worked cooperatively to trap and kill thousands of the dowdy birds that filled the marshes. That was before white men's activities had changed Humboldt Lake from an oasis up to twelve feet deep to a dry basin. The women had spent much of the year making a special kind of milkweed into rope for huge nets which the strongest men would drag across the water to entrap the grey birds. Other men paddled one-man boats made of tule reeds through the water to shoo the birds toward the river's mouth where the nets waited. Although there was much squawking and a few sudden flights, soon those watching could see a predominance of white tail feathers headed north. People on shore caught the frantic birds that tried to escape by land. As each net filled, they carried it to shore where the people killed those birds still alive. After three hours or more of hard work they all helped prepare the birds to eat—some to be fried in grease and enjoyed immediately, others hung to dry in the sun for later use. It was one of the few times the scattered bands came together to feast, socialize and catch up on each others' lives.

Other times Sautaunee reached farther back in their people's history, and on one journey they walked many miles south to the rocky opening of a limestone cave. Their ancestors had lived in such caves, Sautaunee told the children, not so long ago. The cavern, which sheltered them from cold and wind, stretched far back into the darkness and provided places to store belongings. Household baskets, snares for hunting, fiber sandals, bone fish hooks, and extra food could be placed there for safekeeping. With pride, she told the children how their ancestors had destroyed a fierce rival tribe called the Si-ka-das, or Tule-eaters, by trapping them in the cave and burning sagebrush at its mouth until it filled it with smoke and they were suffocated. In this way they gained the right to live in Big Meadow.

She also told them light-hearted tales about their animal neighbors and accounts of the people's fear and curiosity when they saw their first white men. She explained the importance of the spirits, how there were magical powers in the mountains, the animals, in the gray fog of winter and the blue haze of summer. Why women spent a few days alone in a karnee at the edge of the village every month. Why people burned a karnee after a family member died in it. She also told them of the terrible sickness that developed along the river; they called it cholera and even the most skilled Paviotso shamans were helpless to stay its course. Annie long remembered her mother's story of the horror of the people, who fled into the mountains, hoping to escape the plague, only to watch their loved ones continue to drop as they ran. Of how in their terror they did not even stop to care for the dying and the dead.

But when Annie reached school age, such rambles became rare. Lowry first took her to Oreana to live with the Carpenter family, where she lived in a house for the first time. Then he delivered her to the H. C. Emmons' two-story hotel in Lovelock, where she lived while she went to school.

The railroad and the access it provided to California markets had turned settler's experimental plots of wheat and alfalfa into a way of life. Experiments in irrigation brought new settlers. Lovelock boasted a freight house, a telegraph office, and a post office.

Lowry left orders Annie was to speak to no Paiute, be taught to clean her room and make her bed, and be dressed in white, starched aprons for classes in the gray one-room schoolhouse. She was the only Indian child in the school but she did not realize some people considered her inferior. She found the work relatively easy and she might have been happy had she not been desperately homesick. Promised visits home every third week sometimes stretched to three months without seeing her mother and siblings. She tried running away, but Lowry whipped her and returned her to school. Recognizing that running away was useless, she was grateful for two teachers who helped her fit in and accept the routine. Soon she excelled in arithmetic and spelling. She was moved to another household, where she enjoyed helping the owner's immigrant wife learn English. By the time the Lovelock School had grown from one room to a two-story building, she was riding her horse in from the ranch.

After a spill from her horse resulted in a broken arm, Annie found herself again a boarder. Then she overheard her father talking about selling his ranch and moving his stock to Oregon. He said he was taking the boys with him because they could pass for white. He planned to put Annie in a convent school to prepare for an Eastern college. But he planned to leave Sautaunee behind.

Lowry had been a good father in many ways He had demanded the school treat her as well as any white child. He had coached her and her brothers in elocution exercises and taught her to hold up her head and not act "like a Paiute Indian or poor white trash." She had heard rumors of this move before, but this time it was her father's voice confirming her worst fears. She could only think, "He is breaking up our home." She thought of her mother's almost pathetic devotion to the man who had given her a home and realized, "He is leaving my poor broken-hearted mother to shift for herself." Then she thought, "I won't go. He can't make me go."

Later, at home, her father told her all the arrangements had been made. He pictured how she would advance in the convent until he could take her to Virginia and show her off to his relatives. In Oregon, his children could put their Paiute past behind.

Annie staunchly refused to leave her mother and their people. Pleas and promises turned into threats. Finally, when nothing moved the girl, Lowry promised to return for her and her mother after he got settled in Oregon.

The residents of cosmopolitan Lovelock, whose faces represented Scandinavian, French, German, Irish, Chinese and English heritages, gathered at the edge of town to watch as the rancher started his 1,400 head of cattle on the trail to Oregon. A few weeks later, Annie learned he had married a white woman from Idaho, and she knew his promise to her mother was an empty one. Then came word he was on his way back to collect the rest of his belongings. Afraid she was one of those belongings, Annie and Sautaunee fled their dugout home.

In the wide, flat expanse of stunted stage land that surrounded Big Meadow like a sea, there was no real place to hide. Anyone standing upright could be seen for miles. The woman and girl spent their days crouched in the sage, their nights hunting for something to eat. It was a hunt that grew steadily more desperate. They were taunted by thirst, baked by the sun. By the time they were sure Lowry had left for good, they were nearly starving.

Gratefully, the two returned to their ranch dugout. But it was only a day or two before Carpenter, Lowry's partner, told them they had to go; he had bought Lowry's share in the ranch and needed his dugout for hired help. Once again they were homeless. They retreated to the Indian Colony in Lovelock and moved into an abandoned karnee, existing on what scraps the other Paviotso could provide. Annie's days and nights were filled with Sautaunee's wails of grief; in her misery she rolled on the floor and moaned and cried. Annie hardened her heart toward her father and vowed she would never let a white man make her suffer like her mother.

Then the old karnee burned and they lost what few possessions they owned. Shortly after, Carpenter appeared and said Lowry had arranged that Annie must go with him. When she refused, he left to get the sheriff.

Again, Annie and Sautaunee fled. This time they followed the river north, existing on berries and roots for day after day until they had traversed some seventy miles to the town of Winnemucca and Sautaunee's family. Annie got a job working in the kitchen of the town's newspaper editor. Earning her first money, she felt rich enough to have a white woman's dress made and buy real shoes.

She worked for just over a year, grateful that Editor E. D. Kelly's kindly wife helped her learn many things, but when she heard that her father had returned and followed her trail to Winnemucca, she and her mother left without saying a word to anyone or collecting their belongings. Again they trekked the miles to Lovelock, living on what few potatoes the harvesters left in the fields and whatever else they could scavenge. Emaciated, their clothing in rags, they moved in with

Sautaunee's daughter, Toodles, her husband, Sanny, and their two-year-old girl.

Their destitute appearance soon attracted the notice of store-owner Steve Young. A progressive man, who had built the first brick building in Lovelock, he called Annie in from the street one day. Almost too terrified to speak, she managed to answer his query about what they had to eat. At her answer, he told her to pick out a pair of shoes and socks, measured out dress yardage for her and her mother, sacked up some food and told her he would see that Lowry paid the bill. It was a kindness she never forgot, and she would turn to him again over the years. For his part, Jerome Lowry evidently paid his daughter's bills; he just could not allow her to be who she was. With Sautaunee now working in the fields, Annie cared for Toodles and her daughter until the ill and pregnant Toodles died, and Sanny left the toddler, Julia, in their care. They burned the karnee and all Toodles' possessions to prevent the dead's spirit from returning, and with the help of others, cut the boughs to build themselves a new karnee.

Ghosts loomed large in the Paiutes' minds. Even in the new karnee, Toodles name remained unspoken, lest she be called back to this world. Annie believed strongly in Indian healers, but spirits could possess a person for either good or ill.

Annie was summoned to the county seat at Winnemucca to interpret at a murder trial of a man and his sisters who defended themselves by claiming the woman they had killed was a witch. Under threat from the guilty trio's family, she spoke only the words she heard as testimony, instead of telling the facts as she knew them. The experience left her disillusioned to learn "the Indians were as lacking in principle and right dealing as the white man."

Paviotso girls entered adulthood at age fourteen and often began a marriage arranged by their mothers at fifteen. With Sautaunee's consent, Annie's widower brother-in-law, Sanny, began to court her. Annie had a nagging fear of Sanny and did not feel ready to marry. She avoided him as long as she could, but after six months, family pressure made the marriage reality. An accepted Paviotso suitor joined his intended's family and slept closer and closer to his chosen bride for five nights. Although Annie rejected his advances, after the fifth night the family considered them married and she had to accept the fact. Although she eventually came to love him, she always felt she had been given to him against her will.

Sanny worked on the Carpenter ranch and the couple were living in a new karnee when their first son was born in 1889. The winter was unusually severe that year and they lost the baby to croup. Following custom, they burned the karnee. However Sanny built a frame home, and in the next ten years Annie gave birth to three more boys and a girl. But there was as much sorrow as rejoicing in the home because one boy died of cholera and the girl succumbed to bloody flux. Bowing to white ways, they did not burn the house but instead changed the doors and windows. Still, Annie rejoiced in her sons Jessie and Willie, and always took them with her when she washed clothes or scrubbed floors for white people. The pay was low, but that was a secondary concern. She always tried to be at work early because the family would feed them breakfast. When the men of the household had finished the noon meal, the woman took what was left out to the yard, where Annie, often with a youngster in a carrier on her back, worked over a tub. Sometimes, if it was windy and cold, she was allowed to eat in the kitchen, but never with the white family.

The relationship between the Paiutes and the settlers was complex. While they considered the Indians to have no rights and denigrated the people as a whole, they often developed strong personal relationships with the ones who worked for them. They took a paternalistic attitude toward their welfare. White doctors would tend the sick and householders would hand out food, yet they gave little thought to the Paiutes' need to learn for the future. A few exceptional people formed trusting relationships across the racial lines, but most stayed on their side of the line.

Suddenly 3-year-old Willie was ill—desperately ill. Annie and Sanny could see that he was dying. Anne could read and write and she was well aware the whites had great power. But when it came to her son, she turned to the power she knew better—the Indian doctor, or shaman. They were men, and sometimes women, who received their healing powers through dreams of spirits. Spirits of animals, birds, insects, even wind, clouds, thunder and water could tell a shaman how to heal. Each shaman had his own combination of eagle feathers, stones, shells, bones and rattles which he brought in a skin bag. Everyone within walking distance gathered to help with the ceremony, and every action of the shaman and participants had to be exact.

Willie's already stiffening body was laid out by the campfire and the shaman said he would go into a trance and try to bring his spirit back if it had not gone too far. With songs and prayers they watched for a movement of the shaman to be echoed by the little boy's body. Eventually, a small arm moved after the shaman's arm, a shudder shook the large body, then the small, and the shaman began to utilize his eagle feathers as he sang. When the eagle feathers pointed upward and at right angles, he told Annie she could call her son, and Willie came back to them. He would be her comfort and support when Sanny died a dozen years later.

Sanny was working for a ranching family named Holcomb, and the custom was for an Indian employee to add his employer's surname to his single given name. But Annie bowed her back. "Somehow I could not stand another white man's name in my family," she said later. She was observing that white women had more rights than Paiute women, who "had to take a back seat" to their husbands; she was determined to make her own choices. She insisted she remain Annie Lowry, although her children were known as Willie, Jessie, and—the newest addition to the family—Eva Sanny.

Shortly after Eva was born in 1898, Annie received a letter from Jerome Lowry's white wife. Annie's father had died, leaving his wife with a crippled son, and she wanted Annie, whom she had heard was "strong and strapping" to move to Oregon to help care for her half-brother. The woman who employed Annie at the time answered Mrs. Lowry's arrogant letter with some well-chosen words, and she and other white friends urged Annie to claim her share of Lowry's estate. Annie would have none of it. She knew her appearance in Oregon would embarrass her brothers, Robert and Jackson, who were passing for white. She never regretted that choice, and she continued to challenge traditions. In later years, she would invite her relatives and friends for a meal, and when she had only enough chairs to seat the men, she good-naturedly instructed each man to share his chair with a woman so that the women would not be served last as custom decreed.

These years were good ones for the family. They and the other Paviotso worked for the ranchers in the summertime, but when fall arrived, the men went out to hunt and the families continued the custom of the piñon nut harvest. Each year a special leader would scout the trees, and if there was a sufficient crop, the people would gather for a circle dance and appropriate ceremonial prayers before they climbed into the hills and began collecting.

Annie had been ill most of the summer of 1903, and one glorious September day, Sanny suggested that pine-nut hunting might cheer her. Leaving the younger children with his mother, Annie, Sautaunee and Jessie, 14, climbed into the wagon with Sanny and drove up into the East Humboldt Range. Annie cherished Jessie, her oldest son, and thought him beautiful, a sentiment echoed by white women she knew. He was "a shining light" for Sautaunee also, always ready to hear a story about the old days, always ready to lend his hand.

While the group was separated, hunting for a likely grove, Annie saw three Indians on a far slope, one a woman in a pink dress. Thinking it was only another nut-gathering party, she continued the strenuous work of beating the pine cones in a pit until they released the nuts and winnowing out the shells and debris so the nut meats could be roasted and ground into flour. But when they talked with other families later, no one could account for the three strange people. A shaman told them it was a sign that something was going to happen to someone in their party.

Annie thought little of the prediction, but a few days later Jessie hobbled toward her workplace bleeding from a gun-shot wound in his leg. He had saved his money to buy a gun she had forbidden him and accidently shot himself. Panic-stricken, she found the strength to hoist him on her back and carry him the few blocks home. Her employers went hunting for the doctor, who was away in Oreana and did not return until after dark. Although the Lovelock doctor called in a physician from Battle Mountain to assist with surgery, which took place in the doctor's office, the boy died the next evening. This time she had not turned to a shaman to save her son, and instead of following Paviotso custom and burying him in rocks in the hills, Annie buried him in a plot of ground that became the Lovelock Indian Cemetery. Two months later, the grief-stricken Sautaunee passed away, and a few weeks later Jessie's grieving puppy had to be put down. In these dark days, yet another baby girl failed to survive.

Annie and Sanny had two more healthy girls, Mabel in 1905, and Sophie in 1907, which helped distract them from their mourning. Lovelock continued to develop around them. There was extensive irrigation now, and a flour mill. Blacksmith shops, livery stables, and lumber yards lined the streets. But while there were six stores, there were seven saloons and many Paviotso men spent their days drinking and gambling along the street. Private parties made efforts to provide telephones and electricity to residents. Then in the summer of 1909 Sanny was diagnosed with walking typhoid. For weeks, delirious with fever, he raved and moaned night after night. Annie nursed him until he died in January of 1910. Later, Annie designed matching headboards for her son and mother.

They had exhausted all their resources during Sanny's illness. Numb with grief, Annie herself was as thin as a wraith. She had only fifteen cents to her name. She had no food for her three little girls. Well-meaning friends urged her to send her girls to a government orphanage. Some families volunteered to adopt them—one offering Annie substantial payment for a daughter. But Annie refused to consider giving her children away, and 15-year-old Willie stepped into the breach. To buy food for the family, he sold a calf he was raising. He took on the role of head of the family, overseeing his sisters' welfare. Unschooled, he took what work he could find, working as a hand on Carpenter's ranch. As Annie gained strength, she took on more jobs, working at one house in the morning and another in the afternoon. When she could get them, she took two jobs a day, every day of the week. In addition to making all of their clothes, she baked bread. She finished her long days bent over sewing she did for customers by lamplight.

With such a schedule, her only chance to socialize came when friends dropped in to chat as she worked. One visitor, Paviotso John Pascal, was an old friend who reappeared out of her past. Pascal had a good command of English and was known as an expert tracker; he often took jobs with the U.S. Army. Their friendship developed into love, and when they married, Annie was at last able to quit her treadmill of jobs. John supported the family; she discovered he longed to learn to read and taught him how. He worked as a hay hand and a sheep shearer, in addition to trapping. Their years together were good ones. They shared a devotion to their people's way of life and continued the traditional customs.

When Annie, who by now was a large, heavy woman, suffered a stroke in her mid-fifties and became partially blind and paralyzed, a white friend took her to a Reno hospital. It was 1925 and the facility was modern, but the doctors there offered little hope. Wanting to die at home, Annie managed, with help from her two daughters and a friend, to get dressed and board the train to Lovelock. At home, a shaman agreed to treat her, and for four nights they followed a complicated ritual involving eagle feathers, head massage, song and five river rocks. On the fifth morning her daughter, Eva, found her standing and watching the sunrise. Gradually, she regained her strength and returned to normal living.

But Indian medicine soon failed her. Her son Willie had been her mainstay, had insisted his sisters be schooled and watched over their moral well-being. As he matured, he had become a skilled baseball player and played on a white Lovelock team. He used the extra money to pay for Eva to attend Steward Indian School in Carson City. As modern conveniences trickled into Nevada in the early 1900s, he took his family to the weekly moving pictures in Lovelock and they learned to laugh at and love Charlie Chaplin. Willie was married twice and gave Annie two little granddaughters.

Then one evening the young man rode his horse to the store to buy a pound of sugar—so much easier than pounding out lengths of cane—and on the return trip he was thrown and injured. He continued to work when he was able, but after deteriorating for two years he asked Annie about the shaman who had treated him when he was three. The family drove in Willy's car to Nixon to hire the healer. The shaman came dressed in his finery and prepared with an eagle feather wand, tobacco to be smoked by the assembled families, with songs and ritual. But his spirits told him he could do nothing about the lump under Willy's ribs. The next day a white doctor diagnosed a bruised spleen, but he also could offer no treatment. Willie died soon after.

Annie was to suffer still more loss. The husband she treasured, John Pascal, was injured by a run-away team and wagon, and she devoted weeks to his care. Before he died May 18, 1930, they often talked of the beliefs of their ancestors. Annie mused later that Paiute beliefs describe heaven but have no concept of hell. She did not worry about that. She knew without need for teaching, "we get our hell on earth."

"I am a half-breed," she said. "That means I live on the fringe of two races." She knew her white friends considered her "just a plain old Paiute." But the Indians, whom she had chosen over the white world, accused her of feeling superior because she had a white father. Whatever she might wish, she was not wholly Paiute. There were animosities and distrustful feelings among Paiute factions that she was never able to bridge, but she was instrumental in preserving a picture of the culture that was quickly vanishing.

Annie died April 20, 1943. Her obituary in the *Lovelock Review Miner* describes her a "a leader among the local Indian people . . looked to for counsel, and her children, after her, have taken a leading part in community life."

The Paiute people are reserved and secretive; they do not readily share information about their lives or their beliefs. But as she aged, Annie saw the old customs being forgotten. Her children and grandchildren were too busy living like white men to listen to tales of the past. The Paiutes around her seemed entirely foreign from their ancestors. And so she conquered her timidity and began to talk, believing that was the only way her people's historical traditions and beliefs would be preserved. She furnished lengthy information to college student Mabel Reed in 1909, and she was not shy about condemning the degradation and sorrow white man's liquor had brought the Indians. She firmly believed "whiskey has been the downfall of not only the Paiutes, but of all the Indians of the West." Through the years she answered questions from scholars Omer C. Stewart and Robert H. Lowie and others, who considered her a valuable source of information on the Paiutes. And when Lovelock resident Lalla Scott approached her in June 1936 for the Works Projects Administration, she was ready to talk about her life. Scott shaped and added to Annie's personal story to construct *Karnee, A Paiute Narrative,* which was published in 1961 by the University of Nevada Press.

Annie Lowry Bibliography

Archival Sources
Reed, Mabel L. *History of the Development of Lovelock Valley,* BA Thesis TS, University of Nevada, 1909.
U. S. Census, Nevada, Humbolt County, Lake Township, 1880.
U.S. Department of the Interior, United States Indian Service, Lovelock, Nevada, Annual Census, 1910-1911.

Books
Elliott, Russell R. *History of Nevada*, 2nd ed., revised, University of Nebraska Press,1987.
Laxalt, Robert. *Nevada: A History* ,W. W. Norton, 1977.
Scott, Lalla. *Karnee: A Paiute Narrative,* annotated by Charles R. Craig, University of Nevada Press, 1966.
Sherrow, Victoria. *Indians of the Plateau and Great Basin,* Facts on File, 1992.
Underhill, Ruth. *The Northern Paiute Indians of California and Nevada*, U.S. Office of Indian Affairs, 1941.
Wheat, Margaret, M. *Survival Arts of the Primitive Paiutes,* University of Nevada Press, 1967.

Articles
"Annie Lawry (sic), Local Indian Resident Dies," *Lovelock Review Miner,* April 22, (1943).
Basso, Dave, "A History of Pershing County," *Nevada "The Silver State,'* v. II, Western States Historical Publishers, Inc., 1970.
Beck, Leo, "A History of Humboldt County," *Nevada "The Silver State,'* vol. II, Western States Historical Publishers, Inc., 1970.
Life Stories of Our People, Inter-Tribal Council of Nevada, University of Utah, 1974.
"Lovelock Cave," Minnesota State University, www.mnsu.edu/emuseum/archaeology/sites/northamerica/lovelock_cave.html.
Lowie, Robert H. "Shoshonean Tales," *Journal of American Folklore,* v. 37, (1924): 143-44. .
-----."Notes on Shoshonean Ethnography," *American Museum of Natural History Anthropological Papers,* v. 20, (1924).
Park, Willard Z. "Paviotso Shamanism,"*Shamanism in Western North America*, Northwestern University, 1938.
-----."Tribal Distribution in the Great Basin," *American Anthropologist,* v. 60, n. 4, (1938): 622- 38.
-----.*Willard Z. Park's Ethnographic Notes on the Northern Paiute of Western Nevada, 1933- 44,* University of Utah Anthropological papers, n. 114, (1989).
Stewart, Omer C. "Culture Element Distributions XIV, Northern Paiute, *Anthropological Records,* v. 4, n. 3, (1942): 361-446.
-----."Northern Paiute Bands," *Anthropological Records II,* n. 3, (1939): 127-149.
Wheat, Margaret M. "Notes on Paviotso Material Culture," *Nevada State Museum Anthropological Papers,* n. 1, (1959).

Gertrude Simmons Bonnin

National Museum of American History, Smithsonian Institution. Washington, D.C.

Chapter Eight

A LIFE IN LIMBO

Gertrude Simmons Bonnin – Zitkala-Sá, 1876 - 1938
Santee Sioux - American

When 24-year-old Gertrude Simmons named herself Zitkala-Sá in 1900, her choice was symbolic of her divided state of mind. She was half Yankton Sioux, and she wanted the book she had labored over to carry an Indian name that clearly designated her heritage. But she felt enough estranged from her people that she reached out of the Nakota dialect the Yanktons used and chose the Lakota Sioux word for "red bird." The Lakotas were linguistic cousins, as it were, living west of the Yankton Reservation, which was on the banks of the Missouri River in southeastern South Dakota. It was a choice she never explained and only one of several dichotomies in the life of this conflicted woman.

In 1900 she was bright, capable, a rising star in both literary and musical circles in the East. On April 14, the prestigious magazine *Harper's Bazar* had included her picture in its "Persons Who Interest Us" column. Others listed included the composer of an opera, the mother of the Duke of Marlborough and an impressionist who had recently performed at the Waldorf Astoria Hotel in New York City. Praising Zitkala-Sá's "beauty and many talents," which were "attracting attention in many Eastern cities," the editors marveled that until her ninth year, she was "a veritable little savage running wild over the prairie and speaking no language but her own." Yet this "savage" had become a skilled violinist who was a featured performer with the Carlisle Indian School Band, then preparing to play at the Paris Exposition. Education at two Quaker schools in Indiana was credited with accomplishing this transformation. Zitkala-Sá had mastered elementary and secondary studies and moved on to Earlham College in Richmond. There she had won distinction as an orator. She was also a recently published author who had just had a series of autobiographical articles about her childhood and school years printed in the *Atlantic Monthly*. The editors found her writing to display "a rare command of English and much artistic feeling."

They did not explain that the feelings Zitkala-Sá expressed were primarily pain and anger. That she used her skills with a pen and her growing command of English to protest that the education which had liberated her from ignorance of white ways had also alienated her from her heritage. That learning to communicate in English, learning to read, had separated her from her mother and made it impossible for her to live happily at home on the reservation.

Boat traffic on the Missouri had put her people, the Yankton Sioux, in contact with white men in the early 1800s. Less warlike than some other Sioux, the Yanktons were forced to accept the establishment of Fort Randall in their midst in 1856, and by 1857 they were finding game so scarce that they were convinced to cede much of their land to the government. They had been crowded onto a reservation on the north bank of the Missouri about fifty miles upriver from a town the whites had founded before the ink on the treaty was dry. Named for the tribe, Yankton became a center for settlement and commerce in the newly formed Dakota Territory. It was a permanent white presence on the edge of Yankton lives. An agency was set up, annuities were promised and life began to change. They tried to learn to farm. Annuity rations of flour and sugar, if and when they arrived, replaced game, and without sturdy hides to drape their tipis, the Yanktons were soon dependent on inferior canvas from the agency.

Zitkala-Sá described the weather-stained canvas of her tipi home for *Atlantic Monthly* readers, the warm guidance provided by her mother, Taté Iyohiwin Simmons, the freedom to roam and explore and learn about the land and her people's legends. She wrote of the solitary, peaceful breakfasts they had together, because they lived alone. But she did not explain that they were alone because her father, a white man named Felker, had deserted them before the girl was born February 22, 1876. Wanting her children to have no connection with that name, Taté Iyohiwin gave the name of her former husband, Simmons, to her children.

Zitkala-Sá told how her small fingers willingly struggled to create designs of beads, and flattened, dyed porcupine quills to decorate belts or moccasins. She described how she helped her mother dry corn, strips of pumpkin, wild chokecherries and plums for winter eating. She wrote of helping to fetch buckets of water from the river and what a joy it was to chase cloud shadows across the prairie. But the prairie she roamed was cut by roads and the white man's humming wires hung from tall dark posts. She often put her ear against one of the poles and wondered if it moaned in pain from some harm the white man had done it. She also described her mother's grief when she remembered her dead daughter and brother, who had died during a move forced by the white man several years before the child she named Gertrude was born. And her fear that the Yanktons, like the Poncas, still might be sent away from the waters of the Missouri.

By 1884, when Gertrude turned eight, the family had given up the canvas tipi for a log house at the urging of Gertrude's older half-brother, David, who had just returned from three years' schooling at Hampton Normal and Agriculture Institute in Virginia. In March that year, two Quaker missionaries from

White's Manual Labor Institute in Wabash, Indiana, came to their village with tales of a beautiful country full of wonders such as red apples on trees. They were gathering children to take back with them; they would ride on the iron horse to a place called Indiana. To Gertrude, an apple was a wondrous thing, and she begged to be allowed to go and explore this amazing place. Despite her misgivings, her conviction that her daughter would suffer, Taté Iyohiwin gave her permission. Gertrude was small for her age but bright beyond her years, and her mother reasoned that education would be necessary in a future filled with white men. She declared that schooling Indian children was the least the whites could do to repay the Sioux for what they had taken away.

The school days Zitkala-Sá described to *Atlantic Monthly* readers were an ordeal of blazing lights, harsh noises, her comfortable blanket and moccasins replaced by heavy leather shoes and an embarrassingly tight muslin dress. Warned that her long, black braids were to be shorn, a look she associated with cowardice or mourning, she rebelled and fled to a far room where she hid under a bed. Eventually dragged out kicking and scratching, she was tied to a chair and the shears did their work. From then on she felt like "only one of many little animals driven by a herder." Unable to understand or talk to teachers, her misbehavior was sometimes inadvertent, sometimes willfully disobedient. She rebelled when she could against "the iron routine of the civilizing machine." Almost in spite of herself, she did learn English, but she felt her individuality bound "like a mummy for burial." She did not see her Dakota home for three years.

Yet, when at last she returned home, the prairie she had so longed for seemed empty; the freedom from routine meant only long, aimless days. She had learned to love books, and her mother's cabin contained only an Indian Bible. Their once-close relationship was filled with conflict. No longer able to understand her daughter, incapable of filling her needs, Taté

Iyohiwin fled out into the night to cry out her grief. She sought help from the spirits of the dead. Why was her daughter so obsessed with learning from the white man's papers? She had had enough schooling! Why couldn't she be happy at home?

For her part, Gertrude felt immense guilt for her need to learn things beyond her people's culture. "I seemed to hang in the heart of chaos," Zitkala-Sá told *Atlantic Monthly* readers, "neither a wild Indian nor a tame one." She briefly attended the Santee Normal Training School near her home but found it unsatisfying. The stress finally put her on another train heading back to White's Institute for three more years of study. Like the rest of the students, her days were half filled with learning domestic skills the Quakers sanguinely imagined them using in their future homes. She had no such inclinations, but she was also developing musical talents and was allowed to teach music to the primary grades. Those successful years provided a diploma in 1895 and ignited bigger dreams. She had developed notable skill as a violinist, pianist and orator. She gave a graduation speech on behalf of women's suffrage that so impressed a Quaker in the audience that the woman offered to pay tuition so Gertrude could attend Earlham College in Richmond. She was nineteen, now, and wrote her mother for permission. Taté Iyohiwin's answer pointed to neighbors' children who had learned enough English in just three years to talk with settlers; she would not approve yet more schooling.

With regret, Gertrude defied her mother and enrolled at Earlham College that fall. After a miserably lonely first year, she entered an oratorical contest and won first place, and the support of classmates she had thought indifferent. She became active in debating, contributed to the school newspaper, and further developed her musical talents. Buoyed by her classmates' friendship, she traveled to the capital city of Indianapolis to compete in the 1896 state contest. There, seated on the stage of an ornate opera house, she waited her turn to speak. She was the only female contestant, the only nonwhite and last on the program. But when she took the platform, she spoke out freely about the damage the Indians had suffered from white society. She asked for justice, tardy though it might be. She gave a ringing defense of Indian character and actions. But she also acknowledged there were some "treasures of knowledge and wisdom" it profited the Indians to learn from the whites. She finished to polite applause.

As the crowd awaited the judges' verdict, there was a sudden stir. Fans from a rival college unfurled a large white banner. Gertrude was astonished and quickly furious to read words disparaging Earlham and the "squaw" who represented it. Burning with rage, she could only glare defiance at the crowd. But when the judges' decision was read, she was one of two winners named. She felt vindicated, but remained angry at the prejudice displayed, even after Earlham students greeted her return with a grand procession. And she knew in her heart that back on the Dakota prairie, her mother would have scorned her achievement. Facing that fact, her victory had a hollow ring.

Perhaps because of her internal conflict, she fell ill, and in the weeks it took to recover she affirmed her life's work was to help the Indian race. Possibly her success in the white world could inspire others. She decided to leave college and in the summer of 1897 began to teach at the Indian Industrial School in Carlisle, Pennsylvania. She began her tenure with a spirited speech at opening exercises in which she complained Indian history and motives had both been misrepresented. She longed to show the Indians as human beings, and she contacted literary societies, offering to speak and tell the Indians' story. She was soon appearing as a violin soloist and an orator with the Carlisle Band and by 1898 she had attracted enough attention to be depicted by New York photographer Gertrude Kasebier, who posed her in a Victorian dress holding her violin.

When she wrote, "An Indian Teacher Among Indians," the woman who called herself Zitkala-Sá told *Atlantic Monthly* readers only a little about her experiences in the classroom.

164

Carlisle had been founded by Captain Richard H. Pratt, who thought the solution to the Indian problem was to kill the Indian in the child, so that the child could take his place in the white world. The more Gertrude observed the white world, the more she became convinced many elements of the Indian culture were of equal, if not superior, value. Pratt, perhaps to quiet her militant voice, dispatched her out West to recruit both her health and new students.

She did tell her readers about the abject poverty she found on the Yankton Reservation, where many of the Indians' allotted lands had been legally usurped by settlers. And many other settlers, as poor as the Indians, had flowed in and settled in caves across the river, taking what they could not buy. She also described her mother's continuing bitterness against the whites and her repeated warnings they were not to be trusted. Her brother, David, had lost his position as a government clerk when he protested conditions on the reservation. Taté Iyohiwin warned her daughter that the white man offered "holy papers" with one hand and evil liquor with the other. The visit climaxed on a dark night when Taté Iyohiwin stood looking at the multiplying fires lighting white homes. Suddenly her doubled fist shot out at shoulder level. Flinging out her fingers, she sent a curse flying across the river as if she could impale the intruders with her venom.

With deep ambivalence, Gertrude recruited students for Carlisle, believing despite her painful experiences that the Indians' only hope lay in education. She returned to the Carlisle room she thought of as "a white-walled prison," ever more aware of a bureaucracy that sent inspectors who looked only at surface accomplishments and never considered whether the schoolwork they viewed represented "real life or long-lasting death beneath this semblance of civilization." Cut off from the natural world and bereft of its powers of spiritual healing, she longed for a day she could send out all her pain and recrimination like "a flash of zigzag lightning across the heavens."

After eighteen months at Hampton, where she and Pratt had clashing agendas, she decided her hope for inner peace lay in music and writing. She resigned her position to move to Boston and study at the New England Conservatory of Music, her financing provided by the Commissioner of Indian Affairs. She loved her studies, made friends in literary circles and told herself she could best help her people by being successful in the white world. Back in South Dakota, not only her mother felt betrayed by that choice. A resentful relative maintained that since she had turned her back on her people, she had no right to use the name Simmons. Deeply hurt by the accusation, Gertrude had created an identity that was Indian, yet hers alone; she christened herself "Zitkala-Sá".

In the winter of 1900, she was still appearing with the Carlisle Band, dressed, ironically, in a buckskin costume personally provided by Pratt, who evidently understood the public appeal of the culture he was trying to eliminate. Audiences, one of which included President William McKinley, responded to her emotional presentation of the famine scene from "Hiawatha" with tears, then cheers. It was a stellar time for the 24-year-old woman, with her writings in the *Atlantic Monthly* receiving such acclaim that by February of 1901 she had a contract with Gin and Company Publishers for a book of old Indian legends.

She wrote her autobiographical pieces without restraint, without a mentor's refining hand, without an editor's guidance. Critics praised her honesty, but she also had her detractors. Her teachers and Quaker friends were hurt and angry that she wrote only of her bad memories, with no word of thanks to those who had helped her. There was no mention of good times, of kind people who had taught and assisted her. They noted that all Zitkala-Sá had in "literary ability and culture," she owed to her white education and people who had taken her "into their homes and hearts." What was worse, she was championing the Indian culture—praising a lifestyle they had tried so hard to erase. Captain Pratt denounced her efforts in the Carlisle newspaper, *The Red Man and Helper.* One *Harpers' Monthly Magazine* story, titled "The Soft-Hearted Sioux," depicted an educated brave returning to his father's lodge and their pain-filled discovery the boy could no longer feed his starving father because he had been taught not to kill. The Carlisle newspaper censured it as "morally bad." Pratt and the newspaper disparaged her work and accused her of harming the educational work underway for Indian peoples.

Her personal life was equally fractured. She had many suitors, but she had fallen in love with a Yavapai doctor named Carlos Montezuma, whom she evidently met when they both traveled with the Carlisle band. Twelve years her senior, he had a practice in Chicago, and they made plans to marry in November. When the criticism erupted, she confided her pain and anger to Montezuma in letters, but as they corresponded it became apparent their lives were taking different paths.

Zitkala-Sá intended to go back to the reservation, hoping to reconcile with her aging, feeble mother and to collect legends for the upcoming book. She wanted Montezuma to accompany her. He had already tried and failed to practice on reservations and he said he could not succeed there, but more important, he believed the Indians' future lay in assimilating the white culture. She was also unsure she could subjugate her own desires in order to fulfill the confining role of a city doctor's wife, and she had no talent for or intention of maintaining a home. They carried on a stormy correspondence but by the spring of 1901 she had found a position as an issue clerk on the Standing Rock Sioux Reservation in north-central South Dakota. Again in the midst of Sioux who could tell her "their treasured ideas of life," she hoped "to do justice to the abandoned material around me." In August she returned the doctor's ring.

Though she found it difficult to combine work, care for her mother and writing, she felt pressure to preserve the

Sioux legends while the old people survived to share them. Converting an oral tradition to print was challenging. The Indians had long, hard experience in whites using a written page to mean one thing today and another tomorrow. And she knew her people distrusted the written word because, unlike a storyteller, each with his or her own style, the printed page was frozen in time. It allowed no nuances—no inflection in voice, no change in facial expression or posture, no tailoring the tale to a particular audience. Without allowing for this tidbit or that variation, it purported to be the whole truth, when to Indian listeners it could only be an approximation. She struggled with the complexities and provided a manuscript to Ginn and Company, which issued *Old Indian Legends* in October.

Reaching past the controversies of modern Indian life, she interpreted fourteen entertaining Sioux folk tales she thought all children would enjoy. In her preface to the book, she voiced the hope that the children would not only enjoy the stories, but as grownups would find interest in knowing more about native people's "near kinship with the rest of humanity." The sincerity of their belief, she insisted, "demands a little respect." The book was illustrated by an Indian artist from Carlisle and the publisher was already asking for another such book.

She continued to produce stories that she sent back East to national publications. Another Yankton legend was published in *Harper's* in October, and in 1902 she had a story in *Everybody's Magazine,* and an article on Indian schools in a Boston paper. But she was not content to stay in the past. In December the *Atlantic Monthly* ran, "Why I am a Pagan." In the daring story, she boldly rejected what she considered bigoted Christian teachings for the peace and harmony she found in nature. "My heart and I lie small upon the earth like a grain of throbbing sand," she wrote, explaining that she preferred "my excursions into the natural gardens where the voice of the Great Spirit is heard . . . " to Christian dogma. Captain Pratt labeled her work "trash," and her "worse than a pagan."

A fellow employee of the Indian Service, Yankton Raymond Talseface Bonnin seemed to understand and share her love and respect for tribal culture. He was eight years younger than she, but he was capable and ambitious. He intended to devote his life to Indian service. On May 10, 1902, they were married.

The couple spent the next fourteen years on the Uintah Reservation in eastern Utah with their son, Raymond O. (Ohiya) Bonnin, who was born in 1903. The years there, near Fort Duchesne, were frustrating and draining as they tried to help the Indians deal with the challenges of reservation existence. She was depressed at the incidence of typhus and tuberculosis, the poverty, the lack of education that left superstitions intact. Without a position except as a clerk's wife, she drew on her experience at Carlisle and formed a school band. She started a women's basket weaving group and conducted housekeeping demonstrations in reservation homes. She felt deeply the lack of music and books and the literary scene in which she had starred, but her dreams of a literary career seemed over. Finally in 1905, she was hired to teach, an opportunity that came and went over the years. These occasional jobs helped, but her best efforts could not begin to fill the needs.

With settlers pressing in from all sides, she could see the Utes losing their land. And she had land problems of her own. Her mother's continuing resentment of Zitkala-Sá allowed Taté Iyohiwin's older son to persuade her to sell her land without sharing the proceeds with Zitkala-Sá and her half-brother David. Zitkala-Sá spent months on the Yankton Reservation, caring for her mother in her final illness and disputing the land sale, to no avail. She returned to Utah grieving not only for her mother's loss, but the bitter knowledge that she had never been able to mend their relationship.

Then in 1912 a high school music teacher, William F. Hanson from nearby Vernal, approached her with an idea. The 25-year-old teacher was fascinated by Plains Indian culture, the spirituality of their ceremonies, their chants and dances. He wanted to preserve that culture in an opera.

Gertrude immediately suggested that the Sun Dance be its theme. The ritual, forbidden by the government as a "heathen rite," was never-the-less practiced. The religious ceremony had originally been Sioux and she knew it well. Gertrude was always eager to champion Indian culture—ever ready to fight government repression. She began meeting with Hanson, translating chants he had recorded, humming tunes and picking out melodies on her violin while he improvised on the piano. She helped with the storyline, designed to show that Indians experienced the same joys and fears, the same love of laughter and instinct for reverence as any other people. She and Raymond insisted on historical accuracy and appropriate spirit. Through the couple, Hanson had access to an ancient Sioux who lived in their home, to authentic costumes, to the cooperation of the elders, without whose permission the project would have died. Gertrude spent hours and days that led to weeks away from home, delighted to be creating again. *The Sun Dance* premiered in Vernal on February 21-22, 1913. It was an immediate hit and was performed twenty-four times in the next two years, including a Brigham Young University production with 160 cast members. The production garnered favorable notices in the national press, and Gertrude's confidence in her abilities was renewed.

With reawakened energy she decided to join the new Society of American Indians (SAI), an all-Indian group which had organized in 1911 to work for Indians' rights. Her old flame Montezuma was part of the group and she wrote him of her continuing frustration. "I have this eternal tug of war between being wild or civilized. The transition is an endless revolution that keeps me in eternal Purgatory." She struggled with the obligations of being a wife and mother, although she adored her son."I can hardly stand the inner spiritual clamor to study, to write—to do more with my music—yet duty first," she wrote

Montezuma. She and Raymond finally decided the time had come to place Ohiya, now ten, in a Catholic boarding school in the East.

The SAI was devoted to reforming laws affecting Indians, preserving their history and culture, working for citizenship and better education, and self-help among the tribes. It was not enough to wait for churches or government to provide help; each Indian had an obligation to help others. Without funds or salary, she threw herself into organizing local meetings, and in 1915 began a community center that provided hot lunches and sewing clinics. She regularly traveled miles across the million-acre reservation to visit outlying villages. The SAI published a magazine, and she described her projects in *American Indian Magazine*'s pages under the byline Gertrude Bonnin. In 1916 the January-March issue contained a poem titled "The Indian's Awakening." In three pages of evocative verse, she described her traumatic separation from her people, and the joy she experienced as she reconnected with "God and the land," and the souls of her ancestors. For the first time in fifteen years, she signed her name Zitkala-Sá.

In October, she was elected SAI secretary; the next April she and Raymond left Utah to live in Washington, D.C. Raymond studied law until going into the army for World War I. With their son away at school, Gertrude began lobbying Congress and the Indian Office and lecturing for Indian causes. Her theatrical nature led her to give white audiences what they expected—long black braids reaching below the hips of a fringed, beaded, buckskin dress—even as Congressmen addressed her as Mrs. Bonnin. She was casual about the facts of her heritage, claiming full Yankton blood when it suited her—or better yet, the great Sitting Bull as her grandfather—slyly confident none would know a Yankton could not be the granddaughter of a Hunkpapa.

But she spent more hours as secretary, carrying on correspondence, maintaining files, answering "baskets of letters," with only occasional part-time help. In 1918 she became editor-in-chief of the quarterly magazine, writing editorials as well as contributing articles and poetry. She wrote of "Indian Gifts to Civilized Man," and of insults visited on Chipeta, the widow of Ute Chief Ouray. With Raymond in the military—and so many of their members in the service that they postponed their annual convention—she wrote of "five thousand Indian men in the army," a number out of proportion to their percent of the population. Her husband achieved the rank of captain and returned safely to resume the study of law, while she focused her energies on writing for the magazine. She was alert to abuses by the Indian Bureau and detailed an incident when an agent refused to let three educated Indians, including Montezuma, onto a reservation to meet with their people. "Though the riffraff of the white people . . . the very scum of other races . . . were permitted to homestead Indian lands, the "educated, refined and patriotic Indian teaching the highest ideals of democracy is forbidden to meet with his own race. . . ." she raged in a 1919 issue.

She was the first female SAI board member and she reached openly for higher position. She attended SAI conventions, where in 1919 she broke another male precedent by taking the podium. She promoted pride in Indian heritage and thinking and doing for themselves. Emphasizing that "In the Indian home, the mother teaches the children these very principles we are talking about," she urged the male audience to next time bring their wives and sisters.

Her days were exciting, but disagreement over the use of peyote in Indian religious ceremonies soon became a dividing issue. The hallucinatory plant was part of Indian religious ceremonies among some tribes, and Zitkala-Sá, who had seen it used on the Ute Reservation, strongly believed it contributed to lethargy and degeneration in its practitioners. She ignored illness to testify for legislation to forbid its usage, telling a Senate committee that its use resulted in "death, debauchery and orgies." Other Indians considered it part of their heritage and resented her position. This issue and other internal dissension led to the SAI's dissolution in 1920. There were those in the society, including Carlos Montezuma, who protested her focus on the old days. They wanted to be thought of as modern Americans, to erase memories of their tribal past. Zitkala-Sá fought for the Indian's place in modern society, but, before her time, she believed their past and their pride in it was the inherently important center of their identity.

Her personal fortunes fared better the next year. Hayworth Publishing House asked to combine the autobiographical stories she had published in magazines in the early 1900s with her other stories into a book, *American Indian Stories*. The name Zitkala-Sá was again on the cover of a book. Unlike her first book, which contained little of herself, she again voiced her pain and anger at the damage white education had done to the Indian population. These stories were not from the elders, but from her generation, and she used her skills to promote her political agenda. She portrayed Indian religion and Indian justice as superior to those of white society. And she drew a searing portrait of young Sioux trained in white ways who proceeded to cheat their helpless elders out of their allotted lands.

In a final section of the book, titled "America's Indian Problem," she urged Indian citizenship, and used the government's own never-published investigation of the Indian Bureau to document that the Indian "had not even the rights of a foreign resident. The Indian individually does not have access to the courts; he cannot individually appeal to the administrative and judicial branches of the public service for the enforcement of his rights." His property and funds were held in trust, the report continued, and those trusts were a "sham protection." The six-year-old report was still valid, Zitkala-Sá noted, because nothing had changed since it was written.

With the SAI no longer active, she looked outside the Indian community for someone influential to listen to Indian problems. That June she gained a place on the agenda of the General Federation of Women's Clubs annual convention. The two million women represented were a potent force in American society. From a podium in Salt Lake City she reached out to their hearts, detailing the pitiful conditions on Indian reservations across the country. She knew first hand the bookless classrooms, doctor-less clinics, empty bowls and despair.

She was a persuasive speaker. Opera coauthor William Hanson had described her stage presence as "assured," with a musical voice and a "charming and convincing manner." Her facts commanded their attention. She already had the strong support of Oklahoma delegate Roberta Campbell Lawson and other western chapters who had begun to recognize the problems. When she had finished, the GFWC established an Indian Welfare Committee and asked her to be their representative on a task force to investigate conditions in six Oklahoma counties. Gertrude returned to the platform with tears rolling down her cheeks. "It has begun," she cried, "It has begun. Nothing now can stop it. We shall have help."

In the summer of 1923, part of a team of three, including Charles H. Fabens of the American Indian Defense Association and Matthew K. Sniffen of the Indian Rights Association, Gertrude traveled through northeastern Oklahoma documenting case after case of Indians swindled out of their oil-rich land. Local courts would declare the owners incompetent so that judges could appoint legal guardians who proceeded to enrich themselves while the Indians starved. If lies and intimidation failed, the swindlers resorted to kidnaping, rape and murder—and even bringing the dead back to life so they could relinquish their property in the desired manner. Gertrude tended to dramatize what she wrote, but there was no need here. She talked with hungry, tattered victims, attended court hearings and wrote simply what she saw. In barely suppressed fury she called for *"action, immediate action* by the honest and fair-minded Americans of the 20th Century."

The 39-page report, *Oklahoma's Poor Rich Indians: an Orgy of Graft and Exploitation of the Five Civilized Tribes— Legalized Robbery,* was published in February 1924. Where a dry government document detailing the same conditions had failed to catch public interest, the individual stories opened horrified eyes. Oklahoma Indians met in Tulsa and organized to secure corrective legislation. Whether or not the report stimulated the action, American Indians not already endowed were granted citizenship that June. It was a cause for which Zitkala-Sá had long fought. The GFWC established scholarships for Indians, pushed for educational and health centers on the reservation and assisted people living off the reserves. With a change of administration, a new investigative commission named for its chairman, Lewis Meriam, began to survey education, health, hospital and cultural resources available to Native Americans.

But citizenship could not solve all their problems, and in February 1926, the Bonnins organized the National Council of American Indians (NCAI). She hoped to recreate the cooperative effort of Indians working together to improve their lives. *Indian Truth* magazine celebrated her effort at forming an organization that, "bids fair to create increased interest in behalf of the Indians and secure for them added recognition of their personal and tribal rights." The magazine thought "it seems probable that every tribe will be represented."

Gertrude maintained an exhausting travel schedule to western reservations. That year she drove 10,000 miles on the era's primitive roads so that she could bring eyewitness testimony to a Senate committee about conditions there. As always, she continued to champion her people's culture; her organizational letterhead portrayed an idealized Indian village, the antithesis of the squalor she regularly witnessed. She published a newsletter about legislation affecting Indians and tried to help with land claims, school and housing problems. After initial enthusiasm, the NCAI failed to grow, but she devoted the rest of her life to it, trying to assist the many who "are in a destitute condition now and need immediate help."

She long ago had written to Carlos Montezuma, "I am what I am. I owe no apologies to God or men." In 1929 she rose to speak extemporaneously at the Lake Mohonk Conference of Indian Affairs. In this gathering of influential friends of the Indians, she quarreled with a reference to her as a "civilized Indian."

"I don't know what you mean by civilization. We send our little Indian boys and girls to school and when they come back talking English, they come back swearing. There is no swear word in the Indian languages and I haven't yet learned to swear."

Asked about preservation of the Indian home, she said "Home is home wherever it may be, and the children's love for their parents and the parents' love for their children bring a heart tie superior to anything the missionary can do for us."

As she grew older she became more insistent that her methods and goals were the only correct ones, less willing to share control, increasingly sensitive to criticism. She feuded with Indian Commissioner John Collier despite his efforts to protect Indian land and culture, his focus on their right to self-determination. Many of her contemporaries, well on the road to assimilation, wanted all focus on the future. When Zitkala-Sá insisted native beliefs and practices were to be valued, were equal to the white man's culture, she often spoke out alone.

Ill and depressed, grieving over the death of her son, she questioned her life's work. Striving to reform Indian law was an ever-frustrating treadmill without end. She wrote to a friend who praised her service to her people, "But though it took a lifetime, the achievements are scarcely visible." She had been unable to reconcile with her mother. She always felt guilty she could not be content on the reservation and sad that some reservation Indians suspected her motives and goodwill. She had never been able to balance her progressive drive with her need to value and retain the old ways.

She must have been elated to learn late in 1937 that the opera she and William Hanson had written nearly a quarter of a century before was to be presented in the Broadway Theatre by the New York Light Opera Guild. Her old friend, Hanson, was in New York City rehearsing *The Sun Dance* with Guild impresario John Hand. Hand had soloed in the Utah production so many years before and had chosen to revive the production in New York for an April premiere on Broadway. She knew the composition was a celebration of the culture that was her life. She knew 200 professional performers had auditioned to take part. The cast contained Cherokee, Chippewa, Hopi, Mohawk and Yakima, all working together. She may have watched these tribes not only learning the Sun Dance but enriching the performance with their own styles of dancing.

She could not have known 100 members of the New York Society of American Indians attended opening night in full costume. That 3,100 seats were sold out for two performances. That a box of green sage branches arrived from Utah just in time for the aromatic smoke of a sage smudge to be wafted out into the audience when the curtain opened, as they had always done. That opera historian Edward Ellsworth Hipsher would one day praise the opera as "a sympathetic portrayal of the real Indian—a conscientious attempt to delineate the manners, customs, dress, religious ideals, superstitions, songs, games, ceremonials—in short, the life of a noble romantic people too little understood."

She did not know that after her death at 61 on January 26, 1938, Raymond had wired the opera guild, then in rehearsal. Its members, who had accepted her and Raymond, John Hand said, "as though they were actual kin," grieved for her. Hand and William Hanson had driven to Washington for her funeral, where Indian Commissioner John Collier spoke with others who called her "the most sincere and persuasive advocate" and the best defender and fighter for Indian rights. Her tombstone in Arlington National Cemetery includes the name Zitkala-Sá.

That name came to new prominence when the University of Nebraska Press reprinted both of her books in 1985. Her passionate voice, at once strident and evocative, is no longer alone, but now part of a chorus of Indian voices who celebrate their culture.

Gertrude Simmons Bonnin Bibliography

Archival Collections

Society of American Indians Correspondence 1908 - 1929; July 9, Dec. 11, 1908; June 26, Sept. 29, Nov. 8, 1917; Oct. 19, 1918: Feb. 25, 1919: Oct. 29, Nov. 20, 1920; Aug.15, Aug. 28, Dec. 18, Dec. 21, 1923; Jan. 14, Mar 18, April 28, 1824; Jan. 6, 1925; Mar. 31, April 22, 1927; Nov. 28, Dec. 22, 1928; Jan. 8, 1929.

Fisher, Alice Poindexter. "The Transformation of Tradition: A Study of Zitkala-Sá and Mourning Dove: Two Transitional American Indian Writers," Ph.D. Thesis, City University of New York, 1979.

Welch, Deborah. *Zitkala-Sá: An American Indian Leader.* Ph.D. Thesis. University of Wyoming, 1985.

Books

Athearn, Robert. *Forts of the Upper Missouri,* University of Nebraska Press, 1962.

Bonnin, Gertrude, Charles H. Fabens, Mathew K Sniffin. *Oklahoma's Poor Rich Indians: An Orgy of Graft and Exploitation of the Five Civilized Tribes,* Office of the Indian Rights Association, 1924.

Debo, Angie. *And Still the Waters Run: The Betrayal of the Five Civilized Tribes,* Princeton University Press, 1950. (Reprint, 1973).

Hanson, William Frederick. *Sun Dance Land,* J. Grant Stevenson, 1967.

Hepsher, Edward. *American Opera and Its Composers,* Theodore Presser Co., 1927.

Hersberg, Hazel W. *The Search for American Indian Identity,* Syracuse University Press, 1971.

Rappaport, Doreen. *The Fight of Red Bird,* Dial Books for Young Readers, 1997.

Wells, Mildred W. *Unity in Diversity, The History of the General Federation of Women's Clubs,* General Federation of Women's Clubs, 1953.

Zitkala- Sá. *American Indian Stories,* 1901 (Reprint, Foreword by Dexter Fisher, University of Nebraska Press, 1985.)

-----.*Old Indian Legends,*1901.(Reprint, Foreword by Agnes M. Picotte, University of Nebraska Press, 1985.)

Articles

Bataille, Gretchen M. and Kathleen Sands. "Gertrude Simmons Bonnin," *American Indian Women: Telling Their Lives,* University of Nebraska Press, 1984:139.

Bonnin, Gertrude. "A Year's Experience in Community Service Work Among the Ute Tribe of Indians," *American Indian Magazine,* v.4, n.3 (1916):307-10.

Docsteader, Frederick J. *"Gertrude Simmons Bonnin," Great North American Indians,* Van Norstrand Reinhold, 1977.

"Editor's Viewpoint," *The Indian Truth,* v.1, n. 1 (1924).

Fisher, Dexter. "Zitkala-Sá: the Evolution of a Writer," *The Third Woman: Minority Women Writers of the Unites States,* Houghton Mifflin, 1980.

-----"Zitkala Sá: The Evolution of a Writer," *American Indian Quarterly,* v.5, n. 3, (1979): 229- 38 .

"Gertrude Simmons Bonnin (1875-1938)," www.nativeamericanrhymes.com/women/ Bonnin.html.

Gridley, Marion E. "Gertrude Simmons Bonnin: A Modern Progressive," *American Indian Women,* Hawthorn Books ,1974.

Hardy, Gayle J. *"Gertrude Simmons Bonnin," American Women Civil Rights Activists,* McFarland, 1993:80-4.

"Hanson Light Opera Has Premiere Here," *New York Times,* April 28 (1938):26.

Hogan, Linda. "The 19th Century Native American Poets," *Wassaja/The Indian Historian,* v.13, n.4 (1980):24-29.

Jones, Louis Thomas. *Aboriginal American Oratory: The Tradition of Eloquence Among the Indians of the United States,* Southwest Museum, 1965:118-20.

Lukens, Margo. "Zitkala-Sá," *Dictionary of Literary Biography: Native American Writers of the United States,* Brucedi Clark Layman Book, 1997: 331-36.

"Mrs. Gertrude Bonnin," Obituary, *Indian Truth,* Indian Rights Association, v.15, n. 2, (1938): 3.

"Mrs. R. T. Bonnin, An Indian Leader," Obituary, *New York Times,* Jan. 27, 1938.

"NAI Conference Report," *Indian Truth,* v. 4, n. 3, (1916): 3.

"National Council of American Indians Organized," *Indian Truth,* Indian Rights Assoc., v. 3, n.3, (1926): 3.

"Persons Who Interest Us," *Harper's Bazar,* April 14 (1900):330.

Spack, Ruth, "Dis/engagement. Zitkala-Sa's Letters to Carlos Montezuma, 1901-1902," *Melus* Spring (2001).

Stout, Mary. "Zitkala-Sá: The Literature of Politics," *Coyote Was Here, The Dolphin,* n. 9, April (1984): 70-78.

-----"Zitkala-Sá (Gertrude Simmons Bonnin), *Dictionary of Native American Literature,* Garland Publishers, Inc., 1994: 303-307.

Young, Mary E. "Gertrude Simmons Bonnin," v.1, *Notable American Women, 1607-1950: A Biographical Dictionary,* Howard University Press,1971:198-200.

Zitkala-Sá: "A Year's Experience in Community Service Work Among the Ute Tribe of Indians," *American Indian Magazine* v. 4, n.3 (1916): 207.

-----. "Address by Mrs. Gertrude Bonnin, Secretary-Treasurer," *American Indian Magazine,* v.7, n. 2, (1919): 153-57.

-----."America, Home of the Red Man," *American Indian Magazine,.*v 7 n.1 (1919):165-67.

-----. "An Indian Teacher Among Indians,"*Atlantic Monthly,* v. 85, (1900):381-86.

-----. "Chipeta, Widow of Chief Ouray," *American Indian Magazine,* v. 5, n .3, (1917):167-70.

-----. "Editorial Comment," *American Indian Magazine,* v. 7, n. 2, (1919):161-2.

-----. "Editorial Comment," *American Indian Magazine,* v.7, n. 3, (1919): 5-9.

-----. "Editorial Comment," *American Indian Magazine,* v.7, n. 4, (1919):61-63.

-----. "Impressions of an Indian Childhood," *Atlantic Monthly,* v. 85, (1900):37-47.

-----. "Indian Gifts to Civilized Man," *American Indian Magazine,* v. 6, n. 3, (1918):115-16.

-----."The Indian's Awakening," *American Indian Magazine,* v. 4, n. 1, (1916);57-9.

-----."Letter to the Chiefs and Headmen of the Tribes," *American Indian Magazine,* v.7. n. 1, (1919):196-7.

General Federation of Women's Clubs

Roberta Campbell Lawson

Chapter Nine

GUARDING TRADITIONS, EMBRACING CHANGE

Roberta Campbell Lawson, 1878-1940
Delaware – Scottish-American

When Roberta Campbell Lawson assumed her office as national president of the General Federation of Women's Clubs in 1935, and moved to club headquarters, a greystone mansion in Washington, D.C., she told her hometown Tulsa newspaper that she enjoyed living in the nation's capital. Surely, a woman of her energy did find the stimulation of the nation's seat of government invigorating. But she did not tell this reporter that she was sleeping in a window recess so that she could see the stars at night, so that she could watch the sky as dawn broke. That she often stepped out on the balcony of her third-floor office, which overlooked the garden, "to watch and listen to—nothing—the changing moods of nature, perhaps, or the special appeal of twilight."

She was a Western woman, granddaughter of the last chief of the Delaware's Munse or Wolf Clan. As the Colonies were settled in the seventeenth and eighteenth centuries, the Delaware nation was pushed from its original home along the Delaware River. While some of the Delawares moved north to the Six Nations Reserve in Canada, Reverend Charles Journeycake's people, the Munse division of the tribe, had been pushed west to Ohio, then Indiana, then Missouri, and then Kansas. Pressured and persecuted by white settlers in each state, they finally purchased land from the Cherokees in Indian Territory ten years before Roberta was born in 1878. Roberta had grown up in the village of Alluwe in the Verdigris Valley in the northeastern corner of Indian Territory.

There Roberta savored a close relationship with her Delaware grandfather Charles Journeycake. While she claimed only one-eighth Indian blood, she identified more strongly with this aspect of her heritage than any other. With him, she learned to appreciate the crisp scents of pine and sage, the cry of migrating geese, a coyote's yip, the messages in the wind. Although customarily dressed in suit, shirt and black string tie, with neatly trimmed hair and beard, Charles Journeycake's prominent high cheek bones, strong, straight nose and bronze skin bespoke his Delaware heritage, and he talked often of his people's history. The girl easily memorized tribal legends and chants that he shared. He taught her by example to revere items from the past that he treasured, such as the beaded skin tobacco pouch used when the Delawares signed their first treaty with William Penn in 1682. They were the most advanced of any of the Eastern tribes, and another treaty with the Continental Congress in 1778 had provided them a representative in that body. They were a peaceful people who farmed and lived much like the colonists. Yet, after the first, each successive treaty pushed them relentlessly west.

Her mother, Emeline (Emma) Journeycake, daughter of Charles, delighted Roberta with walks across the prairie during which she learned to recognize which root made the best poultices, which bark the best tea, and where to find the herbs to sooth an upset stomach or calm a cough. But Emma knew about far more than herbal medicine. She was one of fourteen children of Charles Journeycake and Jane Scotia, the child of a Delaware woman and a French trader. Charles and Jane believed strongly in education for their family—even daughters, a remarkable stance for their time. Emma and her seven sisters had all been sent to Baptist colleges, at first to

Ohio and later to the first college for Indians in the Territory, Bacone College, which Charles and Jane founded in 1880.

Charles was a Baptist minister; his mother, Sally, had been converted to Christianity, and through her influence he had been baptized into the church after the tribe reached Kansas in 1828. By 1855, he had succeeded his father, Solomon, as chief of the tribe. It was not long before the Union Pacific Railroad and white settlers encroached on their Kansas lands near Fort Leavenworth. Although it was land they had bought, paid for and developed, disgruntled whites stole their stock, broke down their fences, destroyed their timber and plied their young men with alcohol. Chief Journeycake was instrumental in finding a solution. The Munse Delawares contracted with the Cherokees to buy 156,000 acres of land in their northeastern corner of Indian Territory in 1867. He led them as they again abandoned established homes and farms to move south and chose a spot in the unsettled Verdigris Valley, ten miles from any railroad. A village, originally called Lightning Creek, had developed around Charles' and Jane's home.

A few years later, young John Edward Campbell, a Virginian of Scottish descent, came west to seek his fortune after the Civil War. He opened a trading post at Lightning Creek and established a profitable business. The Virginia farmer had been hard put to adjust to life in Indian Territory, and a friendship with Reverend Journeycake eased his way. In addition to the trading post, he began raising cattle on the rich grass that flourished in the fertile valley. What he came to feel for Journeycake's daughter, Emma, grew to be more than friendship. John and Emma were married. In 1878, the year Roberta was born, they built a home, a store and a blacksmith shop. Although the town began with the name Lightning Creek, when Roberta was five, Emma successfully petitioned Congress for a change to Alluwe, a Delaware word meaning "of superior quality."

Granddaughter of a chief, daughter of a prosperous businessman, Roberta led a privileged childhood. There were few schools in Indian Territory and she and her brother, Herbert, seven years younger, were first tutored in a little school house in their own yard. It had extra seats for friends. One friend, a Cherokee boy from a ranch six miles down the Verdigris, would become known throughout the world as humorist Will Rogers. They were to be friends for a lifetime. There was a tennis court, ponies to ride, books, paintings, a piano, and the excitement of never knowing who might drop by. Visitors were warmly welcomed and generously entertained. Roberta loved the country around the trading post and made friends easily with the wide variety of people it attracted. She learned to fish and became an excellent horsewoman, both skills she was to long enjoy.

Her grandparents' home was a meeting place for Delaware visitors, who often came to discuss tribal affairs. Charles built a small church, where he preached every Sunday. Roberta learned to revere her grandfather's teachings and wanted everyone to benefit by them. She admired his ability to communicate his faith not only in his native Delaware, but in the Shawnee, Seneca, Wyandotte and Ottawa languages. He was known as a fearless man, who led his people with wisdom, judgement and dignity. Roberta sometimes failed to live up to his standards. One Sunday when she was six, she became so irritated with another child who was not listening to his sermon and had left her pew to run up and down the aisles, that Roberta stepped out and gave the girl a sharp slap. The deed became a family legend and in later years she enjoyed telling the tale about her excessive zeal.

She was blessed with musical talent and began playing an organ at a young age. By age 9 she was assisting her mother at the Baptist church, by age 11, the Methodist-Presbyterian chapel nearby had enlisted her services. When she grew old enough to be away from home, her parents sent her to a female seminary in Independence, Missouri, within twenty-five miles of the land her grandfather's people had been forced to leave two decades before.

In these early teenage years another incident connected with her grandfather's preaching was more representative of Roberta's innate desire to be helpful. Returning from a shopping trip wearing a new pair of stylish shoes, her carriage passed some roadside campers. Her sympathy aroused by the worn and weary look of the family, she inquired about the mother's welfare and invited her to attend her grandfather's church. When the woman replied she had no shoes to wear to church, Roberta promptly slipped out of her new patent leathers and left them, continuing home in her stockinged feet. Years later she told a reporter that the contentment she saw in that woman's face Sunday after Sunday more than repaid her for shoes that would have been long forgotten, and the memory remained for her "a glowing incentive."

After the private school in Independence, Roberta moved on to Hardin College in the town of Mexico, in northeastern Missouri, where she specialized in music studies. She was an excellent pianist, had a rich contralto voice and also a talent for composing. At Hardin she benefitted from the tutoring of a world-famous composer, Xarver Scharwenka. She would put her lessons to a novel use in the years to come.

On return to Alluwe, her organizational skills began to awaken. She recruited three other young women to form a club that would "promote friendship and culture," and the four of them canvassed the area on horseback.

The early 1890s brought what must have been her first great sorrow. Her grandmother, Jane Journeycake, died in 1893 and Reverend Charles followed her the next year. On his death she inherited the tobacco pouch that had been used when the Delawares met with William Penn more than 200 years before. She had saved Delaware items that interested her since she was a child. Her grandparents' deaths must have enforced in her the need to preserve both the sacred and everyday items that made up their lives.

The area's economic prospects brought a young lawyer named Eugene B. Lawson into Roberta's life. Originally from Shelbyville, Kentucky, Eugene Lawson left home at 19 to teach school in Texas while he also studied law. In 1896 he had been admitted to the bar in Wichita, Kansas. The 25-year-old lawyer decided to hang his shingle in Nowata, a few miles from Alluwe. While he developed his law practice, he served as superintendent of schools.

Roberta was a tall, athletic woman, her black eyes gazing levelly from a face tinged with bronze. A reporter was to write later that she would "never be lost in any assemblage. Her dark eyes and hair, her erect carriage and her definitely strong features stood out as if she had been centered by a spotlight." Her long, black braids were wound around her head, but her somewhat severe appearance was softened by a warm smile and her lively interest in everything and everyone around her. Lawson was soon on her list of suitors.

The surprising discovery that riches lay under the land of this corner of Indian Territory was to change many lives forever. On April 15, 1897, a wildcatting trio composed of William Johnstone, George Keeler and the Cudahy Oil Company, struck oil in Bartlesville, a small town that had formed on a bend of the Caney River a scant ten miles from Nowata. It was also the home of Nannie Journeycake Bartles, an aunt of Roberta, who had married the developer at a time he thought a gristmill and the wheat fields he promoted were the future of the area.

As the exciting news spread that Indian Territory's first commercial well was a reality, people gathered to view the black oil spewing up the wooden tower that was named Nellie Johnstone No. 1. While there was much to celebrate, there were no storage tanks ready and no railway to carry the black gold to a refinery; regretfully the developers shut down the well. But the cap proved to be leaky, and townspeople soon learned that if they came armed with buckets, they could carry away the crude oil to grease machinery, light fires and rub on their farm animals as protection from ticks. Curiosity seekers flocked in, local business boomed, entrepreneurs took a new look, and the surrounding area took on new life.

In 1898, the Bartles moved about five miles north to found the town of Dewey, where Roberta's aunt grandly entertained hopeful oilmen and other fortune seekers in an elaborate Victorian hotel built by her husband. When he finished grading roadbed to the area and the Santa Fe Railway completed construction in 1899, commercial oil production began.

In this exciting atmosphere, Roberta Campbell and Eugene Lawson were married on her twenty-third birthday on October 31, 1901. In 1905 they had a son they named Edward Campbell Lawson. The prospect of statehood raised fervent discussion. The women of the town wanted a library, the businessmen wanted a bank, the children needed a park. Roberta often spent evenings in the law office. While Eugene worked on cases, she studied what communities needed to flourish and how to bring about cultural growth. She worked to establish the library, the park and a music club. Eugene joined forces with his father-in-law to found the First National Bank of Nowata. As their son proceeded through school, they were active supporters of civic causes.

Roberta spent many hours helping develop the YWCA. Believing women ought to know how to be useful citizens, Roberta helped found the La-Kee-Kon Club for Nowata women in 1903. But she did not forget her Indian heritage; it was in these years she became a serious collector of Indian artifacts.

It was a time when most women stayed home to care for their families. Although most were active in a church, many realized they needed something more. In 1890, women had combined two organizations working for suffrage, and that same year the General Federation of Women's Clubs (GFWC) was founded. This group provided one of the few acceptable avenues for women to become educated beyond the home and involved in public life. The La-Kee-Kon Club was Nowata's first women's club, and Roberta served as president for five years.

When Indian Territory and non-Indian Oklahoma Territory merged in 1907 to become the state of Oklahoma, Roberta increased her GFWC activities. She became the Oklahoma federation's first state president and from 1918-1922 she served as a national director. During World War I, her program to bring GFWC members into the war effort brought her an award from the American Defense Society. Through it all, she maintained a close, loving relationship with her son.

She was also active on the federation's Indian Welfare Committee, which was established after Gertrude Simmons Bonnin pleaded for the club women's help in 1921. Roberta Lawson was serving as a director and gave Bonnin substantial support. The two women began working closely together. A joint investigation of Oklahoma Indians in 1922-23 by Bonnin and representatives of two Indian rights associations gave names and faces to those swindled—even killed—for their oil rights. Their 1924 report caused a sensation and alerted the public to the need for reform.

It was during the next four years, as she served as national music chairman, that Roberta became aware that Indian music was in danger of disappearing. With her own special skills and insight, and her knowledge of music theory, she began searching out what other collectors had found. She noted Alice Fletcher's pioneer efforts to record Omaha music, with the assistance of Francis LaFlesche. She had connections that enabled her to record Delaware melodies from the elders still living; she translated native chants and she began to write her own Indian songs. She had her grandfather's book of hymns in the Delaware language and she added another in Cherokee. Her research spread to Zuni, Chippewa, Blackfeet, Sioux, Omaha, Navajo, and Kiowa music and dance. She collected

Indian flutes, drums and rattles, and books and poems both about and by Indians.

By 1926, she had learned enough to publish a small book titled *Indian Music Programs*. It contained outlines for ten programs of Indian music and literature that federated women's clubs around the country could use for their meetings. However, it was much more than that. She described the evolution of Indian music, its roots in nature's sounds and the freedom Indians felt to "compose extemporaneously more than any other people." In writing about the role of music in Indians' daily lives, she also described a child's upbringing, the philosophy and methods of medicine men, and the natives' belief in one Great Spirit and eternal life.

Roberta did not hesitate to point out the dark side of contemporary Indian life. She noted that while "many noble Christian men and women have given their lives for the betterment of the Indian," for every one of these there were "dozens of unscrupulous, designing, intriguing white men" who contributed to the Indians' degradation. She had witnessed more examples of Indians being defrauded and debauched than she could count. "The light of civilization poured in and became the light of a consuming fire that melted glory, institutions, existence and name, " she concluded.

Yet, she had hope for Indian traditions and music. "Love for things beautiful, for the artistic, was born into man just as surely as desire," she wrote. Pointing out that Anton Dvorak's theme of "Largo," from his "New World Symphony," was based on an Iowa Indian theme, she predicted that, "Some day in the American school of music we will find the ladder of musical growth, and Indian music will be the foundation round." She believed that, "Beauties in nature are never wholly lost, neither will Indian music be lost, as long as the pines whisper and sing." Practical woman that she was, she did not depend on the pines' whispers; she created a beaded white buckskin costume and became well known for presentations of Indian music, legends and culture which she performed in many states. Her book found use as a text in many schools.

The years in Nowata had been good to the Lawsons and Eugene had gradually reduced his legal practice to focus on oil exploration. By 1927 the Lawson Petroleum Company had provided the family with a comfortable fortune and prompted a move to Tulsa. They moved into a three-story, red brick house on Sunset Terrace, and the couple widened their social and civic leadership. In addition to being involved in numerous other organizations, such as the Daughters of the American Revolution, the Indian Women's Club, the National Council of Women, and the National League of American Pen Women, Roberta became the only female trustee of the University of Tulsa. She also served as a board member of the Oklahoma State Historical Society and the Tulsa Art Association. She had become a regent of the Oklahoma College for Women at Chickasaw in 1918, a position she would fill the rest of her life. The pull of her Delaware heritage remained constant; she researched her genealogy and in 1927 published an article outlining Delaware history in the magazine *My Oklahoma.*

They had been in Tulsa only two years when the stock market crash sent the nation spinning into the Depression. The next few years were grim as continuing drought sucked life and hope from the Oklahoma soil and sent huge black dirt clouds billowing across the Great Plains. Family after family abandoned homesteads, piled their meager goods into cars and wagons and took to the roads, heading somewhere—anywhere —they might find work. In January 1931, her longtime friend, Will Rogers, now a nationally known and beloved entertainer, began holding benefits to raise funds to relieve the suffering population, especially people in Oklahoma, Arkansas and Texas. Knowing her organizational skills, Rogers asked Roberta to administer the charity fund in Oklahoma. Nothing pleased her more than helping those in need and she eagerly took on the task. Before February ended, she was hard at work.

She was shocked and shaken on June 25 by her husband's unexpected death, a month after his 60th birthday. She and Eugene had worked together for thirty years; they believed in the same causes, and he was one of the few people who could match her in energy and commitment. She was left to run the business with her son, Edward, now 25. To fill the void, she plunged into more activities. With her reputation growing on the national scene, in 1933 and 1934 she was asked to serve on Eleanor Roosevelt's Committee for the Mobilization of Human Needs.

Despite the turmoil caused by the wounded economy, she thought deeply about world peace. She was convinced that education was all that was needed to make people realize they all shared the same basic beliefs. Her Grandfather Journeycake had taught her that harmony would come if one could "link the hearthstones of the world together."

In 1933, she joined the federation's first World Friendship Tour to European capitals, and dressed in her beaded costume, presented several programs of American Indian music in Czechoslovakia. Her study of Native American music had convinced her that a primitive rhythm tied the music of ancient Greek, Russian, and other early peoples together. Through her music, she reached across the language barrier and made connections. The next year she was chosen one of three federation delegates to the Pan-Pacific Conference in Honolulu.

Much of her time in these years was devoted to her now extensive collection of Indian artifacts and literature. As she accumulated items, she carefully cataloged and labeled them and began to display them in glass cases on the upper floors of their home. Grandfather Journeycake had given her the pewter communion set he brought into Indian Territory. The Delaware tobacco pouch was joined by a clay pipe owned by Chief Powhatan and smoked by every U.S. president since Washington. She was able to buy it, pledging she would carry on the tradition. Navajo rugs carpeted the halls and fifty plaques displayed some of her 2,000 arrowheads, a number of which she had spied while enjoying strolls through the countryside. Much older civilizations, such as the Mound Builders, the Cliff Dwellers—even the Aztecs—were represented. She had garments from dozens of tribes, arrows, quivers, war clubs, feather bonnets, moccasins, utilitarian and decorative items from all aspects of daily life. One showcase illustrated the evolution of the tomahawk, another the war club, another bows ranging from children's to those used to bring down large animals.

While she collected with fierce determination, and cataloged her collection with great care, she also enjoyed it. A close friend said of her, "She loves a lark, has a sense of humor, (and) does not take herself too seriously. . . . " In 1932 she told a reporter for the *New York World-Telegram* how she "cut loose" now and then. "First I slip into Sitting Bull's moccasins, then I shake the deer-hoof rattle once owned by Tecumseh's brother; parade around in my feather bonnets, play the flutes and beat the tom-toms. It's a grand way to indulge in self-expression."

She also actively enjoyed her pursuit of Indian literature. While she accepted contemporary materials, carefully screened for accuracy, she was particularly interested in finding "volumes published generations ago." She asked friends and acquaintances and sometimes advertised in the Sunday editions of small-town newspapers in Kansas and Oklahoma. But most of them she found herself when her travels took her to New York City and Washington, D.C. "I like to go through out-of-the-way second-hand bookstores," she explained. "It is in such as those I find my rarest volumes." Among the 500 items in her library were hymn books in Delaware and Cherokee dialects, a history of Indians in New England in the 1600s, a three-volume set of Indian Tales published in 1829—even *Pilgrim's Progress* in the Dakota language. There were books on every phase of Indian existence. She also included biography, novels, poetry and music, both by and about Indians. "It takes time to go through the new and weed out those that deal more in fiction than in fact," she acknowledged. Paintings accurately depicting native life added a rich visual element. She willingly shared her treasures, described by museum personnel as the most comprehensive and valuable private collection in the country, by opening her home to scholars and visitors. Often, parts of the collection were lent to educational institutions.

When she was working for the YWCA in Nowata two decades earlier, a friend had asked why she spent so much time enabling girls when her only child was a boy. "Because someday my son is going to bring me a daughter. . . . Women are mothers of men, and men rise according to the demands of women. When we serve women, we serve all mankind," she replied. The Great Depression changed a woman's "hometown viewpoint," she said later. The challenges it brought "broadened her outlook, strengthened her determination to make a better world for herself and her children, made her realize that she is in reality a part of the government herself and that she can do with it what she will." Roberta had already served several terms on the national board of the GFWC, and in 1935, the Oklahoma State Federation proposed her for national president.

What might have seemed a natural choice—she had been second vice president for two terms and was just finishing her term as first vice president—turned out to be controversial. The eight-day convention in Detroit that June was unusually raucous; the election for president fiercely contested. Underlying the debate about who could best lead as president lay an ugly layer of racism. Her opponent was from Ohio, and some of her Eastern supporters used Roberta's Indian ancestry against her. The usual fun of the campaign, which included banners and lighthearted parodies of popular songs praising the candidates' abilities, was dimmed by bitter words.

Roberta was arguably the best-known, most-admired woman in Oklahoma. She was loved and valued for her generosity of spirit. She had never lost an election in thirty years of club work. Oklahoma women said the state was "loaning to the General Federation her dearest and her best." Southern women supported her wholeheartedly. But the undercurrent of vicious rumors in Detroit came to a head when someone ripped down a Southern banner. The rejection must have caused Roberta pain, but her supporters found her entirely composed, denying bitterness, and the first to urge restraint when the impulse was to retaliate.

Will Rogers had commented in his nationwide radio broadcast and newspaper column about the federated club women: "When you're out to get a job done, just go to them Federated Club Women," he said. "They sure know how to put it over and get things accomplished." But he also mentioned the coming election and decried reports that Roberta's Indian heritage would prevent her election. Some club members took offense, claiming they were indifferent to her ancestry, but their campaign tactics proved otherwise. The Oklahoma delegation countered by bringing forth Rogers' sister, whose hearty endorsement quieted the whisper campaign. On June 10, Roberta was elected by a vote of 846 to 538. Urged by her excited friends to tell them how she wished to celebrate her victory, she immediately responded, "Let's have no celebration. Remember, someone lost."

Central to her leadership abilities lay this unusual empathy for others' feelings. She led with a gentle touch, considerate, self-effacing, always focusing on the goals of the organization rather than her own aggrandizement. She believed the three essentials for leadership were patience, a sense of humor and the spiritual approach. She was a devout woman; the teachings of her grandfather were central to her life. Now leader of two million women in the United States, three million worldwide, she was eager to reach out to each member and through them to influence their families and society. She began her administration with the prayer that she might lead the women in "development of a greater understanding, more tolerance and a deeper consciousness of the golden rule."

With the theme "An Education for Living," she pointed out that club work, if properly directed, can continue and even substitute for a college education. Two of her objectives were practical, educating women on "what the constitution of the United States means to women," the other, education on "how the housewife is taxed and why." But she also had larger ideas. She began work on a congressional bill to establish a National Academy of Public Affairs, "the West Point of diplomatic service," that would provide "a thorough education in our own government formation." It was her dream that such a school would eliminate the spoils system and result in better-trained public servants. She informed nay-sayers the idea had been suggested and supported by George Washington. She also wanted to mobilize GFWC members in the cause of peace, hoping to assemble a peace conference with an agenda "based upon something beside the scrapping of battleships." Such a meeting would be "dedicated to the promotion of friendship, tolerance and human understanding . . . " Aware it was an ambitious plan, she said, "If we shoot at all, we must aim high."

She had scarcely begun her work when she and the nation were shocked and saddened by the accidental death of Will Rogers on August 15, 1935. The nation mourned as if it had lost a son, a brother, a favorite uncle. Unable to be present at a memorial service in Claremont the next week, she gathered a group of Oklahomans where she was, in Minnesota, to give him tribute. "He strove to supplant envy and greed with humanness and understanding," she said . . . "to all who knew him and to the world he loved, he bequeaths a rich heritage of friendship and brotherhood. I mourn the loss of a real friend."

Perhaps taking a cue from her old friend, whose voice had been heard weekly across the airwaves, Roberta initiated a series of radio broadcasts to the nation on NBC in 1937. She had performed her Indian songs on NBC the year before, as always linking legends of peoples from around the world. She was a born educator, and she realized that, "Radio is obviously one of the great avenues of approach to the mind of the people. Thus those who control it have a great responsibility to the maintenance and growth of American civilization."

The half-hour, monthly broadcasts discussed current events, and included music and drama. As the spokeswoman for three million women, she promoted issues as varied as highway safety, the control of cancer, vocational training for women, and uniform marriage, divorce and narcotics' laws. She also spoke out on more controversial topics such as universal fingerprinting, lynching, birth control and syphilis education. She had no patience with the euphemisms of the day, exclaiming, "Let's call it syphilis and do something about it." As part of actor Eddie Cantor's campaign against automobile accidents, she was ahead of her time in wondering, "Are we in the driver's seat or is the machine running us?"

She spent her three-year term of office traveling out from the Washington headquarters to meet with women and encourage them to fight for what the country and the world needed. Personal warmth and charm enabled her to inspire those she met with optimism and purpose. She spent only about one-third of her time in her Washington office where, with secretarial help, she answered as many as 1,000 letters a month. Two-thirds of the year she traveled the states. Often she drove her own car to regional meetings.

Continually, she presented programs of Indian music. Now a recognized authority, she was credited with awakening interest in the history, music, art and legends of the American Indian peoples. Though she admitted she sometimes felt "numb from the knees down" because of the hours spent standing in meetings, she followed her own counsel to "keep right on and on and on, through failure and defeat—doing the next duty, taking the next step, playing the next game through to its finish."

In between she managed visits home to Tulsa to visit her two small grandchildren, meet with the boards of the educational and historical institutions she served, play golf, ride horseback and visit Texas to defend her record catch of tarpon—ten 4-to-6-foot tarpons in one day. Her competitive spirit is demonstrated in the fun she had racing against herself when, as the Oklahoma College for Women's regents' secretary, she signed all that year's diplomas. The registrar stood by with a stop watch as she tried to outdo each previous year's record.

After finishing her term, she denied any political ambitions of her own, but this lifelong Democrat helped organize and worked for the Democrats for Wilkie Committee in the presidential election. The effort to elect the Republican failed, and in fragile health, she returned to her Tulsa home. She had honored her mother, Emma Journeycake Campbell, with a stained glass window in the Nowata Baptist Church, her great-grandmother, Sally Journeycake, with a girls' dormitory at Bacone College, and, in her last illness, she arranged to memorialize her Grandfather Journeycake with a stained-glass window in the Bacone College Chapel. She entrusted its design to a young Indian artist, one of many she encouraged over the years. It was installed in 1941, a few months after her death December 31, 1940, of monocytic leukemia.

Always cognizant of the chain of history, in 1933 she had stood on the University of Tulsa's campus to present the chancellor with a descendant of the elm tree which had shaded the Delawares and William Penn while they signed their 1682 treaty. She had related again the story of the treaty and asked that the elm, a "living link in American history," be known as "The Tree of Friendship and Good Will to All Peoples."

She spent her life reaching out to all people, working for understanding. While she always championed education, she believed, "The end of all education is the development of character, and the test of character is service." She had been honored for her service—seen her photo with Eleanor Roosevelt, Margaret Sanger, Helen Keller and six other women as *Look* magazine's "ten leading women in America," been named to the Oklahoma Hall of Fame, and seen her name honored on a building at Bacone College. But she valued much more the libraries founded by the GFWC, the $1.5 million in loans, scholarships and fellowships given to young people, the girls' clubs she'd organized, the chance to help establish the Foundation for Infantile Paralysis, and especially the opportunity to collect and preserve Indian music, books and artifacts. Her New Year's wish in 1938 had been to "look forward to a greater opportunity (to be) of service to our fellowman and our country."

Today, she is honored by a bronze bust in the American Indian Hall of Fame near Anadarko. Her son, Edward Campbell Lawson, Jr., and his wife, Alice, presented her outstanding collection to the Philbrook Museum of Art in Tulsa. It included more than 1,000 artifacts and 1,005 volumes, and over 700 specimens from prehistoric civilizations. Grandson Edward C. Lawson and his wife remain active in museum activities today.

Roberta Campbell Lawson Bibliography

Archival Collections

General Federation of Women's Clubs Archives:

-----"Autobiography," typescript, #13143, 1938.

-----"Division of Music," Chairman's Report, 1927.

-----"Oklahoma Presents Roberta Campbell Lawson for Advancement from First Vice President to President," 1935.

-----"Oklahoma State Federation of Women's Clubs presents Roberta Campbell Lawson for President," 1935.

-----"Lawson Administration Accomplishments"

-----"Songs for Roberta Lawson Campaign"

-----"State Woman Presented for High Office in National Federated Clubs," 1924.

Ingram, Helen. "Biography of Roberta Campbell Lawson," compiled by the Oklahoma State Historical Society.

Jackson, Effie S. "Roberta Campbell Lawson Interview," Works Progress Administration, v. 33, 1937:113-116.

Lawson, Edward C. "Talk at Claremore Memorial," 8- 22, 1935. Bacone College Archives.

Lawson, Roberta, "Music is my Hobby – American Folk Music,"NBC, radio script, 3-19, 1936, Bacone College.

Lindsey, Lilah. "Memorial to Mrs. Roberta Campbell Lawson," TS. Indian Womens Club of Tulsa, 1941. Lilah Lindsey Collection, University of Tulsa.

-----"A Short Sketch of the Indian Womens Club of Tulsa Oklahoma," MSS, University of Tulsa., n.d..

Pamplin, Mollie Glass."Personal Glimpses," Lawson Scrapbooks, Bacone College, 1985.

"Roberta Campbell Lawson" *Tushka Homan*, Sep. 24, 1935, TS, Oklahoma Historical Society.

Young, Tom. "Roberta Lawson: Keeper of Tradition," Script for 1993 Exhibition, Philbrook Art Museum.

Books

Fugate, Francis and Roberta. *Roadside History of Oklahoma,* Mountain Press Publishing Co., 1991.

Gibson, T. G. and Mrs. J. C. Pond. *History of Oklahoma State Federation of Women's Clubs,* Oklahoma State Federated Women's Clubs, 1969.

Lawson, Roberta C. *Indian Music Programs*, Nowata, Oklahoma, 1926.

Yagoda, Alfred. *Will Rogers,* Alfred P. Knopf, 1993.

Articles

Anderson, La-Vere Shoenfelt. "Delving Into the Neglected Field of Indian Art," *Tulsa Daily World,* Feb. 22, (1931).

Bataille, Gretchen M. and Laurie Lisa, Ed., "Roberta Campbell Lawson," *Native American Women, A Biographical Dictionary,* Routledge, 2001:185-6.

Bland, Sidney K. **"Roberta Campbell Lawson,"** *American National Biography*, Oxford University Press, 1999:299-300.

Bryce, J. Y. "Book Reviews: Indian Music Programs," *Chronicles of Oklahoma*, Oklahoma Historical Society, v. 4, n. 3, (1926): 301.

Cook, Edward. "Journeycake," and "Roberta Campbell Lawson and the Aristocracy of Service," *Love Made Manifest,* Higher Education Publications, Inc., 1994.

Creager, Baron. "Southern Personalities, Roberta Campbell Lawson," *Holland's Magazine,* Nov.(1936):7-35.

Dockstader, Frederick J. "Roberta Campbell Lawson," *Great North American Indians,* Van Nostrand Reinheld Co., 1977:146.

Drennen, Marguerite. "In the Service of Others," *Christian Science Monitor Weekly Magazine,* Jan. 8, (1936):3.

"Eugene B. Lawson, 1871-1931," *Chronicle of Oklahoma,* v. 9,. n. 3, (1931): 489.

"Federation Presidents," *History of Oklahoma State Federation of Women's Clubs, 1898-1969,* Executive Board, 1969.

Ferguson, Mrs. Walter."New Leader Speaks Texas Language," *Fort Worth (Texas) Press,* Jan, 21, (1935):4.

Gridley, Marion E., "Roberta Campbell Lawson, Leader of Three Million Women," *American Indian Women,* Hawthorn Books, Inc. 1974: 88-93.

Hardy, Gayle J. **"Roberta Campbell Lawson,"** *American Women Civil Rights Activists,* McFarland, 1993.

Herrick, Genevieve Forbes. "Women in the News," *Country Gentleman*, Sep. (1935): 59.

Kimborough, Mary. "Stories of Tomahawk, Peace Pipe Behind Indian Collection, *Tulsa Tribune*, Sept. 23, (1936).

Lawson, Roberta Campbell. "The Delawares," *My Oklahoma,* Aug., (1927):15-41.

-----."The Evolution of Indian Music," *Community Arts and Crafts, The Western Art Magazine,* v. 2, n. 5, (1929):15-17.

-----."What Democracy Means to Me – IV," *Scholastic,* v. 31, n. 16, (1938): 7.

-----."The William Penn Elm Tree," *Chronicles of Oklahoma,* v. 11, n. 2, (1933):755-757.

"Mrs. Eugene B. Lawson, Candidate for Second Vice President," "Mrs. Lawson Well Known in Washington," *Oklahoma Club News,* State Federation of Women's Clubs, (1931): 11.

"Mrs. Lawsons Notable Career Ended by Death," *Tulsa World,* Jan. 1, (1941).

"Mrs. Roberta Lawson Plans Official Tour," *New York Times,* Sep. 27, (1936).

"Roberta Lawson Led Clubwomen," *New York Times,* Jan.1, (1941).

Sonneborn, Liz. "Roberta Campbell Lawson," *A to Z of American Indian Women,* Facts on File, Inc., 1998:92-3.

"Tainted' or 'Tisn't?" *Bisbee Daily Review,* (1935).

"Ten Leading Club Women," *Look,* Nov. 23, (1937).

Tulsa Daily World. 2-22, 1931, 6-11, 1935, 7-28, 1935, 8-4, 1940.

Unidentified clippings from Oklahoma Historical Society and Bacone College Archives
"Tulsan is Urged for High Post," April 21, 1934.

"Mrs. Lawson Tells New Yorkers of Warpath She Invented," May 8, 1932.

"Mrs. Lawson Breaks Previous Record for Signing Diplomas," May 25, 1935.

"Tulsa Woman Has Historic Collection of Indian Relics," Sept. 25, 1929.

"City to Honor Mrs. Lawson," June 15, 1935.

"Crusade for Safety on Highways," Nov. 13, 1935.

"Tulsans Included in Hall of Fame," Nov. 16, 1935.

"Seek Appointment for Tulsa Woman" July 6, 1936.

"Leisure Hour Education Federation's Plan for Work," n.d.

"Lawson Indian Exhibit is Given to Philbrook" n.d.

Mary Littlebear Inkanish

Photo courtesy Clark Inkanish Bear

Chapter Ten

CHEYENNE AND NOT CHEYENNE

Mary Little Bear Inkanish, ca.1875-1965
Cheyenne – French-Canadian

About the time Annie Lowry traveled desert sands in her flight from the white world, another teen-aged girl fled across the wastes of western Indian Territory. But where Annie Lowry was putting as much distance as possible between herself and her father's people, Mary Little Bear was fleeing the Southern Cheyenne people who camped across the Northern Canadian River from the Darlington Agency. Mary was fleeing her Cheyenne heritage, determined to deny her mother's bloodline and everything she stood for. She was in shock—desperate to push away from what she had just learned about her mother's duties as Mah-hee-yuna—the Sacred Woman —as her band performed their periodic Sun Dance ritual.

Mary knew only through stories that her proud people had traveled a long and violent journey to reside in white-walled army tents beside the Canadian's northern branch in the early 1870s. Traditionally free to roam the high plains that became Colorado and Kansas territories, the Cheyennes clashed again and again with settlers and soldiers and sometimes achieved small victories. But in the five years between 1864 and 1869 they had experienced swelling white power. It was power fueled by hatred, and the bruising memories of the treatment Colonel

John M. Chivington and his Colorado Volunteers had inflicted on the camp sleeping at Sand Creek in 1864 were still fresh.

The Cheyenne warrior societies had resisted as long as they could, but they had finally been starved into submission. Lieutenant Colonel George A. Custer's devastating attack on Black Kettle's camp on the Washita had begun the year of 1869, and an executive order that made them wards of the government in western Indian Territory had finished it. Still, it was years before the last bands of warriors were subdued, and the army established Fort Reno adjacent to the agency to enhance security in 1874. By the time Mary was born a year or two later, most of her Southern Cheyenne people were reluctantly accepting their fate.

Mary's white father was an unknown quantity to her—a trader named Block who had set up shop at the Darlington Agency in the 1870s. The agency comprised only two or three buildings then—everything in the hot, dry country was new and strange to the Southern Cheyenne and Arapaho people. Living under white rules and regulations was a new and bitter reality. The idea that Cheyenne and Arapaho children belonged in school—whatever that was—had taken more than five years for Quaker missionaries to establish. Even then the school served mainly Arapahos because the Cheyennes resisted the system. The man named Block, who some said was from the far north, had soon become discouraged about serving as post trader to this undisciplined people. Leaving his wife, Little Bear Woman, and the children their union had produced, the trader packed up and left for the East. This is what my people do, he told his young family.

One child was a girl born about 1875; the Cheyenne people named her Ve-Hay-Kah because grey-blue eyes peered from her brown Cheyenne face. Ve-Hay-Kah was Cheyenne for White Girl, and the troubled teenager who was stumbling through the dark had been told from the beginning that she was different. Much as her mother cherished her, much as her maternal aunt and uncle loved her, she was only half Cheyenne. The other Cheyenne children often taunted her and jeered her mixed blood, often excluded her from games "only for Cheyennes," she told her biographers, Alice Marriott and Carol K. Rachlin, years later.

Just now she did not care. Cheyenne was the last thing she wanted to be. Cheyennes were dirty in her eyes. The Sun Dance ceremony was stained with sinful acts—acts the missionaries had taught Mary (the name the teacher gave her) would damn them all to Hell. That the Cheyennes considered the sexual union required of the Sacred Woman and the High Priest the utmost sacrifice a woman could perform for her people was immaterial. That it was undertaken only after eight days of complex and exacting ceremony and suffering did not matter. Sex outside of marriage was immoral. Sex with a family member, when it was required to pass on the sacred power, was not the supreme sacrifice the Cheyenne revered. It was called incest—a word the missionaries spoke with utmost horror. And Mary's mother would perform this horror. The mortified girl was putting as many miles as she could between her and the mother she had always loved and respected.

Mary was slight of build—lacked three inches of reaching five feet—and she felt lonelier than she had ever been, but she was not quite alone. Her closest friend, whom the teacher had named Martha, accompanied Mary in her flight toward the white world. Martha had an adventurous nature and she was ready to leave the Darlington School the girls had been attending. They spoke some English now, their long braids hung down the front of plaid cotton dresses made by the students, and they were learning the strange ways of the white world as explained by the Quakers. Martha wanted to make her place in this new white world, but she had lost faith in her Darlington teachers and was ready to join her friend in this challenge to both tribal and agency authority.

Martha already had challenged tribal customs. She had broken precedent by changing her school name of Martha to Minnie on the first night of the Sun Dance that had proved so traumatic to Mary. It was unheard of to change your own name, but she had honored the traditional custom of presenting four gifts to significant people when a name was changed, and the elders had accepted this new way. Things were changing, but they could not change fast enough for Mary.

She and the newly-named Minnie had planned their flight together, wrapped their few possessions and a little food in their shawls and walked into the darkness hand in hand. It took them two days, moving southwest across some fifty miles of empty, broken country. At times as they walked, the girls discussed the puzzle of the Sun Dance. Mary had observed the ritual all her life. Little Bear Woman had often told her how the aged Shell Woman had proudly named her at a Sun Dance when she was about a year old. Shell Woman had fought beside her man at Sand Creek, so her actions carried particular weight. With no father's name available for the toddler, Shell Woman had chosen what seemed best, Ve-hay-ka. It was not a proud name, but the moccasins on her feet, with the soles completely beaded, the fine new calico dress, and the lavish gifts her mother bestowed on Shell Woman amply demonstrated her family's love for her, her mother told her again and again. And Shell Woman's piercing of Ve-hay-ka's ears was an unusual honor.

"You are a Cheyenne and you are not a Cheyenne," her mother explained as Ve-hay-kah grew old enough to understand, "but remember this. When you were first shown to the people, you had the best we, your Cheyenne family, could give you." The words were engraved on Mary's mind. Seven decades later she would repeat them to Marriott.

Through the years Ve-hay-kah had learned more and more about the Sun Dance ritual and its homage to Maheo, the Above Person, but it was only this summer that she, now a woman herself, had understood the full impact of her mother's responsibilities. She had recoiled with horror and made her momentous decision. Martha—now Minnie—did not feel Mary's horror; she accepted the Sun Dance sacrifice of Little Bear Woman as her sacred duty. A woman willing to sacrifice her own body to strengthen her husband's priestly powers and so strengthen the tribe, could only be admired. Minnie did not understand her friend's shame, but she was more like a sister than a friend, and she supported her in this time of need.

Sometimes, as they walked in silence, Mary's mind whirled, trying to reason it all out. Cheyenne women were the most chaste of the plains tribes. Nubile Cheyenne girls were fitted with a protective cord to guard their virginity when they were with a large group of people. It was essential that a woman be pure until marriage. Yet now her mother was to give her body to her unmarried brother, whom she should not even talk to under ordinary circumstances. How could that possibly be holy? The thought repelled her. Certainly the missionaries knew it was sin of the worst kind. They insisted such damning Cheyenne ways must be stamped out. "I will be white from now on," Mary told her friend. She would follow the white road.

On the third morning the girls looked down on their goal —a large light-brick building amid a small cluster of others sheltered in a grove of white ash that graced a flowing creek. It was a new settlement called Colony, and it looked like an oasis, the grass thick in the bottom land along the clear, cold stream. It had long been a resting place on a westering trail, a country to make a rancher want to settle. The white man they knew as Johnny Smoker greeted the worn, grimy girls from his front porch, the fragrance from his big black cigar pulling them in.

The girls knew and liked John H. Seger. Until recently he had taught school at Darlington, and he had been their first teacher. The short, mustached man had been working with the Cheyenne and Arapaho since 1872. Originally hired as a mason, he had developed a talent for communicating with the Indians, and they came to respect and trust him. He laughed often, and he listened to them when they spoke—never denying them their language—and patiently showing them what they needed to learn. Beginning in 1875, he had built the Darlington School into a complex of dormitories, barns and corrals surrounded by cultivated fields. Students not only studied English, reading, arithmetic and spelling, but the boys also raised successful crops and herds, while the girls learned to sew, cook and clean. Mary knew Seger had better luck teaching the Arapaho, that many Cheyenne refused to work. She was determined no one would ever call her lazy. She was going to be a teacher when she grew up and make lots of money.

Seger was the agency's most successful teacher and in 1886 the agent had asked him to establish this new school at Colony. The school was primarily for Arapahos, but Mary was confident he would allow her and Minnie to stay in the large, two-and-one-half-story brick boarding school. Seeing the complex for the first time, she must have been impressed with its solid look of permanence. Her path to the white world lay before her.

Seger had named the girls, knew both their families and knew of Mary's ambition to be a teacher. When Mary told him passionately that she was no longer a Cheyenne, and both girls stressed they wanted to leave the Indian world behind, he said little. He saw to it that the matron fed, bathed and put them to bed in the dormitory, leaving the difficulties to be sorted out by their respective families in the morning.

The confrontations came a few days later. Mary was to describe the scene for her biographers. Minnie's mother, father and older brother came to take her home. She refused to go and nothing could be said to change her mind. Mary's tense wait came to an end a few days later when Little Bear Woman and her uncle arrived. What Little Bear Woman asked, her uncle made an order: she was to come back to camp with them. Mary threw her father's heritage in their faces. "If I stay here, I will be one of my father's people. Then you can't give me orders to do anything!"

"They have thrown you away," her mother cried. "Come back to your own people, the Cheyennes."

Mary gave a stubborn shake of her head. She might come back someday, she said, but only after she knew more about how her father's people lived. What she already knew was that her mother's part in the Sun Dance was, "wrong, wrong, wrong!" Then she hurled a devastating charge. "You're a wicked woman and I don't want to live with you."

"So be it." Exasperated, her uncle quirted his horse and galloped away. Little Bear Woman looked at her daughter for a long moment. Then she, too, turned and rode away. Mary found comfort in Mrs. Seger's arms until her tears stopped falling. Perhaps later Mary realized the woman spoke no word against Cheyenne custom, only promised that knowing two ways of living was better than one.

The white ways at Colony were even more different than those at Darlington and sometimes Mary thought of the warm companionship in her mother's oblong tent. The old folks talked of how different everything was from the old days when their circles of buffalo-hide tipis were anchored on the free prairie. Now they complained about the white soldier tents they had to use and the agent-ordered wooden privies—but to Mary this was home. Although only a rare family retained a skin lodge, the camp had traditional sweat lodges on the south side of the village. They might be covered with tattered blankets, but they were available for ceremonial cleansing. There were shady arbors in the summertime and shelters of brush to protect the homes from winter winds.

She could picture the members of the Woman's Sewing Society gathering to decorate household items with meticulous sacred patterns of beads or quills. Only the most skilled were invited to join, and her mother was among them. Except for certain sacred symbols, which could be made only after strict rituals had been observed, each woman developed her own designs, and comparisons were constant. Their tongues, working as fast as their fingers, prompted frequent laughter. Other women tackled the laborious job of tanning robes or worked on backrests that made lounging a pleasure. The men hunted when they could, worked with their horses and kept up their societies. Children learned needed skills from the older people and practiced under their patient eyes. There were so many good things about Cheyenne life. So many things she missed.

At the school everything from drinking milk—which the Cheyennes considered only for babies—to learning hymns, and pondering why a man in the Bible named Daniel would be afraid of something called a lion, raised questions in her mind. Maheo, the Above Person, and the Christian god seemed so different. As the months went by, Seger supervised the building of a church and he was soon at work on a house for a missionary expected any day. One minister was Presbyterian, with a glorious voice that made Mary forgive his lengthy prayers, one was a Baptist, one a Kiowa Episcopal missionary and finally the Lake Mohonk Conference of the Dutch Reformed Lutheran Church sent Reverend Reese Kincaide and his wife.

On the wagons with the Kincaids came large wooden crates with contents that Seger said would help the Indians make money to support their new stone church. There were knives and awls and beads, beads, beads. The Quakers and friends of the Indians who gathered at Lake Mohonk knew Cheyenne women were renowned for their fine handwork, and they had decided if they supplied the raw materials, the women could make items to be sold in the East. Half the proceeds of each item would go to the maker and half to the church. Work could take place in the Kincaide's new house in the large front room that the Indians had been so curious about.

Mary had not spoken to her mother since their traumatic parting, but Minnie had sent word back to camp about this opportunity for work. Mary was in the room helping Mrs. Kincaide unpack when a delegation from the Woman's Sewing Society appeared with Little Bear Woman in the lead. The girl froze where she stood, her emotions in turmoil, unable to speak. But her mother walked up and took her in her arms. "It is all right," she said. "You will always be my daughter and I will always love you, no matter what you say." Then Little Bear Woman held her at arm's length and looked at her thoughtfully for a moment. "You are better off here, too, I think," she said. Mary could not talk through her tears, but she knew they were friends again.

The Sewing Society women examined the beads long and closely, exclaiming about their beauty; then each picked certain strands to work on back in the camp. When Little Bear Woman said she would make a long, narrow bag, Mrs. Kincaide suggested she try a shorter, squarer shape that would be more popular with white women for a purse. "Cheyennes don't make that shape," she said doubtfully. But she took the beads and left in deep thought.

When the Woman's Sewing Society gathered again in Reverend Kincaide's parlor—which they were told to call Mohonk Lodge—there was excited and hopeful talk. But when the preacher pulled out a ledger and began measuring and copying each design in color, the room fell quiet. When Mary asked for an explanation, she was afraid to pass the information on to the women. Kincaide intended to keep a record and track sales of each design, so they could all work to reproduce the best-selling items and thus make more money.

Years later, Mary could relate how the idea had shocked them all. Each woman's creation had been her own property: no one wanted others copying her work. Symbolic, sacred designs must be exactly repeated, but in other work the color scheme was each woman's own.

"This is wrong," Little Bear Woman said. There was a shaking of heads; hands reached for their work.

When Kincaide understood what was wrong, he hurriedly explained. Women who made popular designs would earn money. Others, without popular designs, might earn nothing. To be fair, everyone must have a chance to produce the best-selling designs. Hesitantly, Mary translated Kincaide's next words: If a work proved popular, it would become a Mohonk design. The free Mohonk beads could be used only for Mohonk designs. If women wanted to make other things, they would have to buy beads from the traders. But if any of these new designs sold well, they would become official designs, be entered in the book and beads provided.

With a weight on her chest, Mary relayed his words. But her mother's response surprised her. "We have to feed our little children," she said with resignation. "Our old people go hungry, too. Our men have nothing to hunt, and they don't know how to farm." She looked from face to face. "It's up to us to take care of our families. We will use Mohonk designs."

Mary relayed the message to Kincaide, but she could not resist adding. "It's a bad thing to do to them. Something bad will happen." The preacher chided her for being superstitious. But deep down she believed it was wrong.

Gradually Mohonk Lodge became a gathering place, as Seger allowed the girls to join their mothers after classes and learn to bead. Buckskin became too scarce and Kincaide ordered suede; its many colors almost compensated for its thinness, and the colors sold even better than beige items. By the time summer came, Mary was ready to answer her mother's request that she return home to help with her uncle, who was dying of the white man's coughing sickness.

The white family tent had become a square house made from the boards the agency sawmill turned out, and in late summer it was brightened by the presence of a classmate her age, a Caddo boy named Jim Inkanish, who came to help out. His people had come up from Texas, and Seger had let Jim attend the Colony School because his parents did not like the Caddo

214

school at Anadarko. He and Mary had become good friends. At the doctor's urging, Jim spent days prying open the windows Little Bear Woman had nailed shut, so that air could circulate freely. But neither Jim's help nor the doctor's visits could do anything for her uncle. When he was gone, the doctor insisted Mary and her mother burn all his belongings, even clothing they would have given away in the old days. When they had finished, Little Bear Woman slashed her arms and legs in the age-old symbol of mourning. Yet when Mary reached for the knife, she snatched it away. "Not you," she said.

With the need to abandon their home uppermost in their minds, they were grateful when Johnny Smoker arrived in a wagon with an invitation. Mary and Jim were practically adults, but he wanted them back in school at least part time. Little Bear Woman could work in the girls' dormitory as well as Mohonk Lodge, and Mary and Jim could work in the bead room and on the farm respectively, along with taking some classes. It was agreed, and they climbed into Johnny's wagon.

The relationship between Mary and Jim grew closer, and one subsequent Wednesday in August of 1899, the couple set out in another wagon—this time prepared to make their new home in a house on an allotment near Binger, Oklahoma, some twenty miles east of Colony. Mary's hand in marriage had been properly requested, properly granted to Jim Inkanish, and there had been a double ceremony in the stone church with Mary's friend, Minnie, and Robert Cross. Both brides were dressed in white lace instead of buckskin, and Jim's father had offered a house instead of horses, as he would have in the old days. He noted white people said a house lasts longer than a horse, and Mary's mother readily accepted the gift.

Caddo lifestyle was quite different from Cheyenne and differences between their customs also had to be accommodated. Mary's mother explained to Jim's that she would love her new son-in-law as her own son, but she could not speak to him until she had fulfilled her obligations. She stayed at Colony and immediately began working on the beaded moccasins, tipi furnishings and saddle blanket that would allow a Cheyenne son-in-law to accept his mother-in-law's presence.

As Jim did necessary repair work, Mary happily painted the rooms, cut oilcloth for the table and hung pictures on the walls, but she also erected a hut out back for her menstrual days.

Before Little Bear Woman had finished the elaborate marriage outfit, they knew a baby would be arriving in the fall. When it was nearly time, Little Bear Woman and Minnie led a loaded horse up to the door. It was overflowing with riches: a saddle blanket, moccasins, two saddle bags, a bedspread and pillow covers were outshone by a huge horseback cradle that hung from the pommel. Mary was overwhelmed. She had never seen a cradle as beautiful as her "sister" Minnie had crafted in the absence of Mary's paternal relatives. It was old-fashioned, she knew, but she would always love it.

Mary and her mother went to the menstrual hut when labor pains began. Through the day they walked around and around the outside of the hut, until finally Little Bear Woman let Mary enter and kneel over a hole lined with clean, white sand. She grasped a pole planted on each side of the hole and began to pull. In a mist of pain, pulling, gasps and sweat, she felt Minnie's arms pulling and pressing from behind, and soon her wet, sticky son slipped into the world. She had worried the child might have her grey eyes, but she relaxed when she saw he looked all Cheyenne. All the Sewing Society came with gifts, and Mrs. Seger and Mrs. Kincaide brought flannelette to welcome George Inkanish into the world that November of 1900.

As the new century advanced, their world became Oklahoma Territory. But the new name brought mostly grasshoppers and drought. Jim's green fields began to shrivel. As the baby grew into a toddler, Little Bear Woman and Mary continued to work for Mohonk Lodge, and many months the money they made was the family's only income. They turned, as they always had in trouble, to Seger, and he found Jim a job as a teamster in Anadarko, about twenty miles south. They could rent a house at the Caddo Agency.

It was a move that brought even more changes into their lives. In August of 1902, Jim drove Mary to the Indian hospital near Lawton, Oklahoma, where she birthed her second son. She had no birthing hut in Anadarko, and Little Bear Woman had to stay behind to care for George. Instead of quiet, dim seclusion and the touch of familiar hands, she endured this birth on her back under glaring lights with her feet up in stirrups, with white nurses and a white male physician presiding. It disturbed her deeply. She worried how this baby, whom she named Joe, would fare in a world that had greeted him so harshly. She wondered if his grey-blue eyes marked him for a troubled future.

In the next eight years, Mary bore three more children—two boys and a girl—at the Lawton hospital, and life moved into a routine. Jim became an adviser at the Riverside School. Mary's children spoke only English, so they could not converse with Little Bear Woman, although she knew enough English words to chastise them when she was aroused. As the youngsters grew away from Cheyenne ways, Little Bear Woman began to teach Mary Cheyenne customs she wanted to see passed on to future generations. After the noon meal the two women would sit together and talk of old times.

As Mary worked to remember the creation stories and learn the complicated steps of the healing ceremony, she again faced the question of her identity. Later, she told Marriott how deeply torn she had felt. She had to be pure to touch the sacred things her mother was sharing, as she spread the contents of her brother's medicine bundle on the floor. The hawk-wing fan, the maple bowl—which seemed to emit warmth—the horn spoon and buffalo horn could be used to heal a sick person if the ceremony were performed with love and pity. But Mary did not feel pure enough to be the guardian of sacred objects, she told her mother.

Little Bear Woman's response stunned her. "They aren't sacred to you," she said. "these things are sacred to the Cheyennes, and you're a Christian."

"I don't know what I am," Mary wept. "Sometimes I think I'm Indian and other times I know I'm white."

"You'll know someday," her mother said soothingly, ". . . when the time comes, you'll know."

The lessons continued, and Mary continued to puzzle about her place. From the bundle, her mother gave her a four-strand necklace of tiny bone beads, a round shell pendant dangled from it. The shell was round to represent the turtle people— her people—and Little Bear Woman wanted Mary to pass it on to her daughter someday. But Mary feared taking it could bring bad luck since she was not from the turtle people only. Talks with Jim and Minnie brought differing advice, and Mary remained confused. She thought of going back to school to achieve her old dream of being a teacher. Perhaps *that* might make her all white. But doing that would require leaving her children to attend school, and she could not go. She put the necklace in a drawer and covered it with a scarf.

When the agent spurned Mary's attempt to make the rented house like her own by painting the walls, Mary had an unprecedented idea. If they owned their own home, no one could dictate what they did. She summoned her courage and asked the agent if there were laws against Indians owning houses. He knew of none and encouraged her to talk to the county clerk. "You're part white," he said "That makes a difference." That her white blood could be a help and not a hindrance was a startling thought. She mused again about who she was and what it meant.

In one of her conversations with Marriott, Mary described what happened next. One Friday she and Jim walked up the stairs of the two-story, red-brick building and approached the county clerk, seated behind a high counter. Asked brusquely what they wanted, Jim said, "We want to buy a house." When he explained that the agent had said the clerk might know of one they could buy, the official erupted in abuse and sarcastically broadcast their request. The other employees laughed and Mary hung her head. Didn't they already have a house the government paid for? Told Jim's job in Anadarko made it impossible to use that one, he snarled, "Then stay home and work your allotment. . . . Your squaw will do all the farming anyway."

Mary was suddenly furious. Her head shot up. "You make me sick!" she said. "You're all the time talking 'bout lazy Indians and squaws . . .but when one of us, just one, tries to get ahead and do what you say he ought to do, you push him back and you call his wife dirty names." Her breath was coming fast. "You're the ones who make lazy Indians. . . ."

Suddenly defensive, the clerk said, "Look here. I never said you couldn't have a house. You can buy one just like anybody else if you got money and references. . . . Go talk to the bank and tell them what you just told me." He shook his head, "I never knew a sq— , an Indian like you."

The woman who greeted them at the bank was part Cherokee and she deflated Mary's anger with her supportive interest in their request. This time Mary explained, and when Jim elaborated he added a surprising fact. ". . . we got some children. I don't want them to go to Indian schools like we had to. I want them to go to public school." It would mean paying for clothes and books that would otherwise be furnished, in addition to paying for the house, but the two were confident that between Jim's salary and Mary's beadwork sales, they could manage.

They could. The three-bedroom house was all Mary had dreamed of and for seven years life moved smoothly. Then, in 1917, when she was just over 40, Mary was pregnant again. Even the perfect house did not have a birthing hut out back, but this time, urged on by her mother, Mary refused the Indian hospital. Adjusting what she could, she sent Jim and the children to the Riverside dorm for the duration, so that she and her mother could proceed in proper silence and solitude. Josephine, as they named her, had Mary's grey eyes, but Mary was unconcerned. She placed Josephine in the cradle, and the cradle in a crib, and delighted in having a child again. Some years after the crib had given way to school rooms, Josephine decided she wanted to be a teacher. Mary began putting away every spare cent for her education.

Another child entered Mary and Jim's lives in 1928. Their second son, Joe, returned home with his wife and son, William Henry, and Mary watched in pain as Joe sank into alcoholism. Finally his wife left, leaving the youngster, who was called Sonny, in Mary's care. Sonny was a bright, cheerful boy who brought joy into their home. But once again drought shriveled the land, and as the 1930s began the country sank into the nationwide Depression. The older children were grown and gone, and Mary and Jim kept their door open to the many who had much less than they.

No one talked about the Sun Dance anymore, but summer pow-wows, when the people met for dancing and socializing, were a welcome chance to come together. The summer of 1930, when the girl was 13, "sister" Minnie gave Josephine her Cheyenne name. She took her into the center of the dance ring and announced for all to hear, "I name her Mah-hee-yuna."

Mary was shocked. Her mother's name. Cheyennes did not name children after living people. When she objected, Minnie answered that it was not really a name, but a title. It represented the way Cheyenne women gave themselves for their people. She did not want that to be forgotten. Mary's protest was futile. It was done.

And Mah-hee-yuna, Little Bear Woman, left them that winter. Mary and Minnie tenderly bathed and clothed the fragile body and prepared a bucket of food and coffee for her final journey. But Mary did not include the family medicine bundle; it was up to her, now, to keep it safe. After putting Little Bear Woman in the ground in the cemetery west of town, Mary greeted guests gathered back at the house. She would honor her mother's beliefs by cutting her hair short and giving away her possessions. With sewing shears she sawed off her long hair until it lay thick and black around her feet. Mah-he-yuna's tanning tools, her awl, a bundle of sinew and hanks of beads went to her friends in the Sewing Society. Afterward Josephine came to her and said, "Now you will have to teach me."

"I want you to be taught in college," Mary protested. "Let the old ways go. You will live in another world."

Later, Minnie came and sat beside her. "She wants to be a Cheyenne," she said.

"She isn't," Mary said with finality. "I'm half white, and you know it. Her father is a Caddo, and they live more like white people than Indians. She wants to go to college; she wants to be a teacher. That means she'll have to live like a white woman."

Within limits. When Josephine went to her first school dance, Mary sewed her into her underwear, much as her own mother had done.

Mary was wise to be watchful of her pretty teenage daughter. In 1933, the Caddo people heard some of the northern tribes were choosing young women to be princesses. It was a way to promote both business and their heritage. The Caddo Tribal Council decided they should elect one of their own. When the ballot boxes were opened, Josephine had won two votes to one. With Cheyenne buckskins inappropriate for a Caddo princess, Mary and Jim's family outfitted her with a rose blouse and skirt of cotton with a white organdy apron and multiple strings of shiny black beads tied with plaid ribbon. A paisley shawl —a family heirloom—an elaborate hairpiece topping her long braids and new Caddo moccasins completed her outfit. At the parade, the girls, including a Kiowa, Cheyenne and Comanche princess, all riding in shiny new convertibles, so roused Mary, Minnie and the old women watching that they trilled the victory call. When the parade and festival proved a success, it was repeated the next year, and this time Josephine represented the Cheyennes in Mah-he-yuna's buckskin dress.

Josephine gave Mary even more to celebrate when she graduated valedictorian of her high school class and enrolled in the Oklahoma College for Women in Chickasha in 1935. But Mary was even more forward-looking than her daughter. She announced she intended to buy a car so she could visit her daughter at school, sixteen miles east of Anadarko. Using half of Josephine's college fund—vowing to replace it by the time she needed it—Mary bought a used Ford and convinced Field Matron Susie Peters to teach her to drive. The lessons, first in an open field and then on dirt roads, had their exciting moments. Josephine, who had accompanied her mother, learned by observing before Mary mastered the skill, but master it Mary did.

Sonny, who carried Mary's blue-grey eyes, and his friends brought welcome life into the empty house, and Mary was grateful for their schoolboy chatter. His father was sober often enough that he bought the small house behind Jim and Mary's, and he stayed in touch with his wife. But one day when Sonny was about seven, Mary let him accompany his cousins three or four blocks to get some peppermint candy. A short time later the children were crying at her door. Sonny had run ahead and been hit by a car. He was at the local hospital.

Mary hurried there, and after he was stabilized at the city hospital, she drove the brain-damaged boy the thirty miles to Lawton Indian Hospital. Weeks later, when he was declared well enough to go home, she and Jim made the return trip. But the speechless, blank-faced boy they brought home was a stranger who grew only physically. For the next year she worked to teach him like a little child, but while his strength increased, his mind was difficult to reach. When, finally, she could control him no longer, doctors referred him to the Mental Health Institute in Norman. Once again Mary drove the grandson she loved to find help, but this time she had to leave him, screaming and crying, with the white-coated staff. A sobered Joe, who had accompanied them, said, "It's all you can do, Mother." She drove home and only with great difficulty did she eventually make herself drive the Ford again.

The depressed economy that was crippling the nation also slowed Mohonk Lodge sales. One day Mary, her sister-in-law and five other friends were sitting in a companionable group, Mary's fingers busy as usual beading moccasins. Three women were Kiowas, one an Apache, two Caddos and one Cheyenne. Talk of poor sales inspired Matron Susie Peters to suggest a craft society in which members could buy supplies in bulk, be free to make what they wanted and sell their work on their own. When Mrs. Peters offered to advance the money for supplies, the Women's Heart Club became a reality. Soon the women were working with new freedom and satisfaction, no longer bound to a white man's pattern book. After two years of exacting, tiring work, they had enough items, and enough money, to finance a triumphant trip for all to Gallup, New Mexico, for the Intertribal Ceremony of 1936.

The next year Mary received a request from the Riverside Indian School principal that she teach bead work to some of the girls. The federal government had established an Indian Arts and Crafts Board in 1937 to help Indians sell their handiwork, and they wanted them to learn about their old ways. Mary was quick to note the irony. "All my life people been telling me the Indians should forget about beadwork. Now they want me to teach it, all of a sudden? What they want us to do next? Go back to wearing blankets and living in tipis?"

The principal laughed and said she would be paid, which was only right, and with Josephine in her third year of college she could use the money. And so she and a Kiowa friend spent that year driving across the Washita River twice a week to teach the school girls each tribes' bead designs. A display of students' work in the spring raised interest, but there was no money to fund another year. However, a slim, red-haired government anthropologist named Alice Marriott, representative of the Indian Arts and Crafts Board, came to see Mary and asked if she would be willing to teach at other schools. Mary had been named the finest tanner of hides in Oklahoma in 1936, and with the forest service suppling deer hides, Mary taught the young woman she called "Ahneece."—she could never pronounce her "l's" – the laborious, dirty work of tanning a hide. By then the two women were friends.

Marriott took Mary to teach at the Tahlequah Indian School, an institution for the Five Civilized Tribes, 200 miles east. For a month she worked by the creek, instructing twelve teachers to use round stones to stretch, scrape, and rub in a paste of brains, liver and fat until the skin was soft and supple. Most of her pupils despaired before the job was done, and Mary was glad to take her little tin suitcase of tools and go home.

Far away on the west coast, the Golden Gate Bridge was nearing completion, and in late September1939, Mary and Jim drove with Alice Marriott from Oklahoma to San Francisco and then, in fear and fascination, rode a ferry out to the newly-created Treasure Island. Mary's hair was white now, caught nearly into a bun on the back of her head, and the extra pounds she had carried in her middle years had melted away. The couple were to serve as demonstrators in the Golden Gate International Exposition. Although Jim was slowed by arthritis and walked with a cane, he showed how to make bows, arrows and drums. Mary displayed her bead-working technique and the intricately decorated finished items. She also met Frederick Douglas of the Denver Art Museum, who would call on her skills in years to come.

The Pageant of the Pacific brought together all of the American Indians to display and sell their arts and crafts – many native peoples Mary had never heard of—as well as Pacific

Rim nations. They were housed in Navy barracks and came to know a variety of people. A four-acre hall was filled with fur-trimmed Eskimo garments, feathered baskets, pottery, coiled baskets, masks, sand paintings—too many things to absorb it all. Thousands of people thronged through the displays day after day.

A day off spent touring San Francisco enabled Jim to meet Chinese people, whom he had heard might be their ancestors, and Mary to collect shells she had decided would be as pretty on a dress as the artificial elks' teeth they had to use these days. When Alice Marriott noted she would be starting a new style, Mary said matter-of-factly, "Indians can change. They changed from real elks' teeth to imitation when they had to." But their most important purchase was two shimmering silk Chinese shawls for Josephine, who had just wired them she was engaged.

Back home again, they came to know Gerald Red Leaf, a Seneca, whom their daughter had met at Poteau High School where they were both teaching. They planned a wedding for Christmas 1941, after which the young couple would move to Rochester so that Gerald could work on his master's degree in music. But a week after the Japanese attack on Pearl Harbor brought the nation into World War II, Gerald called Mary with the news Josephine had pneumonia. Jim and Mary endured a bus trip to the Talihina hospital in the southeast corner of the state. Mary was just in time to hold her daughter as she took her last breaths. They buried her back home on December 20, robed in her white buckskin Cheyenne dress and the blue Chinese shawl.

Four days later Mary burned the contents of her uncle's medicine bundle. She was convinced it had brought only grief. A stuffed hawk, a bear's paw, a buffalo tail, an otter skin, a deer's leg bone, and a pipe went into the flames. But when she touched the maple bowl, the horn spoon and the beaded necklace, she relented. "I keep these," she said to Jim. Yet when Alice Marriot left to work for the Red Cross, Mary gave the warm wooden bowl into her keeping.

It was late in the year of 1945 when Marriott returned temporarily to Anadarko, and the women were soon talking around Mary's big, round oak table again. Mary was glad to tell Marriott that Anadarko had a new arts and crafts museum, the Southern Plains Indian Museum, with which she consulted regularly. She was certified as a member of the Oklahoma Indian Arts and Crafts Cooperative, an honor only select craftswomen could achieve. An outgoing woman, she had many friends among her people and reached out to others, such as potter Maria Martinez of the San Ildefonso Pueblo, who was scheduled to be the next subject of Marriott's study.

Mary kept both her fingers and her mind busy in the 1940s, donating a total of four objects and identifying several more for the Denver Art Museum. In the last year of the decade, Mary knew great sorrow when she lost her husband of fifty years. She always remembered Jim Inkanish as the best man she had ever known. She was feeling her years; her eyesight was failing and she wanted to make a trip north to see the Northern Cheyennes and the sacred places. That spring Marriott returned from New Mexico and in the summer of 1950, the anthropologist escorted Mary and a small party on a summer visit to the Cheyennes —where Mary contentedly taught beadwork to a people who had lost this knowledge. A Crow Sun Dance and visits to the Northern Arapaho and to Yellowstone Park followed. Before they returned to Oklahoma, Mary donated another seven objects to the Denver Art Museum and again assisted Douglas in evaluating its Cheyenne collection.

As her years mounted, Mary continued to bead and spent hours talking with people from museums and schools, passing on Cheyenne ways and generously sharing her creations—items she could have sold for needed funds. Glasses helped her focus on the numberless pairs of moccasins that passed through her hands, one, a fur-lined pair, was given to the Denver museum's

226

native arts collection. She became known for creating the Inka-Moc and the Inkanish Special Handbag. More and more often, she reverted to the Cheyenne tongue. She also sang her people's songs and related their stories so that a researcher from the Library of Congress could record them.

She had earlier adopted Alice Marriott as a daughter, and at a Labor Day Pow Wow in Colony in 1956, she adopted a new daughter, Carol Rachlin, an archaeologist who was then working with the Sac and Fox people. Carol had earlier been given the name of Laughing Woman and Mary gladly added the young woman to her family. Following the tradition of gift-giving, Mary, whom the scholars called Mama, joined in a naming ceremony which honored Marriott with the name Mah-he-yuna, or Spirit Woman, because she had given her life for the Indian people. Maheo would be pleased, Mary told Alice, that the name would go on. A diminutive figure, her cheeks sunken, her face a network of wrinkles, she attended her last Sun Dance in 1961, singing with the drummers until finally she was leading them, singing old, old songs most of them had never heard before.

In September of 1965, Mary Little Bear Inkanish died at the reported age of 86 in an Anadarko nursing home, tenderly watched over by her son, Joe, and her two adopted white daughters. Her cousin's daughter helped Alice and Carol dress her and paint her face before the family buried her beside Jim and Josephine. The two scholars later collaborated on the story of Mary's life, told as she had remembered it and shared it with them. Joe and his son, Clark, and numerous other family members contributed their memories. *Dance Around the Sun* was published by the Thomas Y. Crowell Company in 1977.

There were some memories Mary never shared, some puzzling gaps in her story. Her biographers never knew about the three children born between Joe and Josephine until after her death. She had never mentioned them in the twenty-five years Marriott knew her. Her memory and known fact cannot always be reconciled, especially regarding the sequence of events. But she is warmly remembered by current Southern Plains Indian Museum gift shop manager LaVerna Capes as an accomplished bead worker, a tiny, soft-spoken presence who loved to talk about how the craft had changed over the years. Her Inka-Mocs have become collectors items, and her legacy lives on in the nimble fingers of Indian women who continue to excel in their people's creative arts.

Mary Little Bear Inkanish Bibliography

Archival Collections

Conversations with grandsons Clark and Garth Inkanish; Eva Williams, curator, and LaVerna Capes, Southern Plains Indian Museum.

First Cheyenne Manual Labor School, "Clothing issued," fourth quarter, 1884.

Records of Donors and Identifications, Native Arts Special Project, provided by Heather Ahlstrom, Research Assistant, Denver Art Museum.

Seger, John. Census of Seger Colony Indians of the Cheyenne and Arapahoe Agency, 6-23-1894.

U.S. Department of the Interior, United States Indian Service, Cheyenne and Arapahoe Agency, Darlington, Okla., Annual Census, Volume by Families, 1877.

Books

Berthrong, Donald J. *The Southern Cheyennes,* University of Oklahoma Press, 1963.

-----.*The Cheyenne and Arapaho Ordeal, Reservation and Agency Life in the Indian Territory, 1875-1907,* University of Oklahoma Press, 1976.

Grinnell, George Bird. *The Cheyenne Indians: Their History and Ways of Life,* University of Nebraska Press, 1972.

Hoig, Stan. *The Cheyenne,* Chelsea House Publishers, 1989.

Marriott, Alice and Carol K. Rachlin. *Dance Around the Sun,* Thomas Y. Crowell Co., 1977.

-----.The Craft Guild of the Cheyenne Women, Oklahoma Anthropological Assoc., 1950.

Seger, John H. *Early Days among the Cheyenne and Arapahoe Indians,* 1956. Reprint, University of Oklahoma Press, 1979.

Articles

Batille, Gretchen, and Laurie Lisa, Ed. "Mary Little Bear Inkanish," *Telling Their Lives,* Garland, 1993:177.

"Hard Time, High Visions: Golden Gate International Exposition," http://bancroft.berkeley.edu/Exhibits/Looking/hardtimes.html. 2005.

Marriott, Alice. "The Trade Guild of the Southern Cheyenne Women," *Bulletin of the Oklahoma Anthropological Society,* v.4, (1956): 19 - 27.

Meserve, Charles Francis."The First Allotment of Lands in Severalty Among the Oklahoma Cheyenne and Arapahoe Indians," *Chronicles of Oklahoma,* v, 11, n. 4, (1933):1040 - 43.

"Notes and Documents," Chronicles of Oklahoma, v. 36, n. 3, (1958): 320.

"Outstanding Craftsman Dies," Press Release, United States Department of the Interior Indian Arts and Crafts Board, Southern Plains Indian Museum and Crafts Center, (1965):Sep 28.

Peery, Dan W. "The Indians' Friend, John H. Seger," *Chronicles of Oklahoma,* v. 10, n. 3 & 4, (1932): 348-68, 570-577; v. 11, n. 1 & 2, (1933): 709-13, 845-68.

"Services today," *Anadarko Daily News,* (1965): Sept. 27.

Strauss, Terry. "Review of *Dance Around the Sun,*" *Society of American Indian Letters,* New Series, v. 2, n. 3, 1978.

AFTERWORD

The Cheyennes believe that a people is not conquered until the hearts of the women are on the ground, Paula Gunn Allen notes in *The Sacred Hoop*. She affirms that Indian people understand "that without the power of woman the people will not live, but with it, they will endure and prosper."

The women profiled in this volume discovered within themselves the power to create new lives that blended the old and new. Their devotion to preserving the old ways, their ability to take advantage of the new, enriched their existence and that of their communities. The twenty-first century finds most indigenous American peoples increasing in numbers, and Indian traditions that once were forbidden, being celebrated for their unique value in the American scene. Writer Joy Harjo, who once found her mixed blood a curse, has "since decided that being familiar with more than one world, more than one vision is a blessing." She recognizes that she makes her own choices. "I also know that it is only an illusion that any of the worlds are separate," she writes.

As each generation seeks anew to inscribe their place in American society, they can look for inspiration to these first-generation daughters, who had to learn the delicate balance needed to walk in both worlds.

GENERAL BIBLIOGRAPHY

Books

Green, Rayna. *Women in American Indian Society,* Chelsea House Publishers, 1992.

Hertzberg, Hazel W. *The Search for an American Indian Identity: Modern Pan-Indian Movements,* Syracuse University Press, 1971.

Lomawaima, K. Tsianina. *They Called It Prairie Light: The Story of Chilocco Indian School,* University of Nebraska Press, 1994.

O'Mera, Walter. *Daughters of the Country,* The Women of the Fur Traders and Mountain Men, Harcourt, Brace and World, 1968.

Prucha, Francis Paul, ed. *Americanizing the American Indians,* Harvard University, 1973.

Articles

Binder, Frederick M. and David M. Reimers, "Indian Schools: 'Americanizing' the Native American," *The Way We Lived,* Fifth edition, Houghton Mifflin Co., 2004.

Evans, Sara. "The First American Women," *Women's American – Refocusing the Past.* Third Edition, Oxford University Press, 1991.

Ewers, John C. "Mothers of Mixed Bloods," *Probing the American West,* University of New Mexico Press, 1962: 62-70.

Morel, Mary Kay. "Captain Pratt's School," *American History,* June, v. 32, n. 2, (1997):26-32, 62-64.

Swagerty. "Marriage and Settlement Patterns of Rocky Mountain Trappers and Traders," *Western Historical Quarterly,* v. 11, n. 2, (1980).

The Author

Nancy Mayborn Peterson grew up in western Nebraska on the North Platte River and Oregon Trail. Moving to the Denver area in 1975 with its wealth of research materials intensified Nancy's interest in western history and she found herself drawn to material about Native American people and their cultures.

Other books by Nancy Peterson include *People of the Moonshell: A Western River Journal, People of the Troubled Water: A Missouri River Journal* and *People of the Old Missury: Years of Conflict.*

Nancy lives in Centennial, Colorado.

INDEX

INDEX

INDEX

For a free catalog of Caxton titles write to:

CAXTON PRESS
312 Main Street
Caldwell, Idaho 83605-3299

or

Visit our Internet web site:

www.caxtonpress.com

*Caxton Pres*s is a division of THE CAXTON PRINTERS, Ltd.